Managing Classroom Behavior

A Reflective Case-based Approach

James M. Kauffman
University of Virginia

Mark P. Mostert
Moorhead State University

Deborah G. Nuttycombe
University of Northern Iowa

Stanley C. Trent
Michigan State University

Daniel P. Hallahan
University of Virginia

Allyn and B
Boston • London • Toronto • Sydney • Tokyo

Series Editor: Ray Short
Series Editorial Assistant: Christine M. Shaw
Editorial-Production Service: Spectrum Publisher Services
Manufacturing Buyer: Louise Richardson
Cover Administrator: Linda Dickinson
Cover Designer: Suzanne Harbison

Copyright © 1993 by Allyn and Bacon
A Division of Simon & Schuster, Inc.
160 Gould Street
Needham Heights, Massachusetts 02194

Library of Congress Cataloging-in-Publication Data

Managing Classroom Behavior: A Reflective Case-based Approach / James
  M. Kauffman . . . [et. al.].
        p.   cm.
    Includes bibliographical references and index.
    ISBN 0-205-14109-9
    1. Classroom management.   2. Classroom management—Case studies
  I. Kauffman, James M.   92-25488
  LB3013. M326 1992   CIP

Printed in the United States of America

10 9 8 7 6 5 4 3 2 1   97 96 95 94 93 92

Contents

Preface

When teachers are not successful in helping students learn and enjoy school, the reason is likely to be, in large measure, the difficulty they experience in managing classroom behavior. Many teachers who become discouraged, feel "burned out," or leave the profession attribute their unhappiness in teaching to their difficulty in managing students' behavior. Managing students' behavior has always been a demanding task, but it has become much more exacting during the past decade. What experienced teachers tell us, what we read, and what we see in schools—every reliable indicator—tells us that disruption, aggression, disinterest in school, social withdrawal, and other forms of undesirable behavior are increasingly common in nearly all schools. Without effective strategies for dealing with unacceptable and troublesome behavior, teachers are unlikely to have a career in teaching and even less likely to enjoy and be successful in their chosen profession. Furthermore, students are very unlikely to learn what they should when their teachers are unhappy and feel defeated.

We understand both the immensity of the challenge of students' behavior in today's schools and the importance of preparing teachers for that challenge. This book represents our efforts to help prospective and in-service teachers meet that challenge as reflective practitioners of the profession of teaching. Our experience in working with students of teaching, whether in preservice training programs or in the field, has led us to the conclusion that the typical expository style of textbooks and the typical lecture-discussion format of courses are inadequate.

In the late 1980s, we began experimenting with a different approach—the case method of teaching, which has been used for decades in schools of business and law. We found much in the case method to recommend it, and we became convinced that it could become the model for some, but not all, of the courses we teach in education. The case-based approach, it seemed to us, was a "natural" for an applied course in classroom behavior management because successful management requires the kind of reflection and analytical skills case analysis demands. Nevertheless, we discovered that teaching cases without readings that provide a foundation of basic concepts about reflection on behavior management issues was also unsatisfactory. For a course in classroom behavior management, we found no texts that presented the information we found most pertinent in a manner designed to encourage reflective analysis of teaching practices. This book was born, in our minds, of necessity. Over a period of several semesters, we collected and wrote cases of our own and used them in our teaching. The cases included in this book are ones we have taught and found useful in helping teachers think through the complexities of dealing effectively with troublesome classroom behavior.

In Part I, we provide an overview of basic concepts that our experience leads us to believe are essential to classroom behavior management. Each chapter begins with an advance organizer—an outline of the major headings, giving the reader a preview of the questions we will be addressing. The body of each chapter is organized around a common framework: (1) An opening statement about the topic of the chapter, (2) vignettes illustrating problems of the type we will be discussing, (3) the major questions on which we are asking the reader to reflect, (4) consideration of the questions for reflection, and (5) a brief chapter summary. At the end of each chapter, we list references providing the basis for many of our statements and providing resources for further study.

Our intention is not only to present basic concepts succinctly but to induce in readers a process of self-questioning that carries forward from the first chapter to the seventh and that is intimately connected to how one analyzes cases. We have not prepared a "cookbook" or behavior management manual. Rather, our approach is based on the assumptions that asking good questions is a prerequisite for finding good answers and that the preparation of reflective professionals requires primary attention to question-asking. Thus, although we make some specific suggestions regarding behavior management, we raise more questions than we answer. Our writing style, we hope, is both readable and conducive to reflection. We have deliberately written without the usual number of reference citations and used reference notes to indicate specific sources that are especially pertinent to our statements. We hope our readers will pursue the concepts, strategies, or issues we address by consulting references and resources at the end of the chapter.

In Part II, we offer cases for analysis. Some are cases we have written following interviews with teachers, others were written by teachers or intern teachers themselves. All the cases are factual—they are not hypothetical, and the only changes in the facts of the cases are those necessary to protect the identities of the individuals about whom they are written. We have not chosen cases that are tied to specific chapters in Part I. Based on our experience, we believe that such categorization of cases is artificial. Each case suggests problems and analyses to which most or all of the chapters in Part I are relevant. One aspect of the case-based approach that is frustrating, yet that makes case-based teaching and learning particularly challenging and exciting, is the multitude of perspectives from which one can view any given case and the multiple problems each case presents. That is also one of the strengths of the case-based approach—it reflects the real-life complexities we do not ordinarily encounter in brief vignettes, hypothetical examples, and straightforward exposition of principles.

Case-based teaching is relatively new in teacher education. Consequently, you may not have any prior experience in case analysis. The process of case analysis is one you can learn only by doing it. Your instructor will lead you and your fellow students through the analysis of cases by asking you to prepare study questions and guiding your discussion of various aspects of the cases. Some of our cases are divided into parts: Part A and Part B. For these cases, Part A is included in this book. Part B, a continuation of the case, will be provided by your instructor after you have discussed Part A and tried to predict what might happen next.

If your experience is anything like that of the students with whom we have used these materials, you will find case-based learning highly intriguing and rewarding. We hope you enjoy both parts of this book and find them useful in thinking about how you manage students' behavior.

We acknowledge with thanks the teachers who shared their experiences to make the compilation of these cases possible. Preservation of their anonymity is necessary to protect them and the other individuals involved. We are also grateful to the University of Virginia's Commonwealth Center for the Education of Teachers and to its director, Robert F. McNergney, for providing the encouragement and support that helped bring our efforts to fruition.

J.M.K.   M.P.M.   S.C.T.   D.G.N.   D.P.H.
Charlottesville, VA

Part I

Developing a Reflective Approach to Problems

C h a p t e r **1**

Identifying Behavior Problems

Questions for Reflection
Could this problem be a result of inappropriate cirriculum or teaching strategies?
What do I demand and prohibit—and what should I?
Why do certain behaviors bother me, and what should I do about them?
Is this behavior developmentally significant?
Should I focus on a behavioral excess or a deficiency?
Will resolution of the problem solve anything else?

Managing classroom behavior is a complex task, one that requires self-questioning and careful reflection that even the best teachers must work to acquire and maintain. This self-questioning and reflection should begin as soon as a teacher becomes concerned about the behavior of a student or group. First impressions about a problem can be misleading. Our experiences in classrooms with children and youth lead us to believe that even outstanding teachers sometimes jump to conclusions about what the problem is rather than taking a more reflective, analytic approach to identifying it. As a consequence of not being sufficiently reflective and analytical, a teacher can waste a lot of time and energy dealing with a problem that is not the most important while neglecting a more significant problem. Consider two teachers' reflections on their initial mistakes in identifying problems (see vignettes, Sally and Sam, page 4).

Effective teaching requires much more than keeping students' behavior under control. Yet, without reasonable control over students' classroom behavior, a teacher will have no chance of being effective. Behavior management skills are necessary but not sufficient for good teaching. Because behavior management skills are necessary, some educators and parents make the mistake of judging the competence of a teacher solely on the basis of how well the class is controlled. Because these skills are not sufficient, other educators and parents misjudge a well-managed class as an indication that the teacher is more concerned about control than teaching. We hope that as you

3

Sally: Kevin was a first-grader who drove me nuts by doing all kinds of things that were not just irritating but kept me from being able to teach effectively. It seemed he was always out of his seat when he was supposed to be working. He grabbed things from other kids and pestered them when they were working. He yelled out things to me when I was across the room. He whined. At first, I thought if I could only keep him in his seat I'd be making a lot of progress. So I devised a plan for rewarding him for working at his desk—at first, you know, for just a couple of minutes at a time, then for gradually longer periods. And he began staying in his seat more. But I realized after a while that the other problems weren't getting any better and that there was a bigger problem. The bigger problem was noncompliance. Kevin just about never did what I told or asked him to do, and staying in his seat to do his work was just one of those things. When I finally figured out that getting him to be reasonably obedient was the real problem, I started teaching compliance as a skill in short lessons. Then I really saw a change in all these things that at first I saw as separate problems. I wish I'd gotten the bigger

picture right away, before I spent a couple of weeks on just keeping Kevin in his seat.

Sam: A couple of years ago, the kids in the high school where I taught often wore hats. A lot of the boys wore a baseball hat or painter's hat just about everywhere they went. The school administration didn't have any rules about wearing hats, so I had to make my own. I have this "thing" about wearing hats in homes, restaurants, schools, and so on. It seems impertinent to me. The way I was raised, you just don't do it. I think it's disrespectful, and I just want to grab these guys' hats and tell them to keep them off until they get outside. So I spent a lot of my time and psychic energy on hats. I made a strict no-hats rule in my classroom, and I enforced it successfully most of the time. But I ended up having some serious conflicts with kids, too, especially because I was the only teacher in the school who strictly prohibited hats. I wish I'd been able to see at the time that the real problem was my intolerance for a cultural custom that differs from mine. Sure, I have a right to my feelings, but the real issue was how I could exercise control of myself, not a custom of these kids that many see as harmless.

study issues in behavior management you will carefully examine your own concerns and values about controlling the students you teach.

- How much control is enough?
- How do I judge the amount of control necessary in a given circumstance?
- What means of control are legitimate?
- How do I learn to relinquish and regain control?

To a large extent, these and similar questions can not be answered for you. They are matters that you must address for yourself—as a teacher exercising informed, professional judgment.

Questions for Reflection

We suggest that when you believe a behavior problem in your classroom needs attention and correction you begin at the beginning—by asking yourself questions that will help you focus on what the problem really is. Only after you have identified it accurately can you feel secure in analyzing the problem and planning ways to manage it. The questions you need to ask yourself include the following:

1. Could this problem be a result of inappropriate curriculum or teaching strategies?
2. What do I demand and prohibit—and what should I?
3. Why do certain behaviors bother me, and what should I do about them?
4. Is this behavior developmentally significant?
5. Should I focus on a behavioral excess or a deficiency?
6. Will resolution of the problem solve anything else?

Could this problem be a result of inappropriate curriculum or teaching strategies?

As teachers, we have a tendency to overlook the fact that what and how we teach can contribute directly to our students behaving in ways that we find irritating, perplexing, or unacceptable. This tendency comes, in part, from the difficulty of keeping the student's perspective in mind while concentrating on teaching. It is easy to forget how frightening new tasks can be, how overwhelming assignments and expectations can look, how boring and mindless requirements can seem, how devastating criticism can be, or how irritating it is to be unengaged in activity and spend long periods simply waiting. It is easy to fall into the trap of assuming that because *most* students learn what we are trying to teach, *all* students can, or that all students will respond similarly to our teaching methods.

Consider life in the classroom as a student might experience it. For example, imagine yourself as a student who sees no point in what she or he is being asked to learn, one who finds the materials or instructions utterly confusing, one who sincerely believes that she or he can not do what is expected, one who is expected to repeat again and again a lesson already mastered, one who is expected to listen attentively once more to instructions he or she has heard and comprehended and followed many times already, one who often hears criticism but seldom receives recognition for work well done. Under these circumstances, students are prone to misbehave—to talk to and distract their neighbors, daydream, become irritable, make hostile remarks, and so on. Adults, including teachers themselves, respond in like manner to these conditions. Think of your own behavior, or the behavior of some of your colleagues, in poorly taught classes, at "boring" faculty meetings, or "useless" in-service sessions. Adults, too, are vulnerable to inappropriate behavior, given certain conditions.

Before assuming that there is more to the problem, reflect on questions like these:

- How relevant to or functional in the student's life is the curriculum?
- Do I have the option of teaching something more relevant and functional?
- To what extent could I individualize instruction?
- How successfully is this student or group performing in the curriculum?
- Am I using an approach to teaching that provides too little structure, too much direction, too little positive feedback, or too much criticism?
- How frequently do my students have an opportunity to respond to academic tasks?
- What percentage of the time are they actually actively engaged in learning?
- How and how much could I change the teaching strategies I use?

Behavior problems are not always a result of poor choices of curriculum or teaching strategies, but these must be the first factors we examine. No other questions are appropriate until we can conclude that the what and how of instruction are not the likely source of the problem. That is, we should not proceed until we are satisfied that what we are asking students to learn is important to their lives, that they are being challenged by assignments but not overwhelmed by failure, that they have frequent opportunities to respond as well as listen, that they are performing with a high degree of success and receiving frequent positive feedback about their performance. These are essential elements of effective instruction. If they do not characterize what happens in the classroom, then the first order of business is to put them into practice.

We are aware of the difficulties teachers can encounter in using effective teaching practices. The best efforts of excellent teachers sometimes fail to convince students of the importance or relevance of the subject matter. Sometimes teachers are given little or no control over what they are to teach, the materials they are to use, or the instructional methods they are to employ. In such cases, it may be difficult to resist pressures from administrators or supervisors who impose curriculum and methods on a system-wide or school-wide basis. Sometimes teachers are faced with overwhelming problems in being able to meet the instructional needs of individual students. They may have too many or too diverse a group of students to be able to serve them all adequately, or they may be told not to expect relief or assistance. Advocacy for additional resources to meet students' needs may fall on deaf ears or receive hostile responses. Teaching is not an easy profession. It sometimes demands risk-taking, sometimes dictates compromise, and always requires struggling with dilemmas. You might ask yourself other questions:

- If I am uncertain about whether my teaching strategies or curriculum are contributing to behavior management problems, what steps could I take to resolve my uncertainty?
- How might I evaluate whether my teaching approximates the best practice?

A summary of the fundamentals of good teaching as a leading research group describe them is found in Table 1–1. You may wish to compare the descriptive statements in the table with your own practice.

TABLE 1–1   Highlights of Research on Good Teaching

From studies of the Institute for Research on Teaching and those of others, we have a picture of effective teachers as semiautonomous professionals who:

- are clear about their instructional goals;
- are knowledgeable about their content and the strategies for teaching it;
- communicate to their students what is expected of them–and why;
- make expert use of existing instructional materials in order to devote more time to practices that enrich and clarify the content;
- are knowledgeable about their students, adapting instruction to their needs and anticipating misconceptions in their existing knowledge;
- teach students metacognitive strategies and give them opportunities to master them;
- address higher- as well as lower-order cognitive objectives;
- monitor students' understanding by offering regular appropriate feedback;
- integrate their instruction with that in other subject areas;
- accept responsibility for student outcomes;
- are thoughtful and reflective about their practice.

Source: Porter, A. C., and Brophy, J. (1988). Synthesis of research on good teaching: Insights from the work of the Institute for Research on Teaching. *Educational Leadership, 45* (8), p. 75.

What do I demand and prohibit–and what should I?

Assuming that you are satisfied with the what and how of your academic instruction, that they do not set up circumstances under which students' misbehavior is predictable, you should next consider your expectations for students' behavior. You will need to consider what you demand of your students and what you will not tolerate in two areas: academic performance and social behavior. You will also need to question your expectations for both the class as a group and for individual students. The specific behavior demanded and prohibited varies considerably from teacher to teacher. Some teachers have very different expectations for individual children, compared to those they hold for the class as a whole. In some cases, management problems are not so much students' behavior as their teachers' inappropriate expectations.

There is much greater agreement among teachers about what behavior is prohibited than what is demanded. That is, teachers find it easier to specify what they will not tolerate than to specify the appropriate behavior they demand. Perhaps this is a result of our culture's focusing on punishment as the primary means of behavior control. Yet knowing what to demand of students–and, therefore, what to reward with recognition and praise–is a key to good behavior management.

Adults' expectations for children are matters of constant debate in American culture, and teachers' expectations for their students are a central point of controversy.

- How do teachers arrive at their expectations for their students?
- To what extent are they biased by labels or stereotypes?
- Are they based on cultural standards that discriminate unfairly against some students?
- Are they based on cultural traditions that are not necessary for, or are even inconsistent with, effective teaching?

With these questions in mind, we consider the kinds of academic and social behavior most teachers demand and prohibit.

Demands

Most teachers demand a set of academic and social behaviors that describe a good or "teachable" student.[1] For example, most teachers indicate that the following types of behavior are critical for success in their classrooms: following their established classroom rules, listening to their instructions, following their written instructions and directions, complying with their commands, doing in-class assignments as directed, avoiding breaking classroom rules even when encouraged to do so by peers, producing work of acceptable quality for his or her skill level, and having good work habits (e.g., making efficient use of class time, being organized, staying on task). Far less agreement is found regarding demands for behaviors such as these: using social conventions appropriately (e.g., saying "thank you," "please"), volunteering for classroom activities, working on projects with other students, sharing materials with others in a work situation, and initiating conversations with peers in informal situations.

Prohibitions

Teachers generally agree that they will not tolerate certain types of behavior in their classrooms. Among those behaviors considered intolerable by the vast majority of teachers are the following: inappropriate sexual behavior, stealing, physical aggression, destruction of property, behaving inappropriately to correction, refusing to obey classroom rules, disturbing or disrupting the activities of others, self-injury, lewd or obscene gestures, ignoring teacher warnings or reprimands, creating disturbance during class activities, cheating, and being verbally aggressive toward others. Considerably less consistency among teachers is found in teachers' intolerance of behaviors like the following: pouting and sulking, asking irrelevant questions or making irrelevant remarks, refusing to play games with others, ignoring the social initiations of others, or refusing to share.

Opinions about teachers' expectations—what they demand and prohibit—vary widely among educators and the public. One commonly heard criticism of teachers' expectations is that they are too low, that teachers get about what they expect from students and they expect too little. Another criticism is that teachers' expectations are too traditional and self-serving. According to this criticism, teachers set expectations for their students based primarily on the way they themselves were taught. Furthermore, their expectations are designed primarily to make their job more comfortable rather than to create effective environments for learning and to avoid criticism in a system that places a high value on conformity. This stifles innovation and maintains the status quo in schools. Another criticism is that teachers' expectations are not sensitive to cultural and ethnic differences in behavioral styles or norms, thus they are unnecessarily restrictive and oppressive. In any given situation, we must consider the extent to which these criticisms are justified.

A major concern of educators is that teachers' expectations should not be too high or too low. Expectations that are too high are problematic because students and teachers are too frequently confronted with failure. Students become demoralized because they almost never are able to measure up to the teacher's standards. Teachers, too, become demoralized and drop all expectations because they lose confidence that their students can succeed. Expectations that are too low do not challenge students, convey to students the idea that they are not capable of meeting higher standards, and result in low achievement and frequent misbehavior. Low expectations become self-fulfilling prophecies.

High expectations for some students will be too low for others, depending on what they have experienced and learned. Getting the expectations just right requires a high degree of knowledge and sensitivity to students' abilities and histories of success and failure. "The same high expectations for all students" may sound egalitarian and be consistent with some educators' philosophy. The problem with the same expectations for all, however, is that individual differences are ignored.

Nearly every teacher insists on some basic rules of the classroom that apply to all students.[2] It is as if the teacher has said, "If you want to be a part of this classroom, then there are certain things you have to do and certain things you must not do." Yet most teachers have more specific expectations for one or more individuals in the class. For certain students, the teacher may interpret the standard expectations differently or articulate a different set of demands and prohibitions. Having different expectations for different students presents a dilemma, however, for, on the one hand, having the same expectations for everyone ignores individual differences and, on the other hand, individual expectations could be based on favoritism or negative bias. This is not an easy dilemma to resolve. It is part of the extremely difficult task of creating classrooms and schools that are both sensitive to individual differences and consistently enculturating.

Another major concern is that expectations must be communicated clearly and consistently. Sometimes behavior problems arise because the teacher has not articulated clearly and frequently what is demanded and prohibited in the classroom. The teacher may feel that her or his expectations have been communicated, but if the students are asked they cannot state what their teacher expects. Perhaps the teacher has never discussed, posted, or reviewed any classroom rules. Some teachers and administrators have so many rules that students cannot reasonably be expected to remember them all. We have been in schools in which the rules were several single spaced typewritten pages in length and in classrooms where 20 or more rules were posted. This kind of rule "overkill" does not result in effective communication of expectations.

Sometimes teachers state one set of expectations verbally but in subtle ways convey a different set of expectations through their nonverbal behavior. For example, a teacher might state that students need to raise their hands and wait to be called on before speaking, yet respond to students who call out answers. A teacher might also say that showing respect for others in the class is expected but respond to some students with sarcasm. Teachers may also fall into a pattern of changing expectations from day to day so that students are never quite certain which rules are in effect or how they will be enforced.

Very likely, you will be able to state what you demand and prohibit in your classroom. Once you have done so, however, you will need to reflect on several questions about those expectations:

- Are my expectations justifiable, and if so, on what grounds?
- Have I clearly, repeatedly, and consistently communicated those expectations?
- Are they biased against certain groups of students?
- Do I hold the same expectations for everyone, or do I make exceptions for certain individuals?
- If I make exceptions, how do I justify and communicate them?

Why do certain behaviors bother me, and what should I do about them?

We have been discussing expectations as if they are somehow objectively determined with little reference to teachers as individuals with highly personal, emotional responses to children's behavior. This is due to the fact that to a great extent teachers must be able to take a detached, objective view of their behavior and that of students. Nevertheless, teachers must maintain a high level of self-awareness and understanding of how their personal responses to behavior affect their interactions with students.

Our expectations for behavior—what we consider polite, proper, crass, threatening, profane, annoying, unacceptable, and so on—are a result of our upbringing in a particular culture and family, our exposure to other cultures, groups, and individuals, and our personal values, biases, preferences, and sensitivities. Some of our expectations are based on what we believe children need to learn if they are to have friends, be employable, and avoid incarceration or institutionalization. These expectations might be considered universal in American culture. Other expectations, however, are based primarily on more limited social conventions or personal preferences. Sometimes it is difficult to judge whether an expectation is based primarily on broad social or cultural norms or on personal preferences.

Student teachers and those new to the profession are sometimes unprepared for the "tacky" or "trashy" behavior many children may exhibit in the classroom. Many children engage in behavior that may seem intended to challenge, threaten, badger, humiliate, irritate, agitate, or disgust others, including their teachers. Behavior of this type may indicate that a child has serious emotional problems, but often it does not. Furthermore, different individuals may find certain behaviors annoying, offensive, or threatening while others do not. The language children use at school, particularly certain forms of address and various words that some consider vulgar, is a type of behavior about which teachers often have very different opinions. One teacher may bristle at a student's use of the word "nerd" or "dork," while another may feel these words are a legitimate part of all youngsters' vocabulary. The mannerisms of certain children may elicit excruciating tension in one teacher but be easily tolerated by another. The way we respond to a given type of behavior may say a lot about how we have been reared and enculturated in school ourselves. It may also say a lot about how secure and competent we feel as a teacher. Sometimes it merely indicates a hypersensitivity to certain characteristic behaviors of an individual child.

Given that certain behavioral characteristics may "set us off," how should we deal with them as professional educators? All of us find certain idiosyncrasies of others particularly grating and have our pet peeves, and it is legitimate to have especially intense reactions to some types of behavior that others may be able to tolerate far more easily. Yet teachers must be very careful not to foist their personal standards on their students and not to become peevish or tyrannical in response to personal irritations. They must also be aware of how certain types of behavior may make them defensive and distract attention from important issues. Behavioral standards and personal preferences raise issues of the rights of students and teachers, teachers' responsibility to exercise self-control, and recognition of developmental risk.

- When do you have a right to impose your personal standards on your students?
- When do your students have a right to behave as they wish?
- How do you determine whether your expectations are consistent with broad social or cultural demands or primarily idiosyncratic?
- How do you recognize that you react intensely to a particular student's behavioral characteristics, yet avoid treating this student unfairly?

These are often not easy questions to answer, and they frequently demand careful reflection. You may need to solicit the opinions and suggestions of other teachers, an administrator, a parent, or others more detached from the situation to help you weigh these issues.

Imagine that you have become aware that a behavior irritates you primarily because it offends your personal values or sensitivities. You consider it inappropriate or bothersome, but you realize that in the broader social context it is trivial; you consider it "tacky" and grating, but you know that it is essentially harmless. It might be wearing a hat indoors, as Sam described in the vignette on page 4, or it might be a child's tone of voice that you consider grating or disrespectful. What should you do about it? You might try to change it. On the other hand, you might try to learn to live with it. Perhaps it isn't worth trying to change; maybe it isn't something you feel you can learn to tolerate. In either case, considerable self-control might be required on your part to deal effectively with the situation. Sometimes teachers find that managing their own behavior—learning techniques of self-control—is the better solution to dealing with irritating student behavior. Unfortunately, some teachers seem not to learn to ignore irritating but unimportant misbehavior, and they become embroiled in conflicts about trivia.

Also unfortunately, some teachers learn to ignore or tolerate behaviors that they should not. They allow students to behave in ways that have serious consequences. Some types of behavior should not be ignored or tolerated because they entail developmental risk for students. That is, these behaviors are signs that students have serious problems that are likely to become worse without effective intervention.

Is this behavior developmentally significant?

Developmentally significant behavior problems are those that have serious long-term consequences for children. That is, if the problems are not resolved, it is highly likely that the children who exhibit them will have increasing difficulties in becoming self-sufficient, reasonably well-adjusted adults. Many of these behaviors are seen by teachers at school. It is extremely important that teachers recognize the seriousness of these behaviors and intervene as early and effectively as possible to change them. Although there may be other types of developmentally significant behavior, most of them fall into one of four primary categories: academic failure, aggression, depression, and problems with peers.

Academic Failure

Children who fail to acquire basic academic skills in the early grades, those who fail grades or earn failing grades in courses, and those who drop out of school are at high risk for social and economic difficulties. In fact, failure to learn basic skills in reading and math in the early grades is likely to lead to later failure and dropping out. At least a moderate level of success in academics is necessary for most children to develop a healthy self-image. Students who are not academically competent are often shunned or rejected by their peers. Thus identifying a student's skills that lag seriously behind grade level and taking steps to bring them up to grade expectations are critically important.

At first thought, identifying and remediating deficient academic skills as early as possible seems a straightforward task. A little reflection, however, will bring out some of the persistent problems in defining and dealing with academic failure.

- How do I establish performance expectations for a particular grade level or age of student?
- How far behind grade expectation is far enough to merit special attention? That is, how much failure does a child have to experience or how far behind the rest of the class must a child fall before I become seriously concerned?
- If I perceive that a student is falling significantly behind, how should I intervene?
- How can I tell whether my efforts to help are merely making matters worse?
- When I've exhausted my own knowledge in trying to improve the student's performance, whom should I consult?
- Under what conditions should I conclude that I don't have, and can't acquire quickly enough, the skills or resources necessary to address the problem effectively?

These are only a few of the questions you must consider in dealing with academic failure. Questions such as these have sparked much controversy among educators for many decades, and the answers are not obvious. Nearly all educators agree that a teacher has an obligation to see that every child in her or his class experiences frequent success and achieves at the highest level possible. Nevertheless, nearly everyone who has been a teacher has experienced failure in dealing with a student's failure—despite our best efforts, we have not been able to help a student experience an acceptable level of success in our classroom and approximate the achievement of the peer group. The way we assess our limitations and deal with our failures as teachers is extremely important for the education profession, and even more important for the futures of the students we are assigned to teach.

Academic failure usually brings with it a variety of behavior problems.[3] Children who do not keep up with their peers in academics seldom have a strong sense of personal worth and dignity. They have little to lose, and sometimes much to gain in the way of attention from peers and adults, by getting into trouble. If they do not become persistently annoying to others, they may withdraw from social interaction and become morose. In either case, they are laying the groundwork for further academic failure, which leads to increasing tendency to aggression or depression or both. Breaking the vicious cycle of academic failure and maladaptive behavior may require attention to multiple aspects of the problem. Besides academic remediation, the teacher needs to be ready to intervene in other developmentally significant behavior problems.

Aggression

Numerous writers have noted that aggression is endemic in our country—"as American as apple pie," as some have put it. Violence is the primary active ingredient in the popular media. Hostile aggression and other antisocial behavior, both physical and verbal, is pervasive in many neighborhoods and schools. Homicide is one of the leading causes of death among adolescents and young adults. Because of its pervasiveness in our culture, and because of the long-held misconception that it is not a highly significant indicator of mental illness, hostile aggression is often ignored. We are not referring here to the adaptive assertiveness that is necessary for survival in a humane society. We are referring to hyperaggressive behavior that harms others or destroys property, drives others away by threats or intimidation, prompts counteraggression, and is incompatible with learning prosocial behavior or academic skills. It is behavior that is inappropriate for one's age and the social circumstances in which it occurs.

Extremely aggressive behavior carries an extremely high risk of other developmental problems. The earlier in life a child's behavior is highly aggressive (compared to other children of the same age), the longer a child's history of aggressive acts, the more different settings in which a child is aggressive (e.g., playground, classroom, bus, home, neighborhood), and the more varied a child's aggressive acts (e.g., hitting, kicking, biting, pinching, scratching, throwing things, threatening, extorting), the worse the prognosis for later adjustment and achievement.[4] Thus, early intervention to stop aggression and teach more prosocial behavioral alternatives is critically important.

If a child stands out from his or her peers as being highly aggressive, we are doing the child and our society no favor by ignoring it, assuming that the child will outgrow it, or justifying it on grounds that the expression of aggression may help to reduce it. Engaging in aggressive antisocial acts is not good for children; it does not help them develop appropriate behavior, but increases the likelihood of further aggression, maladjustment, and social and academic failure. Effective means must be sought to stop it and replace it with more adaptive, self-enhancing behavior.

As is the case with the other topics we've discussed, easy answers to most of the questions raised by students' aggression are not to be found, although we can offer a few with considerable confidence.

- What aggressive acts fall within the developmentally appropriate range for youngsters of a particular age, social background, and gender?
- When is aggressive behavior acceptable because it falls within the student's cultural norms, although it violates the teacher's expectations?
- How much aggression should be tolerated in a regular classroom, given the teacher's best efforts to reduce it, before the student is excluded from the regular class?

Questions like these will likely stir controversy among educators for many decades to come.

Nevertheless, we feel confident in stating that hyperaggression is a developmentally significant type of behavior that teachers must take seriously. The more clearly a child is verbally and physically aggressive than the norm for his or her age, the more we should be concerned for the child's future. We also feel confident in stating that educators' responses to students' aggression must not be counteraggressive. That is, truly effective interventions in aggression do not involve adults' aggression against students.[5] The response to aggression must be, to the greatest extent possible, nonviolent and instructive. We discuss this matter further in subsequent chapters (see especially Chapter 3).

Depression

Only within the past couple of decades have developmental psychologists, mental health professionals, and educators begun to understand the nature and extent of the problem of depression among children.[6] Suicide and suicide attempts by children and adolescents have increased dramatically during the past 20 years, and suicide is now one of the leading causes of death among adolescents and young adults. Furthermore, studies of the thoughts and feelings of children and adolescents have revealed that they become depressed in much the same way adults do and that depression is a far more frequent problem among minors than previously thought. Depression is often a problem related to aggressive behavior, social withdrawal, hyperactive and inattentive behavior, and academic failure.

The signs of depression in children and adolescents may be similar to those in adults. Any radical change in behavior should be taken as a signal that the student may be experiencing depression. If a student exhibits one or more of the following characteristics over a period of weeks, he or she should be evaluated for depression by a mental health professional:

- inability to experience pleasure, or depressed mood
- sudden change in appetite or weight
- disturbance of sleep (insomnia or constant drowsiness)
- exaggerated, excessive, or retarded physical movement

- loss of energy, feelings of fatigue
- feelings of worthlessness, self-reproach, excessive guilt
- inability to think, concentrate, or make decisions
- talk about suicide

Signs of depression are often ignored by teachers. Frequently, depressed students do not disrupt the class (although this is not always the case), so it is easier for the teacher not to become involved with their behavior. Ignoring depressed students may compound their problems, however, because depressed students often feel isolated, neglected, or "invisible." They often have given up on themselves and see themselves as unworthy of other people's concern.

How should you respond to students whom you suspect are depressed? Perhaps the most important thing you can do is persist in attempts to establish communication with these students, to reach out to them and let them know you have noticed them and are not going to give up on them. You should also ask others to help—a school psychologist or counselor who can evaluate students and, if necessary, make referrals to mental health professionals. In some cases, you may encounter problems that call for difficult personal or professional judgments. Some depressed individuals are extremely manipulative and are masters at getting others entangled in their problems in ways that are not helpful. If possible, you should seek the advice of a mental health professional who is familiar with the student.[7]

Problems with Peers

Children and adolescents who do not have friends their own age or who are in frequent conflict with their peer group are at high risk for other developmental problems. Those who have serious academic problems are not typically popular among their peers. Those who are aggressive are, understandably, typically rejected by their classmates. Those who are depressed often cut themselves off from social interaction with others. Whatever the reason, the student who ends up a loner is not headed down a developmental path likely to lead to personal fulfillment and satisfactory adult adjustment.

Healthy psychological and social development depends on friendships—close, mutually gratifying relationships that involve giving and receiving support in dealing with life's vicissitudes. Teachers frequently overlook or downplay the importance of peer relationships in school. The focus in schools tends to be on individual achievement and deportment, with social relationships relegated to a secondary or even minor role. When thinking about a student who is exhibiting problem behavior you should inquire about his or her friendship patterns and social interactions:

- To what extent is this student accepted or rejected by peers?
- Does this student have friends, including a best friend?
- When this student interacts with others, who initiates the interaction?
- How sensitive is this student to influence, positive and negative, from the peer group?

These and more specific questions should help you assess the extent to which peer problems are an issue, a topic to which we return in Chapter 5.

Finally, we note that academic failure, aggression, depression, and problems with peers are not mutually exclusive categories of behavior. Academic failure often is accompanied by aggressive behavior, depression, poor peer relations, or all of these. Not all depressed students are socially withdrawn; a substantial percentage manifest aggressive behavior as part of their depression. The prognosis usually is worse for an individual with multiple, interrelated problems. Students who fail academically and are aggressive and depressed are at particularly high risk for severe and protracted personal problems.

Should I concentrate on a behavioral excess or a deficiency?

When we think of behavior management, we typically think first of things we want students to stop doing–behavioral excesses. A student who exhibits highly aggressive behavior is one we're likely to see as needing to stop doing aggressive acts. Just as important, however, are the things students do not do but should–behavioral deficiencies. The aggressive student needs to learn alternative nonaggressive ways of interacting with others. Trying to reduce excessive behavior without at the same time increasing deficient behavior is a common tactical blunder that contributes to many teachers' behavior management difficulties.

Because it is so easy to focus on getting rid of maladaptive behavior and forget the importance of teaching alternative adaptive behavior, some have suggested always thinking of "behavior pairs." A behavior pair includes both a behavior that should be increased and one that should be decreased. For example, completing school work might be paired with not paying attention to work. This pairing would help the teacher focus on what is desired and what should be rewarded (completing work), not just on what is undesirable (inattention). The pairs chosen must be opposites–things that are very difficult or impossible to do simultaneously–so that increasing the desirable behavior is virtually certain to decrease the undesirable behavior.

The pairing of behaviors to be increased and decreased helps the teacher avoid thinking only of the negative side of how the student should behave. This is critically important because effective and humane behavior management relies very little on punishment and is primarily a matter of supporting desirable behavior.

Before assuming that you have identified a behavior management problem with sufficient clarity, ask yourself these questions:

- How do I want this student to behave?
- Can I describe in positive terms what I want the student to do?
- For each behavior I want the student to stop or decrease, have I identified an alternative behavior that I want the student to learn or exhibit more often?

Will resolution of the problem solve anything else?

Some behavior management problems seem overwhelming because there are so many things that need changing. It is hard to know where to begin. Some problems seem insurmountable because the behavior is so extreme. It is hard to know how much change is reasonable to expect. When faced with such problems teachers can easily become hopeless or adopt strategies that are self-defeating. They may begin attacking problems at random or choose to work on trivial behaviors, or they may reach the unfortunate conclusion that unless they are able to resolve a problem completely their efforts have been wasted. An important skill in behavior management is identifying problems in ways that help one know where to begin and how to judge progress. We offer two caveats about managing difficult behavior problems. First, you should not expect to solve all problems at once. Second, you should not expect to resolve all problems entirely.

The more difficult the management problem, the more important it is to address first things first—to look for key behaviors that, if changed, will make the greatest difference overall. People who are very experienced in managing difficult children are able to identify the behavior in a constellation of problems that holds the key to generalized improvement. For example, Gerald Patterson and his colleagues, who have helped hundreds of families achieve better control of aggressive children, have found that not minding (disobedience to parents and teachers) is a key behavior. Rather than starting with other aggressive acts, Patterson and others have found that it is often better to start dealing with an aggressive child by working on compliance or obedience. Furthermore, experience shows that it is wise to begin a behavior management program by concentrating on one important behavior and dealing with it very consistently. The temptation to deal with multiple problems at once must be resisted. Thus if you are confronted by a child or class with multiple problems you should ask yourself the following:

- Can I identify one behavior that seems likely to be the key to general improvement?
- If I resolve this one problem, what else is likely to change?
- How can I develop a consistent, effective plan for attacking this key behavior?

Teachers are typically judged harshly by others, and they sometimes fall prey to harsh self-judgment. And teachers, like most of us, are impatient with behavioral change that is slow or incomplete. Sometimes it is difficult to know whether the amount of change achieved in a behavior is worth the teacher's effort or whether change is occurring rapidly enough to meet a reasonable goal.

- Has the change in behavior made a significant difference in the classroom, even if the change is not total and complete?
- Is the change worth my investment of time and energy?

- How much more change should I try to accomplish?
- What is a reasonable goal?

Teachers vary considerably in what they see as worthwhile progress. Too often, in our judgment, teachers devalue progress or behavioral change because they expect themselves to accomplish a radical and permanent transformation of a pupil or their class.

Summary

Skillful classroom behavior management requires that teachers first engage in careful reflection about the nature of the problem. Before attempting to analyze a management problem in detail or develop a management strategy, teachers must consider their own behavior, values, sensitivities, and knowledge about pupil behavior. The behavior management problem may be a consequence of inappropriate curriculum or teaching strategies. Teachers' demands and prohibitions may be poorly communicated or overly lax, strict, or inappropriate for the class or certain students. Teachers must examine the reasons that certain behaviors of pupils are bothersome and decide whether self-control (personal tolerance) or intervention to change the pupil's behavior is more appropriate. Some types of behavior, especially academic failure, aggression, depression, and problems with peers, carry particularly high risk for continuing developmental problems. Teachers must be particularly concerned about these. In thinking about the nature of behavior problems, teachers must take care to give at least as much concern to what they want students to do as they give to what they want students not to do. In dealing with multiple behavior problems, teachers must begin with a single important behavior. They must attempt to find a key behavior that, if changed, will be likely to produce more generalized improvements. Teachers must also weigh carefully their goals and standards for judging success.

References and Resources for Further Study

The following references provided the basis for many of our statements in this chapter. You may wish to consult selected references for additional information on specific topics. Our reference notes for this chapter refer to sources in this list.

Curriculum and Teaching Strategies

Brophy, J. and Good, T. L. (1986). Teacher behavior and student achievement. In M. C. Witrock (Ed.), *Handbook of Research on Teaching* (3rd ed.). New York: Macmillan.

Kameenui, E. J. and Simmons, D. C. (1990). *Designing Instructional Strategies: The Prevention of Academic Learning Problems.* Columbus, OH: Merrill/Macmillan.

Porter, A. C. and Brophy, J. (1988). Synthesis of research on good teaching: Insights from the work of the Institute for Research on Teaching. *Educational Leadership, 45* (8), 74–83.

Simmons, D. C., Fuchs, D., and Fuchs, L. S. (1991). Instructional and curricular requisites of mainstreamed students with learning disabilities. *Journal of Learning Disabilities, 24,* 354–360, 353.

Wallace, G. and Kauffman, J. M. (1986). *Teaching Students with Learning and Behavior Problems* (3rd ed.). Columbus, OH: Merrill/Macmillan.

Teachers' Demands and Prohibitions

Kauffman, J. M., Lloyd, J. W., and McGee K. A. (1989). Adaptive and maladaptive behavior: Teachers' attitudes and their technical assistance needs. *Journal of Special Education, 23,* 185–200.

Kauffman, J. M., Wong, K. L. H., Lloyd, J. W., Hung, L., and Pullen, P. L. (1991). What puts pupils at risk? An analysis of classroom teachers' judgments of pupils' behavior. *Remedial and Special Education, 12*(5), 7–16.

Kerr, M. M. and Zigmond, N. (1986). What do high school teachers want? A study of expectations and standards. *Education and Treatment of Children, 9,* 239–249.

Walker, H. M., and Lamon, W. (1987). Social behavior standards and expectations of Australian and U.S. teacher groups. *Journal of Special Education, 21* (3), 56–82.

Walker, H. M. and Rankin, R. (1983). Assessing the behavioral expectations and demands of less restrictive settings. *School Psychology Review, 12,* 274–284.

Wong, K. L. H., Kauffman, J. M., and Lloyd, J. W. (1991). Choices for integration: Selecting teachers for mainstreamed students with emotional or behavioral disorders. *Intervention In School and Clinic, 27,* 108–115.

Developmentally Significant Behavior

Guetzloe, E. C. (1991). *Depression and Suicide: Special Education Students at Risk.* Reston, VA: Council for Exceptional Children.

Kaslow, N. J. and Rehm, L. P. (1991). Childhood depression. In T. R. Kratochwill and R. J. Morris (Eds.), *The Practice of Child Therapy* (2nd ed.) (pp. 43–75). New York: Pergamon.

Kauffman, J. M. (1993). *Characteristics of Emotional and Behavioral Disorders of Children and Youth* (5th ed.). Columbus, OH: Merril/Macmillan.

Kazdin, A. E. (1991). Aggressive behavior and conduct disorder. In T. R. Kratochwill and R. J. Morris (Eds.), *The Practice of Child Therapy* (2nd ed.) (pp. 174–221). New York: Pergamon.

Lloyd, J. W., Hallahan, D. P., Kauffman, J. M., and Keller, C. E. (1991). Academic problems. In T. R. Kratochwill and R. J. Morris (Eds.), *The Practice of Child Therapy* (2nd ed.) (pp. 145–173). New York: Pergamon.

Loeber, R. (1982). The stability of antisocial and delinquent child behavior: A review. *Child Development, 53,* 1431–1446.

Patterson, G. R. (1982). *Coercive Family Process.* Eugene, OR: Castalia.

Patterson, G. R. (1986). Performance models for antisocial boys. *American Psychologist, 41,* 432–444.

Poland, S. (1989). *Suicide Intervention in the Schools.* New York: Guilford Press.

Stark, K. (1990). *Childhood Depression: School-Based Intervention.* New York: Guilford Press.

Reference Notes

1. See Kerr and Zigmond (1986) for research with secondary level teachers and Walker and Rankin (1983) for research with elementary teachers.

2. Kauffman et al. (1989) and Wong et al. (1991) discuss differences among general education teachers' demands and prohibitions.

3. See Kauffman (1993) for discussion of the relationship between academic failure and other characteristics of children and youth with emotional or behavioral disorders.

4. See Loeber (1982).

5. See Kazdin (1991) and Patterson (1982, 1986) for elaboration.

6. See Kaslow and Rehm (1991).

7. See Guetzloe (1991), Poland (1989), and Stark (1990) for suggestions for teachers.

Chapter 2

Analyzing Behavior Problems

Questions for Reflection

What are my assumptions about why students behave the way they do?

What are the most important explanations of the misbehavior?

Are there causes of the misbehavior that I can control to a significant degree?

How should I define the behavior I am concerned about and identify its antecedents and consequences?

How might I identify the probable cognitive and affective aspects of the misbehavior?

How should I measure the behavior problem and changes in it?

What is a reasonable goal?

Skilled professionals in all fields analyze problems carefully before attempting to solve them. Physicians, engineers, lawyers, and merchants, as well as teachers and school administrators, are typically more successful when they are able to figure out why a problem exists and how bad it is before they start doing something to change it. People with little knowledge of a field of study or professional practice sometimes become impatient with a competent practitioner's approach to a problem because they believe the analysis should be simple and quick. The competent practitioner knows that apparently simple problems can be unexpectedly complex and understands that time spent in analysis can save time in the long run and prevent embarrassing, costly, or tragic errors. Here are two examples of teachers' reflections on their analysis of behavior problems (see vignettes, Sally and Trisha, page 22).

If you approach a behavior management problem with the questions we posed in Chapter 1, you have already started the process of problem analysis. You will have begun eliminating wrong explanations for the behavior and be ready to analyze in more detail the extent of the problem, its possible causes, and where you might find a point of leverage in changing it. Understanding the possible and probable cause (or

Sally: When I first started working on the problems I had with Kevin, I wasn't aware of how often he failed to do what I told him. Actually, I had quite a few kids in my class who were noncompliant pretty frequently, but Kevin was really by far the worst. The thing that helped me most when it came to getting a handle on the problem was keeping track of my directions and Kevin's compliance for a while. I kept a daily record of how often I told Kevin to do something and the percentage of times he did what I told or asked him to do.

It was a little extra work to remember to keep track of my directions and his compliance, but it wasn't too bad. I was surprised by the numbers—by how often I was giving him a command of some sort and by the low percentage of the time he obeyed me. He seemed to me to give me the most trouble during reading, which he doesn't do very well, especially when I was working with another group. He also had lots of trouble during less structured activities, like lunch break and art. So I focused my record keeping on reading and lunch period, which included noon recess. I carried a little card in my pocket, and every time I told or asked him to do something I just made a tally mark. Then, if he complied within about a minute I circled the tally. I divided the card into two sections, the top for reading and the bottom for lunch period.

By keeping track, I had a daily record of how often I was telling him to do things and how often he complied in those two situations. I did this for about five days

before I started the compliance training, so I had a pretty objective basis for judging whether the training was making a difference on compliance in reading and math. Of course, subjectively I felt things were getting a lot better too, but the data on the cards helped me confirm that he really was improving.

Trisha: It took me a while, but I finally figured out something that was a really effective reward for Sammy, this kid who was such a whiner and a crier. He was so spoiled by his mother and grandmother that there just seemed to be nothing I could offer him that he was interested in working for. Then one day I was talking to him about other things and he said something about not liking the name Sammy. He said his name was Sam, like his daddy's name, and that's what he wanted to be called. He thought Sammy was a "baby name," as he put it, and he didn't want to be called that anymore. So then I thought, aha! There's something he maybe cares enough about that I can use it as leverage to get him to stop crying. This is a kid who would have 10 or 15 crying fits just about every day, most of them lasting for just a couple of minutes but some going on for an hour. I think we really turned the corner with him when I had a little talk with him about his crying and his name and I told him I'd have to call him Sam, and so would all the other kids, as long as he wasn't crying. If he cried, we could call him Sammy, but otherwise we'd use his grown-up name.

"Trisha" is based on Kaufhold, S. and Kaffman, J.M. (1974). Sammy: Frequent crying spells. In J. Worell and C.M. Nelson, *Managing Instructional Problems: A Case Study Workbook* (pp. 188–193). New York: McGraw-Hill.

causes) of behavior is often critical to choosing means for trying to change it. Measuring the level of the problem and having a way of judging progress are essential for making good decisions about whether to try a different strategy and when to consider a problem resolved. Setting clear and reasonable goals helps teachers avoid getting discouraged or becoming overly optimistic. In brief, as you analyze problems you need to ask yourself important questions about your assumptions and intentions.

- What are my assumptions about why students behave the way they do?
- Can I identify causal factors that I can change?
- What is sufficient evidence that I am making progress in changing behavior?
- Exactly what am I trying to accomplish?

These and other questions are part of a careful analysis of behavior management problems leading to well planned strategies for change.

Questions for Reflection

We suggest that after you have made an initial identification of a behavior management problem you analyze the problem further before planning an intervention strategy to change it. Your analyses should include possible causal explanations for the misbehavior, measurement of its level and trend, and the goals you hope to accomplish. A careful analysis will greatly increase your chances of devising a management plan that is effective and efficient. The questions you need to ask yourself include the following:

1. What are my assumptions about why students behave the way they do?
2. What are the most important explanations of behavior?
3. Are there causes of the misbehavior that I can control to a significant degree?
4. How should I define the behavior I am concerned about and identify its antecedents and consequences?
5. How might I identify the probable cognitive and affective aspects of the behavior?
6. How should I measure the behavior problem and changes in it?
7. What is a reasonable goal?

What are my assumptions about why students behave the way they do?

All of us make certain assumptions about why people behave as they do. These assumptions are important because they are often the basis for our attempts to change behavior. Examining our assumptions about the causes of behavior is important because beliefs are related to actions; what we do may change as a result of a change in our beliefs. But what we do also affects what we believe. Beliefs and actions influence each other, along with other factors in one's environment.

Historically, philosophers, religious leaders, and scientists have offered a variety of explanations for human behavior. Their explanations might be grouped into four basic categories:

- Biological—physiological or biochemical factors, such as brain damage, disease, or malnutrition.
- Environmental—events in the objective external world, such as the consequences of behavior, the settings in which it occurs (e.g., signs or signals that certain behavior is expected or prohibited), and the examples provided by others.
- Psychological—internal mental characteristics or phenomena, such as thoughts, feelings, or emotional states.
- Spiritual—supernatural or mystical forces, such as god(s), devil(s), or other spirits.

Present-day explanations also include all four of these categories of variables. None of these categories is entirely discounted by most people, although most of us give more credence to some than to others, particularly in cases of highly unusual behavior. In analyzing a behavior problem it is important first to clarify the basic assumptions with which you approach human behavior.

- How do I typically explain people's behavior?
- What is the basis for my beliefs about behavior?
- To what extent are my beliefs based on scientific evidence about the causes of behavior?

The general notions you have about the causes of human behavior will likely influence significantly how you attempt to explain the misbehavior about which you are concerned.

What are the most important explanations of the misbehavior?

Most people believe that there are multiple causes of human behavior, some of which are more important than others for explaining particular acts or patterns of conduct. For example, a person might believe that biological, psychological, and environmental factors are all involved to some degree in causing human behavior. However, in explaining why a given student behaves in a particular way in the classroom, this person might also believe that the most important causes are psychological (e.g., feelings of self-efficacy, predictions of the consequences of behavior) and environmental (e.g., the consequences of behavior and signals that certain behavior is expected). A task of the teacher is to identify the most likely and most relevant explanations of classroom behavior for individual students and specific circumstances.

We suggest that teachers pay particular attention to explanations of behavior that are supported by ample empirical research and offer a teacher the possibility of a reasonable measure of control. Concentrating on relevant and reliable explanations means, in our opinion, that the teacher will pay particular attention to environmental and psychological causes. They are the causes most directly related to teaching and the ones that are supported by the most scientific evidence. We are not suggesting that other explanations have no relevance or validity, simply that in most cases the greatest research support and opportunity for the teacher's control are likely to be found in explanations having to do with environmental and psychological variables.[1]

Some of the potential causes of behavior problems are things that teachers can not control, at least not directly. Nearly all of the possible biological reasons for misbehavior are matters for which the teacher can only make a referral or ask for assistance from a health care professional or social worker. Sometimes misbehavior is a result of brain dysfunction, disease, or problems of diet or health. The teacher must be aware of these possibilities and refer the student for evaluation by qualified health care providers. Sometimes misbehavior is a result of abuse or neglect at home or is related to other home or family conditions over which the teacher has no direct control. Again, it is extremely important for the teacher to be aware of these potential sources of problems and request evaluation or assistance when needed.

Being unaware of or ignoring potential causes of problem behavior can result in unfortunate outcomes. For example, missing or ignoring signs of malnutrition, seizures, abuse, and so on will result in failure to address critical aspects of the problem and could frustrate the teacher's attempts to ameliorate it. Teachers must be keenly aware of possible causes of behavior problems other than those that are most obvious. This requires extensive knowledge of child development and a high level of sensitivity to children's life circumstances.

When analyzing a behavior problem you should consider the range of possible causes and try to make sure that no plausible explanation for the behavior is ignored.

- What possible reasons for the behavior can I identify?
- Have I asked for evaluation by other professionals to eliminate certain explanations for the behavior that might be important?

We offer two cautions: First, possible or plausible causal factors often remain matters for speculation. In many cases, the precise causes of misbehavior can not be identified with certainty. Furthermore, there are typically several plausible causes, not just one. Second, finding the cause or causes does not necessarily lead directly to an effective intervention. That is, the cause does not necessarily tell us the "cure." Some causes can not be reversed (e.g., brain damage, a history of abuse). Some interventions are effective even though the cause is not known. For example, stimulant medication may benefit a hyperactive child even though the cause of the hyperactivity can not be found. Consistent consequences may result in improvement of an aggressive student's behavior even though we can only speculate about the causes of aggression.

Where does this leave you as a teacher who is trying to analyze a behavior problem? We reiterate two points that we made earlier. First, it is important to recognize the possible range of causes of students' behavior and request the services of other professionals who may be able to rule out certain causal factors or obtain help that you, as a teacher, may not be able to provide. Second, you should give your greatest attention to the causal factors that you can alter.

Are there causes of the misbehavior that I can control to a significant degree?

Teachers often can make a difference in the lives of their pupils by getting involved in matters that extend beyond the classroom or school. For example, some teachers make repeated home visits for the purposes of understanding and improving the home lives of their students by working with parents. Others are able to make a significant contribution to improving students' lives by counseling students or obtaining health and social services for them outside the school environment. We caution that teachers can become overinvolved in their students' lives and neglect their own needs (and those of their own families). We also recognize that there are limits to parental involvement in behavior management (see Chapter 7). Furthermore, circumstances such as living in a community far from the school in which you teach may preclude your extensive involvement with your pupils outside the classroom or school. Yet, you might ask yourself whether there are circumstances or conditions outside your classroom or school that may be contributing to a pupil's misbehavior and that you might be able to change.

Clearly, conditions and events in the classroom and school can contribute to behavior management problems. As we mentioned in Chapter 1, the curriculum and teaching strategies teachers use, the demands and prohibitions of teachers and administrators, and the influence of peers are critical factors that can set the stage for appropriate or inappropriate student behavior. Of all the possible factors that can contribute to behavior problems, events and conditions in the classroom are the factors over which the teacher has the greatest control. Furthermore, a substantial body of empirical research suggests that teachers can often improve their students' behavior substantially if they change certain classroom conditions.

Of all the questions you could ask yourself about the causes of behavior, we believe the single most important one is this: What is happening in my classroom that might contribute to misbehavior?[2] There are a variety of ways of examining events and conditions in the classroom and their possible effects on behavior. In our opinion, the most useful way of analyzing what happens in the classroom is to define the behavior of concern as an observable event and then examine what happens immediately before it occurs (antecedent events) and after (consequences).[3]

How should I define the behavior I am concerned about and identify its antecedents and consequences?

Defining a behavior problem is not always as simple as it first appears. Many times, students exhibit a wide array of "trashy" behaviors that are irritating and divert attention from the central issue (recall, for example, Sally's description in Chapter 1). Sometimes it is difficult to focus in on the problem and describe it as a particular behavior the student does or does not do. Nevertheless, precise description of what the student does or does not do is extremely important in identifying antecedents and consequences and devising an intervention plan. Moreover, precise description is important for measurement of the problem—assessing its severity and evaluating progress or success.[4]

Defining Behavior

Defining a problem as something a student does or does not do requires that you observe carefully just how the student behaves and describe it clearly as an action. You must describe the behavior objectively and precisely enough that nearly anyone else observing the student independently could state whether or not the behavior occurred. You must take care not to describe the problem as your reaction or interpretation (e.g., "He irritates me") or the student's internal state (e.g., "She goes off into her dream world"), as these are too subjective and measurement of them will be too unreliable. "She cries," "She looks off into space with a blank expression," "He rummages in his desk," "She talks without permission," or "He does not complete his homework" are behavioral definitions that are probably objective enough that, with some clarifications, two or more independent observers could agree about whether they occurred in most instances.

If you have defined a behavior precisely and objectively, you will be able to observe when it begins and when it stops. That is, the behavior will not be described as a state of being ("unmotivated," "hostile," or "reticent," for example) but as a measurable event or episode (e.g., "slept," "cursed or hit someone," "did not respond to direct question"). A good test of whether you have defined a problem appropriately for our discussion here is to ask yourself one of these questions:

- Could I count occurrences of this behavior so that I could state how many times it occurred today?
- Could I measure the duration of these episodes so that I could state how many minutes of the period the student was engaging in this behavior?
- Could I glance at the student and tell whether or not the student was engaged in the behavior at that instant?

Once you have defined the behavior so that you can observe its occurrence accurately, you will be able to observe what happens just before and just after it occurs. As we discuss further in Chapter 3, the events that occur just before and just after a behavior can have a powerful influence. In fact, one explanation of behavior is that it is almost entirely a function of its antecedents and consequences. We urge you to take careful note of the events surrounding the behavior you are concerned about, because you may be able to alter these surrounding events and thereby modify it.

Identifying Antecedents

You might begin by noting the antecedents. What are the events or conditions that immediately precede instances of the problem behavior? You may need to keep anecdotal records or other written notes in order to describe a pattern of when, where, and under what conditions the behavior most often occurs. Your objective in examining the antecedents of the behavior should be to anticipate it—to predict it accurately. If you find that the behavior occurs only under certain conditions or immediately after certain events, then you might be able to resolve the problem completely or in part by changing the antecedents. For example, if you find that the student nearly always exhibits the problem behavior when you give an instruction or make a request, you might try varying the way you present the task to avoid the problem. Sometimes giving a student a choice rather than a direct instruction (e.g., "Which of these pages would you like to do first?" rather than "I want you to complete these two pages") will make a significant difference in his or her compliance.

We are not suggesting that the antecedents of troublesome behavior can always be identified or that you can always alter them. Sometimes the antecedents may be internal events or states. For example, a student experiencing high levels of anxiety or having a psychotic condition may be responding to perceptions or thoughts that you can not observe directly. Sometimes the antecedents are things you can not change. For example, you may find that the student exhibits the problem behavior whenever there is an announcement on the school intercom, a condition that you are not able to alter. At the least, however, identifying the antecedents should help you anticipate problems and know where and when to focus your intervention.

Identifying Consequences

Equally as important as noting the antecedents is identifying the consequences—events that occur after the behavior you are concerned about. What does the student "get" out of the behavior? You must remember that appearances can be deceiving; the student may appear to get nothing or to receive only negative consequences for the behavior, yet persist in doing it. A rewarding consequence, or a punishing one, for one person is not necessarily the same for another. You must also look for multiple consequences.

Sometimes the "payoff" for behavior has several components, and the nature and sequence of these components can be highly significant. In the classroom, for example, a student may frequently misbehave in ways that result in criticism or punishment from adults (perhaps including restrictions or extra work) and the scorn of peers. A consequence of this kind of behavior is the attention—often the undivided attention—of one or more adults, several peers, perhaps the entire class. Although the misbehaving student seems to earn only punishment, the attention that goes with the punishing consequences may be a sufficient reward to outweigh the intended effect of the punishment. For some students, seeing adults get upset is a very powerful rewarding consequence. Enticing the teacher into an emotional outburst may, for these students, be well worth enduring any punishment adults are likely to devise.

Identifying Chains of Events

Antecedents, behaviors, and consequences occur in continuous strings or chains of events. To analyze relationships among them, you may need to keep a running record of the sequence of events. Here is an example, drawn from a case written by John Shearer, "Foul Language: Classroom Trouble" included in *The Intern Teacher Casebook* (edited by Judith H. Shulman and Joel A. Colbert, ERIC Clearing House on Teacher Education). It recounts a sequence of events in a junior high school classroom. The incident involves a student's (Richard's) use of language that the teacher (John) considered foul:

1. John asks for volunteers to name sources of pollution
2. Richard raises hand, says "I know, teacher! Farts!"
3. boisterous laughter and noises from class
4. John calls class to order, cautions Richard
5. Richard flails arms in air, says "Teacher, teacher! Malcolm just told me to [sexually graphic phrase]!"
6. howling, whistling from class

We could label the first three events in this sequence in what is called an ABC analysis. For example, we might label these events as follows:.

Antecedent	Behavior	Consequence
J asks for volunteers	R raises hand says " . . . Farts!"	laughter, noises from class

We might go on to label the next three in a similar fashion:

Antecedent	Behavior	Consequence
J calls for order, cautions R	R flails arms, makes sexual comment	class howls, whistles

Notice that in such analyses a given behavior can be both a consequence for the behavior it follows and an antecedent for the next behavior in sequence. Thus the teacher's behavior can be a consequence for the student; likewise, the student's behavior can be a consequence for the teacher. We might have chosen to diagram a sequence of ABCs as follows:

Antecedent	Behavior	Consequence
R raises hand says " . . . Farts!"	laughter, noises from class	J calls for order, cautions class

In interactions, individuals provide consequences and antecedents for each other in an ongoing chain of events. Where we start the analysis—which event we choose to label antecedent and whose behavior we choose as the focus—depends on our purpose. The purpose of an ABC analysis is to clarify the sequence of classroom events from a particular perspective, either the student's or the teacher's. It helps us understand what each party is responding to and what each is getting out of the interaction. ABC analyses are usually done for the events surrounding a specific behavior problem episode.

Doing an ABC analysis requires that the sequence of events be recorded accurately. Few teachers will have the help of someone who can observe classroom interactions and record them accurately, although sometimes a classroom aide or support staff (e.g., school psychologist, consulting teacher) can do so. If you must do the analysis yourself, you should attempt to jot notes to yourself whenever possible and reconstruct the sequence of events as soon after the episode as possible. Recalling the exact behaviors and their sequence is critically important. We suggest that if you plan to do an ABC analysis you use a form similar to the one shown in Figure 2-1.

Whenever you are perplexed by classroom behavior, you may need to answer these questions:

- What is the precise sequence of events surrounding this problem?
- Can I clearly identify the ABCs of the interactions that are troublesome?

ANTECEDENTS	BEHAVIORS	CONSEQUENCES

FIGURE 2-1   Form for Recording ABC Analysis

Answering these questions is particularly important for resolving the negative interactions that are called coercion.

Identifying Coercive Interactions

Antecedents, behaviors, and consequences sometimes are characterized by an escalating pattern of aversiveness. That is, starting with an antecedent that is aversive (unpleasant or painful, something the person would like to escape from or avoid), two parties attempt to control each other by increasingly powerful negative consequences. Positive consequences are not an outcome of these interactions. For example, abused and aggressive children often behave in ways that are extremely irritating to adults; they seem to "ask for" punishment, and adults typically oblige by providing it. Their irritating behavior typically is followed by harsh reprimands, if not physical abuse from parents, which sets the stage for even more highly irritating acts. They and their parents become embroiled in a battle that someone "wins" (usually the parent when the child is younger) by being more obnoxious, threatening, or brutal and forcing the other party to stop. This type of interaction is known as coercion.

Coercion is sometimes a feature of classroom interactions between teachers and pupils and of interactions among classroom peers. The pupil may find the teacher's expectations and demands aversive and attempt to avoid them by misbehaving. The teacher finds this aversive and restates the demands or increases them, perhaps threatening or punishing the student. The student feels challenged to become more obnoxious, tempting the teacher to respond with more severe punishment or threats. This kind of coercive interaction continues until either the teacher or the student "wins" or an uneasy and temporary truce is made. Following is an example of a coercive classroom interaction.

- teacher asks student to complete page of math problems
- student says, "I don't know how to do this crap!"
- teacher says, "Yes you do, we just did some problems like these yesterday. Get started now."
- student slams book closed, saying "Ain't doin' it!"
- teacher goes to student's desk, opens book, hands student pencil, says in angry tone, "Get started now!"
- student shoves book off desk
- teacher squeezes student's shoulder, growls "Pick that book up, young man!"
- student jumps to feet, says "Get your hands off me, bitch! You pick it up! You can't make me do nothin'!"
- teacher yells, "That's it! I've had enough of this! Pick that book up and get to work now or you're outa here to the office!"

Many students are masters at drawing teachers into these power struggles; they know how to start wars of will, and often how to win them. Students sometimes lay coercive "traps" for teachers by engaging in irritating conduct, knowing that many teachers will respond to them by engaging in a power struggle, often over minor misbehavior. The more skillful the teacher is at behavior management, the more tactics she or he has for ending the struggle early, typically by finding a way to disengage and avoid stepping into the trap. Clearly, coercive interactions are not desirable, although they are common in many classrooms. Understanding the process of coercion is important in finding ways to deal effectively with it. We discuss the underlying process—negative reinforcement—in Chapter 3.

Becoming keenly aware of coercive interactions is critically important to successful use of more positive behavior management strategies. In analyzing the ABCs of your classroom interactions, you should be especially concerned about those that involve a coercive process. Ask yourself questions about the early stages of the interactions.

- How do these interactions start?
- At what point could I avoid the process by disengaging from it?
- How could I start a different interaction that does not end in a power struggle?
- How could I try to replace coercive interactions with ones ending in positive consequences?

Sometimes you might discover that in trying to find answers to these questions you need to consider your own thoughts and feelings and those of your students.

How might I identify the probable cognitive and affective aspects of the behavior?

Teachers who are expert in behavior management pay attention to more than what students do. They recognize that thoughts and feelings are intimately connected to the way people behave. They would like students to think rationally and feel good about themselves, and they know that helping students develop cognitive skills and appropriate affective responses is part of their responsibility. Furthermore, finding out what students think and how they feel, and reflecting on one's own cognitive and affective reactions, can provide useful insights in finding a resolution to behavior problems. We are not referring here to analyzing unconscious motivations or hidden meanings. Rather, we are referring to paying attention to what students say and their reactions to situations that reveal their thought processes, preferences, and emotional responses.

Teachers often suspect that students' thoughts and feelings cause them to misbehave, and often they would like to change the way students think or feel about things. Someone else's thoughts and feelings can not be manipulated directly, however. Furthermore, changing the way students think or feel will not *necessarily* change the way they behave. Teachers can directly manipulate many of the antecedents and consequences of students' classroom behavior, however, and in this way they may be able to alter thoughts and feelings. But how does one identify the thoughts and feelings that might be involved in behavior? The simplicity of the answer belies the complexity of the task: by watching and listening.

Observing and interpreting the affective components of students' behavior requires sensitivity to subtle individual differences and changes in posture, facial expression, and voice. Students who are the easiest to manage are likely to be also the easiest to "read." Those who are difficult to manage and interpret often express themselves in atypical ways or send mixed signals—verbal and nonverbal messages that contradict each other. In fact, they often put teachers in a quandary by saying one thing and doing another.

Teachers often learn much about students' thoughts and feelings indirectly through casual conversation. Perhaps most teachers could learn more by asking students directly what they think or how they feel about their own behavior and important aspects of the classroom and school. Some students are reticent in expressing their feelings; others tell teachers what they think they want to hear; a few may make deliberately misleading statements. Teachers must be aware of these possibilities. Nevertheless, asking students is often better than relying solely on indirect interpretations.

One important benefit of finding out what students think and feel about themselves and aspects of their school experience is that it often gives the teacher a clue about rewarding consequences for behavior. Trisha's reflection on Sam (at the beginning of this chapter) provides an example of a teacher's identifying a student's feelings about something that could be used as a highly effective consequence. In Chapter 4 we discuss other benefits of talking with students about their behavior. For purposes of analyzing a behavior problem, however, we suggest you ask yourself these questions:

- Are students giving me clues to their feelings about themselves and the classroom?
- Have I listened and observed carefully to detect the emotions that accompany their behavior?
- Have I asked them directly what they think and feel about specific events or conditions?

How should I measure the behavior problem and changes in it?

Measurement is a fundamental requirement of many professional activities. Physicians, engineers, and economists, for example, typically rely heavily on measurements related to their analyses of problems and base their professional recommendations and judgments of success on measured outcomes. In education, measurement of students' academic skills is an accepted part of professional practice. Measurement of problem behavior is expected as an integral part of an intervention plan.

We recognize that there are many different types of measurement ranging from subjective impressions to extremely precise quantitative assessments. Choosing the most helpful and efficient type of measurement and choosing to measure the right things are keys to competent professional practice. Your choice of measurement may depend on how you answer several questions related to the problem behavior.

- How serious do I believe the problem is?
- How am I going to judge the success or failure of my intervention?
- To whom do I need to communicate about the problem and my success or failure in dealing with it?

Ordinarily, the more serious you believe the problem is the more concerned you should be about devising a precise way of measuring it. For minor problems, subjective impressions may suffice; for major problems, objective data are critical. More precise and objective measurement is needed for more serious problems for three reasons: (1) the consequences of the problem and its resolution are greater for both the student and the teacher, therefore greater care in assessment is required; (2) the more serious the problem the more likely the teacher will need to communicate objective, reliable information about it to others; (3) subjective impressions can be very misleading.

Subjective impressions about behavior and changes in it are often included in summary reports of student progress. Some teachers keep diaries in which they record their impressions or reactions to students' behavior. These subjective, nonquantitative statements may be useful, but they have severe limitations in cases of serious behavior problems. Teachers seldom define problem behavior as precisely as we have suggested they should when they record only their subjective impressions.

A systematic anecdotal record is a more precise level of measurement. Such a record requires that the teacher jot down observations about the student's behavior whenever it occurs or at regular times (e.g., daily). Anecdotal records can be quite helpful, but they do not allow one to make a careful assessment of the problem unless they include sufficient detail to allow an ABC analysis. An ABC analysis is actually a very careful anecdotal record in which specific events are recorded in time sequence to describe a behavior and its antecedents and consequences. A still more precise and quantitative level of measurement is often needed, however.

Direct daily measurement is extremely helpful in assessing serious problems and evaluating the effects of interventions. Measurement of this type requires that the teacher define the behavior as an objectively observable act, as we have suggested, and record occurrences of the behavior to establish its quantitative level. We cannot detail the methods of direct daily measurement here (you may want to consult one or more of the references at the end of the chapter). However, an example may show some of the advantages of such methods. We use the case of Trisha's work with Sammy, described in a vignette earlier in the this chapter. We do not provide all the details of Sammy's case but focus on those aspects related to direct daily measurement.

Sammy was a third-grader who, Trisha realized, had a serious problem because he frequently disrupted the class with loud crying and wailing. His peers teased him when he cried, contributing further to the problem. Trisha knew Sammy cried a lot, but she didn't know how to describe how much he cried or how to measure changes in this problem behavior. She knew that his crying episodes sometimes lasted only a couple of minutes and that others lasted for as long as an hour.

We considered how Trisha could measure Sammy's crying in such a way that she would have a more objective basis than her subjective impressions or general description ("He cries a lot!") for describing the seriousness of the problem and changes in the behavior. Trisha could have measured the duration of each crying episode by jotting down the time (or starting a stopwatch) when each crying episode started and again when it stopped. This would have had certain advantages, as she could then have described total crying time in minutes per day, percent of the day spent crying, and number of episodes per day. Because she was responsible for the entire class and had no aide or other person who could keep such a record, however, we needed to find a measurement system that she could manage, but one that would still give her an objective description. Trisha agreed that she could keep an index card handy and make a tally mark for each crying episode. This gave her the number of episodes per day, but not their duration. She kept a daily log sheet, on which she wrote down the number of tallies for the day.

By the time we began working with Trisha to resolve Sammy's crying, she had already tried several approaches: comforting, ignoring, and reprimanding him. None of these seemed to bring about improvement, although Trisha had no objective basis for judging the effects of her attempts to get Sammy to stop. She had given up on the problem until she could think of something new to try. We suggested, therefore, that she first record Sammy's crying episodes under "baseline" conditions, before she tried anything else. After recording his crying episodes for ten days, she reported that Sammy cried an average of about 17 or 18 times per day (see Figure 2–2). She felt that reducing the number to 6 or 8 times per day would be a reasonable goal. Next, Trisha tried totally and consistently ignoring Sammy when he cried. After five days of ignoring, the average was still about 15 (14, 15, 17, 15, 16 times per day), a little lower but not very close to her goal. Then she discovered that Sammy wanted to be called Sam. She designed an intervention in which she and his peers called him Sam—except when he was crying, when they tried to ignore him but could call him Sammy. Trisha also asked Sam to record his own behavior by entering his behavior on her graph each

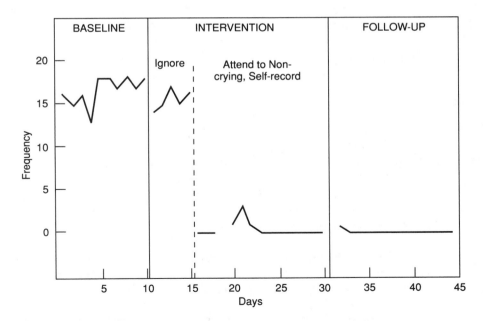

FIGURE 2–2 Sammy's Crying

day. The number of crying episodes then dropped to nearly zero (0, 0, 1, 4, 1, 0, 0, 0 for the next eight days). Trisha continued counting for a while longer (during follow-up) but eventually was satisfied that the problem had been resolved.

Trisha's direct daily measurement helped her plot Sammy's progress more objectively and quantitatively than her subjective impressions. Her subjective impressions were useful, but her objective measurement gave her subjective perceptions a firmer base. Another method Trisha used was plotting her data daily on a graph, which is commonly done as a part of direct daily measurement. Her graph, shown in Figure 2–2, gave her a quick, easily interpretable picture of what was happening with Sammy's behavior.

What is a reasonable goal?

The ideal behavior management strategy resolves the problem immediately, completely, and permanently without creating any new ones. We nearly always have to settle for something less than the ideal. As teachers, we try to help our students learn patience and persistence and how to obtain gratification from partial successes. Teachers should be models of these characteristics by setting goals for themselves and their students that challenge but do not overwhelm. What does this mean for how you should approach setting a goal for the outcome of your intervention in a behavior management problem? We can not answer this question directly because it is a matter for careful reflection in the individual case.

We can, however, suggest that goals are more likely to be reasonable when teachers define the problem behavior precisely and devise a way of measuring it objectively and accurately. Precise definition and quantitative measurement often help teachers notice progress that they might not perceive if they rely on more global, subjective impressions.

Summary

Careful analysis of a problem prior to designing a plan for attacking it is an accepted part of professional practice. Analyses of behavior management problems should include examination of one's assumptions about the causes of behavior, as beliefs may significantly affect the choice of intervention strategies. Some explanations of behavior are more important than others for teachers. We suggest that teachers should focus on the causal factors that have the greatest support in empirical research and offer teachers the greatest opportunity for control. For teachers, classroom events are usually the most important causal factors. Analysis of classroom events should begin with precise definition of the problem behavior. Particularly important in analyzing the problem is identifying antecedents (events immediately preceding the behavior) and consequences (events immediately following). Sequences or chains of antecedents, behaviors, and consequences (ABCs) may be described to clarify interactions from a particular individual's perspective. Coercive interactions, in which each party struggles for control by presenting increasingly aversive consequences for the other, are especially important to analyze carefully. The cognitive and affective aspects of behavior should be identified through careful listening and observation, as they may provide clues for resolving behavior problems. Analyzing behavior problems requires that the teacher select an appropriate approach to measurement. Direct daily measurement allows the most precise level of assessment and is particularly useful in evaluating the effects of interventions. Precise definition of behavior and accurate measurement of it helps teachers set appropriate goals for behavioral change.

References and Resources for Further Study

The following references provided the basis for many of our statements in this chapter. You may wish to consult selected references for additional information on specific topics. Our reference notes for this chapter refer to sources in this list.

Causes of Behavior

Achenbach, T. M. (1982). *Developmental Psychopathology* (2nd ed.). New York: Wiley.

Bornstein, P. H. and Kazdin, A. E. (Eds.). (1985). *Handbook of Clinical Behavior Therapy with Children*. Homewood, IL: Dorsey Press.

Kauffman, J. M. (1993). *Characteristics of Emotional and Behavioral Disorders of Children and Youth* (5th ed.). Columbus, OH: Merrill/Macmillan.

Van Hasselt, V. B., Strain, P. S., and Hersen, M. (Eds.). (1988). *Handbook of Developmental and Physical Disabilities*. New York: Pergamon.

Definition and Measurement of Behavior and ABC Analysis

Alberto, P. A. and Troutman, A. C. (1990). *Applied Behavior Analysis for Teachers* (3rd ed.). Columbus, OH: Merrill/Macmillan.

Kazdin, A. E. (1984). *Behavior Modification in Applied Settings* (3rd ed.). Homewood, IL: Dorsey Press.

Kerr, M. M. and Nelson, C. M. (1989). *Strategies for Managing Behavior Problems in the Classroom* (2nd ed). Columbus, OH: Merrill/Macmillan.

Kerr, M. M. Nelson, C. M., and Lambert, D. L. (1987). *Helping Adolescents with Learning and Behavior Problems*. Columbus, OH: Merrill/Macmillan.

Morris, R. J. (1985). *Behavior Modification with Exceptional Children*. Glenview, IL Scott, Foresman.

Nelson, C. M. (1981). Classroom management. In J. M. Kauffman and D. P. Hallahan (Eds.), *Handbook of Special Education* (pp. 663-687). Englewood Cliffs, NJ: Prentice Hall.

Reference Notes

1. See Achenbach (1982) and Van Hasselt et al. (1988) for further discussion of causal factors.

2. See Kauffman (1993) for extended discussion of classroom causal factors.

3. See Kazdin (1984) and Morris (1985) for further description of the role of antecedents and consequences.

4. See Alberto and Troutman (1990), Kerr and Nelson (1989), and Kerr et al. (1987) for more on the definition and measurement of behavior.

C h a p t e r *3*

Changing Behavior

Questions for Reflection
Have I tried the simplest and most obvious strategies?
What approaches to helping students change their behavior are most likely to be successful?
How might I use the five operations of a behavioral approach?
How can I capitalize on the cognitive and affective aspects of behavior change?
Is my approach positive and supportive of appropriate behavior?

Attempts to change behavior, whether by parents, teachers, politicians, or employers, have traditionally been impromptu. As reliable scientific evidence regarding behavioral change is accumulated and professional practices are more widely shared and evaluated, behavior management is becoming less improvised and more plannned. Today it is possible for teachers to select from a wide variety of strategies for managing classroom behavior. Some are "packaged" as programs, books, or workshops under special titles or trademarks (e.g., *Assertive Discipline, Teacher Effectiveness Training, The Self-Control Curriculum*).[1] Others are presented in textbooks or resource manuals that focus more on underlying principles and their application to unique circumstances. Our approach is to present principles and suggest some initial questions teachers might ask themselves in selecting a management strategy. We also offer some specific suggestions and cautions for using specific strategies. This implies that teachers will not thoughtlessly follow a standard plan or passively accept whatever is offered but, rather, use their knowledge of behavior principles and best professional practices to select strategies with a high probability of success. Our intention is to foster reflective professional practice rather than provide a "formula" or "recipe" for teachers to follow. Mary and Tom provide examples of the kind of thinking we hope to encourage (see page 40).

The wide range of methods and materials for behavior management available today requires a self-questioning strategy on the part of teachers. What have I tried,

Mary: Two years ago, I went through a truly horrible time. I had one of the most difficult groups of kids I've ever taught. I was in terrible shape physically, psychologically, and financially. My whole world seemed to be a mess. I had back problems. My two grown kids both lost their jobs and came back to live with me. My husband had run away. I was deeply in debt. Maybe it was understandable, but I was not positive with the kids in my class. I was cranky. I yelled at them a lot. They got on my nerves. I was unhappy, and so were they. One day my supervisor was in my class and gave me one of those looks—you know, like, What's the matter with you? That was enough to make me stop and think about what was happening in my class and how I'd gotten into a lot of negativism, criticism, nagging, and other depressing kinds of interactions. My life outside school was bad enough, but my experiences in my classroom were just adding to my exhaustion. I knew I had to pull myself together and not let my personal life outside the classroom determine the way I behaved in school. It was really, really hard to do that! For a while, I kept an informal tally (on an index card) of my positive and negative statements to kids. Then I worked hard on being more positive when kids were doing what I wanted them to. I talked about this with my aide, too, and she helped me by watching for kids who were doing what they were supposed to and signaling me to let them know I noticed and approved. Fortunately, I got things turned around to the way I usually teach, with lots more positive than negative interactions with my students.

Tom: My sixth-grade group ate lunch in my room. They brought their lunch trays into the room from the cafeteria. After they ate, they were supposed to go out into the hall to scrape their trays into a waste can and stack their trays on a trolley. Even though I thought I had stated the rule clearly—no more than four students at a time in the hall—I had a lot of difficulty with too many kids going out together. Once five or six of them got out into the hall together, they started horsing around, shoving, pushing, doing gross things with the leftovers, and so on. Naturally, this made a lot of noise and led to problems with teasing, threatening behavior, spilled food, and soiled clothing. Finally, it occurred to me that what might work was some sort of "pass" or object to make the rule easier to monitor, something tangible that would regulate traffic for me. So I got four pieces of bamboo to use as "batons" or passes. The rule was that you could go out to scrape your tray only when you had a baton. The kids actually thought it was kind of fun because they made a game of passing the baton to the next person of their choosing. It worked for this group, but I was aware that it could have created problems, too. Kids could have started doing bad things with the batons. We could have had fights and teasing and hard feelings over who got the baton next. But we didn't. Other things could have gone wrong. But they didn't. If it had backfired—and I was ready for it to do just that—I wouldn't have lost much, if anything, by trying. What I learned was that sometimes little gimmicks work, especially in regulating kids' turns or movement. After all, why do you suppose some stores have customers take a number so they know when it's their turn to be waited on?

and how well have I implemented what I've done? Have I overlooked the simplest potential solution? What reasons do I have to believe that this approach might be successful? Given what I know about child development and this particular problem, what would be an inappropriate strategy? Have I fallen into a pattern of negative or coercive interactions in trying to manage this problem? Am I employing best professional practices in dealing with this situation? These are only a few of the questions teachers must pose for themselves in tackling a behavior management problem after they have made an initial identification and analysis.

Questions for Reflection

When you have reached the point of planning a strategy for changing behavior, it is important to make a wise choice from the options you might try first. Sometimes the simplest and most obvious yet effective strategies are overlooked. We recommend that you consider how you might approach the problem from both behavioral and cognitive perspectives. Whatever the theoretical basis for the strategies you choose, it is critically important that you focus on what you want the student to do and provide a positive, supportive environment for appropriate behavior. You should ask yourself at least the following questions:

1. Have I tried the simplest and most obvious strategies?
2. What approaches to helping students change their behavior are most likely to be successful?
3. How might I use the five operations of a behavioral approach?
4. How can I capitalize on the cognitive and affective aspects of behavior change?
5. Is my approach positive and supportive of appropriate behavior?

Have I tried the simplest and most obvious strategies?

Amid the demands of teaching and the availability of relatively sophisticated or technical information regarding behavioral change, it is easy to forget that simple, direct approaches can be effective. When simple strategies work, they have the advantage of saving time and energy. They also tend to be more "natural" and may avoid the problems associated with highly technical or "artificial" approaches, including difficulties in implementation and failure to obtain long-term improvement in behavior. They are also easier to explain and defend to parents, administrators, and other teachers.

We are *not* suggesting that you take a simplistic approach to behavior management—an oversimplified view that justifies the use of discredited or unethical strategies (e.g., lecturing, sarcasm, corporal punishment). Many classroom behavior problems are complex and have no simple solution. Experience and research show, however, that such simple things as clear and consistent instructions and other uncomplicated strategies sometimes quickly and effectively resolve seemingly intransigent problems.

Simple things may seem obvious to someone else who is taking a fresh look at a situation, but they are easy to overlook when you are the teacher responsible for managing a difficult child or class. We suggest that before attempting a more complicated or elaborate approach you try to get a fresh look at the problem yourself, through self-questioning and reflection, to see whether a simple strategy might work: What is the simplest, most direct approach I could take to this problem? Have I overlooked an obvious tactic that might work? If I have tried a simple, direct strategy, have I implemented it well and consistently?

If a simple approach resolves the problem, you will have saved a lot of time and energy; if it doesn't, you will have lost little or nothing. We cannot catalog all the simple, direct, and effective strategies teachers might use. Teachers constantly amaze us with their creative but simple, direct solutions to common problems. We can, however, suggest several categories of interventions that are often overlooked. These include instructions, examples, and choices.

When faced with the problem of a student who either does things he or she should not or fails to do what is desired, we believe the simplest, most direct approach a teacher can take is using instructions—telling the student what is expected. You may at first think that this approach is unrealistic because the student obviously has been told how to behave. After all, most students who present behavior problems have been talked to quite a lot. Nevertheless, you might reflect on your communication with this student and consider whether you have used instructions in the most effective way:

- Have I made the instruction as simple and clear as possible? Adults often clutter and complicate their instructions with too much verbiage. Consider the differences between following: (1) "It's time to get ready to go out to recess, so pick up everything and put it away and get ready to go, because, like I've told you, we're not going to go out to recess until everything's cleaned up and put away where it belongs and you're in your seats." (2) "It's time for recess. Put your things away so we can go."
- Have I given the instruction in a clear, firm, nontentative, but polite and nonangry way? Adults are more likely to get compliance when they speak as if they expect compliance and treat the student with respect. Questions are not instructions. For example, "Could you do this problem now?" indicates that you would like the student to do the problem but leaves you vulnerable to the response "No!" An alternative way of expressing your expectation might be "Please try this problem now."
- Have I made certain I have the student's full attention before giving the instruction? Students sometimes don't follow instructions because they never really "hear" them. Do not make the mistake of assuming that instructions are being received and processed when the student is doing something else or not looking at you when you give them. Sometimes it is helpful to have the student repeat the instruction to make sure it was heard.
- Have I given one instruction at a time? Sometimes adults are unaware that they are piling instruction upon instruction without waiting for compliance with the first before giving a second. When repeated instructions are given in a short period of time, the student will likely perceive the adult as nagging.

- Have I been careful not to give too many different instructions? Students often feel they are ordered about constantly. Instructions will be more effective when they are carefully considered and only essential ones are given.
- Have I waited a reasonable time for compliance before assuming that the instruction will not be followed? It is easy to make the mistake of demanding instantaneous obedience. Giving the student the "room" of a few minutes often avoids noncompliance.
- Have I monitored compliance? Students with behavior problems often "tune out" adults because they are convinced no one will notice whether they obey. They are accustomed to adults assuming that instructions will be ignored.
- Have I provided appropriate consequences for compliance? Positive consequences for compliance, perhaps in the form of attention, recognition, or praise will probably increase the likelihood that your instructions will be followed in the future. Adults often forget that reasonable compliance with instructions is learned—it needs to be rewarded consistently when it is a new behavior for the student, one we hope the student will acquire.

Depending on your responses to these questions, you might want to consider modifying your use of instructions. We have not exhausted the questions you might ask yourself. You might consider using models (drawing attention to other students who are following instructions), self-instruction (giving yourself audible instructions, then following them; asking the student to give himself or herself instructions and follow them), and making compliance with your instructions a kind of "game" (e.g., by interspersing "silly" or humorous instructions with serious ones).

We do not suggest that you train students to obey instructions without thinking. Unless students comply with most of the teacher's instructions, however, little learning will take place. Pupils who are highly noncompliant are at a severe disadvantage in school. They frustrate their teachers, but more importantly they cut themselves off from many opportunities to learn. Helping students become reasonably compliant with classroom instructions is therefore a critical task of teachers.

Instructions depend on understanding the language used to describe an action or series of actions. We often take for granted that someone we are teaching will understand our instructions because they seem simple enough to us. "Oh, just write a little batch file and put it in the root directory" or "Now make sure you reduce the sauce before adding the mushrooms" may seem perfectly clear to some of us, but to others these instructions are as dense as Mississippi mud. We have a much better chance of doing what is expected if someone models the action for us, that is, if we are *shown* how to do it while we are given step-by-step instructions and feedback. We might need to be shown repeatedly or we might do better if we have a chance to practice under supervision before we're expected to know what to do the next time we hear the instructions.

Examples are simple but indispensable tools in teaching. For some reason, we often forget that this is the case even when we are teaching children social and interpersonal behavior. We forget that the social skills we assume are second nature are unfamiliar, even mysterious, to some youngsters. "You need to pay attention" may mean little or nothing to many students with serious attention problems. Many of these children must be shown examples of what they typically do when they are not paying attention and how they might behave if they were paying attention. We and others have found that in teaching students to pay attention to their work it is typically necessary to (1) demonstrate for them the way they behave when they are not paying attention (e.g., looking around the room, playing with an object), (2) model for them the kind of behavior involved in paying attention (e.g., reading, writing answers, looking at the teacher when the teacher is talking), and (3) have them practice the behavior involved in paying attention and give them feedback on their performance. Being polite, sharing, waiting your turn, and so on are examples of other types of behavior that some students may not understand without being shown examples.

When instructions are not working, we suggest that you ask yourself this question: Could I provide an example, model, or demonstration that would make my expectation clearer to this student? Can I show this student step-by-step just how I want him or her to behave? You might reflect further as follows.

- Have I provided both correct and incorrect examples and labeled them? Examples of desirable or correct behavior are essential. Typically, students will understand better what they are to do if you show them what is *not* correct as well as what *is* correct performance. Correct and incorrect examples must be labeled; that is, you must tell the observing student what is correct and what is incorrect (or appropriate, not appropriate).
- Have I demonstrated each step clearly and in sequence? Remember that unfamiliar tasks are difficult for most of us to learn. The student will likely not acquire the skill you are trying to teach if you fail to give examples that are both clear and complete.
- Have I made sure the student is "with" me all the way? Watch for lapses in attention or points of confusion. Examples, like instructions, are useless if the student isn't paying close attention or doesn't comprehend what is happening.
- Have I given corrective feedback when the student makes an error? Students will learn slowly, if at all, when they do not receive feedback about how they are doing.
- Have I maintained a positive instructional atmosphere? No one likes to be taught by someone who is impatient, uses sarcasm or ridicule, or otherwise causes embarrassment. Be careful to choose a time and place for giving examples that will avoid making the student feel inadequate or humiliated in the peer group. Maintain a supportive, positive attitude and recognize progress, even if it is slight.

Examples or models provided by the teacher can be extremely effective teaching tools. In addition, the models of behavior provided by peers can be extremely influential. We discuss peer models further in Chapter 5. Suffice to say here that showing students how you want them to behave is a simple but often effective means of teaching. It is a strategy that has been used by master teachers in all fields for thousands of years.

One of the simplest but frequently overlooked techniques of managing problem behavior is giving people choices. Not only children in classrooms but individuals in all kinds of social situations are likely to behave more constructively when they perceive that they have the power to make choices that are important to them. Conversely, people often behave badly when they feel "boxed in," perceiving that they have no choices. Students are likely to be less resistant to their teachers' instructions and control when they can choose certain features of their instruction or classroom environment. The savvy teacher makes wise choices about the choices students are allowed to make for themselves.

Too few choices breed resentment and resistance to authority. Too many choices induce a kind of paralysis, leaving a person frustrated and unable to make a decision. For obvious reasons, some individuals should not be allowed to make certain choices. We know that if some individuals are given certain choices they are highly likely to make very bad ones. The teacher, then, is faced with this question: For a given individual, how many choices—and which ones—are appropriate?

Master teachers understand that choices must be structured for students to prevent catastrophic consequences and to foster interest and personal responsibility. That is, they must try not to allow students to make choices that will close off future options (e.g., deciding not to attend school or not to complete assigned work). On the other hand, teachers must try to encourage students to make wise choices and to present options that will heighten students' interest, satisfaction, and judgment. This requires (1) helping students understand and be able to predict the consequences of their choices and (2) constructing appropriate options where students have not ordinarily had them.

Students sometimes make choices in situations that you cannot control or structure. Under such circumstances, you can only try to help students make good choices. Our point is that *constructing* options is a simple strategy that can be used very creatively and often successfully to manage behavior. The kinds of options we are referring to may appear to some teachers to be trivial, but to students they may be significant. They may involve such simple choices as which assignment or problem to do first, what color paper or pen to use, or where to sit for a particular activity. Students might be allowed to choose one of two or more tangible rewards or special activities when they have earned it or to choose a friend with whom to work. When teaching, and especially when teaching a "difficult" student, you will be wise to ask yourself the following questions.

- What appropriate new options can I give this student? There are nearly always new choices that a student might be allowed, thereby increasing the student's stake in the classroom activity.
- Do I know that I can live with the choice the student makes? Be careful not to construct an option that is intolerable or unacceptable.
- Have I constructed an array of options that is consistent with the student's developmental level? The student's age, preferences, and decision making characteristics are important to take into consideration. The number and nature of options must be matched to the student's interests and ability to make choices.

What approaches to helping students change their behavior are most likely to be successful?

Teachers have many choices for approaching behavior management problems. More skillful behavior managers are aware of more options and able to make better choices among them. Regardless of the number of alternative approaches you may know about, it is important to be able to articulate your reasons for choosing one approach rather than another. Following are the primary questions we suggest you ask yourself when considering the choice of a particular approach.

- Is this approach consistent with professional practices? Teachers must be constantly aware that their practices must reflect sound professional judgment. The fact that a particular approach has been used or suggested by other teachers does not *necessarily* mean that it is appropriate. Teachers must studiously avoid practices that are prohibited by law or school policy and those that are questionable on ethical grounds.
- Does my own experience or that of colleagues suggest that this approach might be effective? Teachers themselves are often good judges of what is likely to work and what is likely not to work with a given class or student. We caution that some teachers find it easy to reject useful suggestions out-of-hand based on their personal biases; some cling to approaches that are familiar to them but are not very successful. Nevertheless, the judgment of experienced and highly skilled teachers must be viewed as an important test of the value of any suggested approach.
- What technical assistance can I find for helping me implement this approach? Guidance from colleagues, consultants, technical manuals, or professional publications is often a critical factor in determining whether an approach is successful. Trying to implement procedures on a seat-of-the-pants basis often leads to disappointment, sometimes to mistaken judgment about the value or workability of the approach. Some approaches are failures, even when skillfully implemented; some are failures because their implementation was flawed. When you select an approach to a problem, you should attempt to make sure that you use it skillfully.
- What empirical research supports this approach? In our view, support from empirical research should be a critical factor in selecting an approach to behavior management. Testimonial evidence alone ("I tried this, and it works!" or "I don't believe it's ever effective, because I've never been able to make it work!") does not seem to us as reliable as teachers' opinions that are supported by evidence obtained in carefully controlled research studies. Because we take the position that accumulated evidence from empirical research is the single best criterion for selecting strategies, we describe approaches based on the research literatures of behavioral psychology and social learning, particularly as they apply to the classroom.

How might I use the five operations of a behavioral approach?

Research in behavioral psychology has produced a wide range of techniques for changing human behavior. Here we briefly describe only five basic operations that provide the core strategies for building all others.[2] With an understanding of these basic operations, teachers are able to create sound techniques for intervening to increase or decrease specific behaviors. We refer to "operations" because we are discussing "operant" behavior—actions that "operate" in the environment to produce certain outcomes. The operations we describe are ways of modifying the social environment so that specific behaviors will produce predictable consequences.

The five operations we describe here are all based on the principle that the events immediately following a behavior—its consequences—determine to a large extent how likely it is to occur again. Positive and negative reinforcement involve using consequences to *increase* the probability or rate of a behavior; extinction and punishment, whether by response cost or presenting aversives, involve using consequences to *decrease* the probability or rate of a behavior. Each of these operations has advantages and disadvantages, and some should be used more frequently than others. In most classroom situations, teachers' interventions will involve combinations of operations.

Positive Reinforcement

Positive reinforcement is the staple of good behavior management, and it is a concept with which most teachers are familiar. It means that when the student behaves in a specific desirable way the consequence(s) will be positive—something the individual student is willing to work to obtain. Positive reinforcement has the effect of increasing the behavior that produces such consequences. Providing rewards for appropriate behavior is extremely simple in principle, but putting positive reinforcement into practice in ways that are effective and self-enhancing for the student sometimes requires great creativity and finesse on the part of the teacher. Teachers are sometimes unsuccessful in using positive reinforcement because they neglect the fine points that are critical in using the operation effectively. Following are questions you need to ask yourself if you wish to use positive reinforcement to increase the kind of behavior you would like to see a student exhibit more frequently.

- Am I sure the consequence I am using is a positive reinforcer (reward) for this student? Not everyone finds the same consequences reinforcing; what is rewarding for one person may not be for another. To use positive reinforcement successfully, you must provide a consequence that is attractive to the particular student whose behavior you are trying to improve. Finding the right consequence is sometimes difficult. It must not only be something attractive to the student; you must be able to control access to it. You might consider several categories of *potential* reinforcers:

1. social, e.g., attention, praise, touching (these are among the most natural reinforcers);
2. activity, e.g., talking with friends, reading, playing a game or sport, caring for pets, tutoring a peer, playing a musical instrument, working at the computer, watching a video (this category is nearly inexhaustible for the creative teacher and might be seen as only slightly more artificial than social reinforcers);
3. tangible, e.g., edibles, toys, clothing, money (or any other type of token that has no inherent value but can be exchanged for other desired reinforcers; tangibles are often considered highly artificial reinforcers).

- You might identify reinforcers by asking a student what he or she is willing to work for, by observing the student's preferences, or simply by trying out things you think might work. The ultimate test of whether a consequence is a positive reinforcer for a given individual is whether he or she will work to get it. Bear in mind, however, that you can offer a potential reinforcer in ways that will make it useless, that is, that destroy its appeal. If you require too much for earning a reward, if you offer the reward in too small or too large amounts, or if you are inconsistent in providing the reinforcer, for example, you may be unsuccessful. Finally, sometimes students receive consequences that appear to be punishing, not reinforcing, yet they continue to behave inappropriately. In many cases, some aspect of the apparent punishment, perhaps the attention or the emotional behavior of adults who are upset, are actually rewarding consequences of misbehavior that outweigh the intended punishment.
- Does getting the reinforcer depend on the student's exhibiting the appropriate behavior? Reinforcers are typically useless unless they are made *contingent* on the behavior you want to increase. "Contingent" means that the reward is available when, and only when, the behavior is exhibited. If the reinforcer is available freely without performance, then the individual is unlikely to be motivated to earn it; earning it means that it is not available until after the appropriate behavior is exhibited. Teachers often experience failure in attempts to reward students' appropriate behavior with attention because they fail to respond differently to desirable conduct and misbehavior. When students get attention—either positive or negative—regardless of how they behave, they are unlikely to learn to behave as you would like them to. If you can not control when the student has access to the reinforcer, then you probably can not use it to improve behavior. You must attempt to use reinforcers that are under your control—things you can regulate.
- Is the reinforcer available soon after the student performs the appropriate behavior? Much of our behavior is controlled by immediate consequences. Smoking and overeating are common examples in which, even for many successful and well-adjusted adults, immediate positive consequences take precedence over long-term negative consequences. As people develop psychologically, they are able to tolerate greater delays in gratification and are controlled to a greater extent by long-term consequences in most areas of their lives. Young children and those whose psychological development is lagging, however, typically will not respond to rewards that are delayed for more than a very short time. Teachers often underes-

timate the importance of immediacy in using positive reinforcement effectively. Often, finding a way to decrease the interval between appropriate behavior and reward will be key to making positive reinforcement effective. Remember, too, that for many students the behavior that is rewarded is the one that occurs immediately prior to their receiving a reward. Regardless of what you *intend* to reward, the reinforcer will likely strengthen whatever behavior the student has just exhibited. We offer this caution: Be very mindful of the timing of your reinforcement.

- Am I providing an appropriate unit of reward for the expected unit of behavior? Reinforcers are, in effect, like wages; they must be fair and effective compensation for performance. Fairness is not necessarily judged by what is typical. It is far more complicated than that. Perhaps the best way of determining what is fair is negotiating it with the student. Especially with young and developmentally delayed students, and especially when the student is learning a new skill, we recommend that you require only a little performance for reinforcement. Frequent small rewards are typically more effective than infrequent large rewards.

- Is the reinforcer a "natural" consequence or, at least, paired with one? "Natural" reinforcers are ones that exist, or should exist, in a humane environment and effectively influence the behavior of most individuals. Most people agree that praise, recognition, and healthy recreational activities are natural reinforcers. "Artificial" reinforcers are those contrived for special purposes when natural consequences have failed (e.g., token systems in classrooms designed to remediate serious behavior problems). Natural reinforcers are preferred because they are likely to maintain behavior after artificial incentives are withdrawn. Artificial reinforcers are sometimes critical to initial success in changing behavior, and they should not be shunned when they are necessary. When they are used, however, they should be paired with (i.e., delivered concurrently with) more natural rewards. For example, social attention such as praise should nearly always be given along with tangible reinforcement. In this way, natural consequences are likely, with time, to take on some of the power of artificial incentives.

- Am I careful to respect entitlements? One of the more difficult ethical and legal issues involving positive reinforcement is the question of the conditions and privileges to which students are entitled regardless of how they behave. People may disagree about whether every student has a fundamental right or entitlement to certain activities (e.g., recess, all classroom privileges) or whether they may be made contingent on a standard of classroom conduct. Activities and privileges that are considered entitlements can not be made contingent on desired behavior, and thus can not be used as rewards. We can not draw the boundaries of classroom entitlements for you; we can only urge you to be aware of the issues and take precautions against ethical and legal questions being raised. One precaution is making sure that your principal approves of any contingency that involves making any "standard" activity contingent on a student's behavior. Another precaution is using *additional* activities or privileges *beyond* those granted routinely to all students as reinforcers whenever feasible. A final precaution is reviewing the conditions of your students' lives from the perspective that every student has the right to be treated fairly and equitably and to receive recognition and rewards for appropriate behavior.

A problem that most teachers anticipate, and many experience, is the claim of entitlement to reinforcement by a student who has not behaved appropriately. That is, a student may deny that he or she has not met the criterion for reward or argue that he or she should receive the same reward as another student. In some cases, teachers become so weary of the carping of students who do not earn rewards that they eliminate special contingencies for students or groups with special needs. Some teachers become so frustrated by claims of entitlement that they conclude positive reinforcement simply is not worth the hassle. When teachers abandon positive reinforcement contingencies because of this problem, the students are winning a contest of wills, but both they and their teacher are losing opportunities for more constructive interactions.

We have two suggestions for responding to inappropriate student claims of entitlement. First, you should be certain that every student in your class has a reasonable opportunity to earn frequent, meaningful rewards. Students' complaints sometimes mean that the opportunities for reward are simply too few, and you may need to alter your reward system accordingly. If rewards are scarce and given disproportionately to a few, students may have a legitimate complaint. If the same contingencies do not apply to everyone, you may need to explain briefly and in simple language that different students need and earn different rewards. Second, you should not become embroiled in arguments or long discussions about rewards. If you are confident that the reward system is fair to everyone in the class, then you have no need to offer repeated justifications or respond to nagging. Let one simple explanation of why the reward is given suffice; ignore further complaints.

Negative Reinforcement

The term negative reinforcement is frequently misunderstood to mean punishment. The term actually means reinforcing (strengthening) behavior by removing or preventing something unpleasant. That is, negative reinforcement strengthens whatever behavior allows the individual to escape or avoid a negative consequence. A few everyday examples may help to clarify how negative reinforcement works. Normally, we take analgesics to remove (escape from) pain; taking such pills is a behavior maintained by negative reinforcement. We buckle our seat belts to avoid a negative consequence—injury or death; buckling up is a behavior that is negatively reinforced. Students may study for a test at least in part to avoid negative consequences such as embarrassment or a low grade; studying is a behavior that may be maintained in part by both negative reinforcement (avoidance of failure) and positive reinforcement (getting a good grade or earning privileges as well as—we always hope—the intrinsic satisfaction of learning).

Ordinarily, negative reinforcement should not be a prominent part of classroom behavior management for two reasons. First, negative reinforcement relies on the presence or threat of negative (aversive) consequences. While some negative consequences or their threat are an unavoidable part of everyday existence, including a reasonably demanding learning environment, good teaching and management does not rely primarily on threats. Second, deliberate negative reinforcement sets the stage for coercion—the use of force or intimidation to achieve one's objectives. A coercive relationship is one in which both parties vie for control by increasing the level of pain or discomfort of the other, as we suggested in Chapter 2. Whoever wins the contest is negatively reinforced; the losing party withdraws his or her pressure, providing negative reinforcement for the winner. Coercion is, unfortunately, a part of the family life of many students with behavior problems. To make coercion a part of their school experience adds insult to injury.

When devising a behavior management program, ask yourself the following questions about negative reinforcement: What part does negative reinforcement play in my students' motivation to learn and behave appropriately? Are there ways in which I can rely more on positive reinforcement and less on negative reinforcement to motivate my students? Am I becoming engaged in coercive interactions—power struggles—with my students? Power struggles are sometimes difficult if not impossible to avoid. Nevertheless, they are a sign that your behavior management strategies need close scrutiny and, possibly, revision.

Extinction

One way of eliminating behavior, whether desirable or undesirable, is to eliminate its reinforcement—an operation called extinction. When a behavior no longer produces the desired effect (positive or negative reinforcement), it will eventually fade away (be extinguished). Using an extinction procedure assumes that you can identify the reinforcer for the behavior you are trying to eliminate and that you can terminate the reinforcer. The concept of extinction is indispensable in a behavioral approach to classroom management, but the procedure is never appropriate as a sole strategy.

Extinction has two major disadvantages as the primary focus of an approach to reducing problem behavior. First, it is a slow process, especially for a behavior pattern that has become well established. Second, when an extinction procedure is first implemented, the behavior is likely to become worse before it starts to improve. When people do not get what they have come to expect as a consequence of their behavior, they first try harder to produce the usual result. For example, if a child is used to getting what he wants by throwing temper tantrums, his tantrums will at first become more severe when adults place them on extinction (i.e., resolutely refuse to give in to them). Furthermore, extinction by itself is of little value. It does little or nothing, without reinforcement for desirable conduct, to improve behavior. The central feature of a skillful behavioral approach is a combination of shifting reinforcement away from undesirable behavior (i.e., extinction) and toward desirable behavior (i.e., positive reinforcement). The critical concept in the approach is making sure students receive ample positive reinforcement—but only, or at least overwhelmingly, for behavior that is appropriate. When using extinction, the following are important questions to ask yourself.

- Have I identified and effectively terminated reinforcement of the undesirable behavior? Occasional reinforcement during extinction is likely to make the behavior even worse. Try to make sure that you keep the behavior from resulting *at any time* in its former consequence.

- Am I offering strong positive reinforcement for alternative appropriate behavior? Remember, positive reinforcement for the behavior you want to encourage is a key to making extinction work.

Response Cost Punishment

Like negative reinforcement, punishment is a term that is often misunderstood. Punishment does *not* necessarily mean causing pain, either physical pain or serious psychological distress. Punishment means providing a consequence that decreases the likelihood that a behavior will be repeated. True, punishment *may* involve causing physical or psychological distress, but the punishment procedures that are most effective for most individuals do not cause such trauma. The most effective punishment typically involves withholding or withdrawing a positive reinforcer contingent on a specific misbehavior. Punishment of this kind means that misbehavior "costs" something, hence the term "response cost." It may mean the loss of money (i.e., a fine) or other possession or the withdrawal of a privilege (e.g., loss of a specific amount of time for TV viewing, recess, or another valued activity).

Punishment of any kind, including response cost, can be abusive if it is excessive or capricious. Nevertheless, it appears that rearing children who are reasonably socialized and maintaining a humane social structure require the judicious use of punishing as well as positively reinforcing consequences. When you are contemplating or evaluating the use of punishment, ask yourself the following questions.

- Have I made every effort to use positive procedures to manage this student's behavior? Punishment should never be your first resort. Consider it only after you have devised a behavior management scheme that emphasizes positive consequences for desirable conduct.
- Am I generally positive toward my students, giving very frequent praise and other forms of positive attention to them when their behavior is appropriate? Punishment is most effective when it comes from people who are typically warm and loving toward the individual when his or her behavior is acceptable. If you are generally irritable or negative toward a student, your attempts to punish are likely to backfire. Punishment is most effective when it represents a stark contrast to the typical interactions between teacher and student.
- Am I able to administer punishment matter-of-factly, without a display of anger, and without nagging, threats, or moralizing (trying to induce guilt through sermonizing or shaming)? Displays of anger and lectures that accompany punishment will almost certainly have exactly the opposite effect you intend. Repeated warnings are actually nagging or threats, which are counterproductive. If you are going to give a warning before punishing, give only one. After the student has been punished, do *not* lecture him or her; pick up classroom activities as if nothing had happened and emphasize positive consequences for appropriate behavior.
- Is the punishment immediate, fair, and consistent? Delaying punishment, like delaying reinforcement, reduces its effectiveness. Effective punishment is reasonable—not trivial, but not out of proportion to the seriousness of the offense. And

predictability is a critical feature of effective punishment. The student must know what behavior will result in punishment, and the punishment should be consistently applied for that behavior.

- Does the punishment quickly produce behavioral change? Effective punishment does not take a long time to work. If a change in behavior for the better is not quickly apparent (after it is administered a few times), you should revise or discontinue it. It is better not to punish at all than to persist in ineffective punishment (which is abuse). Punishing more severely is seldom the answer. Changing the nature of the consequence or making punishment more immediate or consistent is more likely to produce good results.
- Have I communicated my punishment procedures to all concerned parties? The student(s), parents, and your school administrators should know what punishment procedures you intend to use. Your best insurance against legal entanglements and unprofessional conduct is to keep concerned parties fully informed and your procedures open to inspection by others.

Punishment by Presenting Aversives

Punishment may be accomplished in one of two ways, by either withdrawing valued commodities (as described in response cost) or by presenting aversive consequences such as reprimands, isolation, or noxious stimuli. Using noxious or painful consequences places the teacher in extremely dangerous territory, both legally and ethically, and our advice is to steer well clear of using them. However, reprimands and *brief* social isolation may be appropriate when used carefully and skillfully along with the positive procedures we have discussed. All the questions and caveats we offered in our discussion of response cost apply as well to the operation of presenting aversive consequences. In addition, consider the following regarding reprimands.

- Do I keep my reprimands brief and to-the-point? Lectures and general criticisms tend to be wasted words, if not inducements to further misbehavior. "Randy, stop talking to Rachel" is preferable to "Randy, I've told you I will not tolerate this kind of behavior, and I want you to stop it right now and pay attention to your work. Now shape up!"
- Do I keep my reprimands as private as possible? Private reprimands are ones given so that few if any of the student's peers can hear what is being said. Public reprimands are those that nearly everyone in the class can hear. Private reprimands, for which the teacher goes to the student and speaks quietly but firmly, are usually most effective. Public reprimands may sometimes be necessary, but more is lost than gained when the teacher uses primarily loud, public criticism or rebuke.
- Do I make sure I have the student's attention and attempt to get eye contact before reprimanding? Like instructions, reprimands will be ineffective if they are delivered to a student who is otherwise occupied. Use the student's name. Look directly at the student when speaking, and use a direct, firm, but not angry tone of voice. There should be no misunderstanding about the fact that you are displeased with the student's behavior, but you should not be visibly upset.

Brief social isolation is sometimes referred to as "time out." Nearly every teacher is familiar with the term, yet many teachers misuse the procedure in attempts to punish misbehavior. The technical meaning of time out is time out *from positive reinforcement.* That is, it means an interval during which positive reinforcement can not be obtained. The implication is that positive reinforcement is readily available, except when the individual is in time out. As such, time out does not *necessarily* require physical isolation; it may not involve removal of the student from the group, only a period during which the student will be ignored or not allowed to earn the typical rewards for appropriate behavior. It may, however, involve placing the student for a brief period in a place where he or she is unable to interact freely with others and obtain attention and other positive reinforcers. When time out involves placing a student in a separate room, it becomes a highly controversial procedure and one that is easily abused. We recommend that you not use any such isolation procedure without the explicit approval of your school administrator and the student's parents and with consultation from a professional with extensive experience in appropriate use of the procedure. Brief social isolation of a less radical nature, such as having the student "sit out" of a game or move to another seat in the classroom, is less risky. Even with this kind of time out procedure, however, you should be sure to keep our previous questions and cautions regarding punishment in mind. In addition, remember that longer time outs are not typically more effective than shorter ones. The *maximum* effective time out period is usually not more than 5 minutes. To use time out appropriately, you will need a timer to signal when the time out period has ended; you must *not* allow yourself to forget the student in time out. Finally, recall that time out means time out from positive reinforcement, not merely time out of the classroom or time out of your sight. Attempts to use time out often fail for one of two reasons: (1) the "time in" environment offers little positive reinforcement, so being excluded from it is not punishing, (2) the "time out" environment is one in which the student obtains unintended reinforcement. The latter is often the case when the student is placed in a hallway or office, where interesting observations of and interactions with others are typically available.

How can I capitalize on the cognitive and affective aspects of behavior change?

A behavioral approach provides anchor points for devising specific management techniques. The five operations and combinations and variations of them are a core that enables teachers to plan explicit strategies. Nevertheless, the nuances of behavior management require that the teacher also approach students as thinking, feeling individuals. In fact, the teacher who ignores the way students think and feel about their behavior and about management techniques is doomed to be ineffective. Sensitivity to meanings and emotions is required for effective behavior management. We briefly highlight the importance of cognitive and affective aspects of talking with students, choosing consequences for students, teaching self-control, and teaching social skills.

Talking with Students

In Chapter 4 we elaborate on the importance of teachers' verbalizations to students. Here we merely wish to point out that the success of the strategies we have discussed may well depend on how the teacher presents them. Students' understanding of contingencies and their emotional responses to them will be determined in part by just what the teacher says and how she or he says it. Words and tones that convey a positive attitude, respect for the student, self-confidence, and firm expectations that the student will behave appropriately will make a significant difference in the teacher's probability of success. What really matters to students? How do they feel about important aspects of school and the classroom? It should seldom be the case that a student can say, "No one ever asked me."

Choosing Consequences for Students

"Different strokes for different folks" is a cliche that applies to selecting effective reinforcing and punishing consequences. Sensitivity to the student's preferences, which can be obtained only through careful observation and listening, is essential in choosing consequences of behavior that will have the desired effect. Talking with students about their behavior and its consequences is necessary. Nevertheless, talking is not enough. Watching and listening with understanding sometimes reveal that students' words do not reflect their true feelings. Many a student has fooled a teacher by saying "I don't care." Sometimes verbal bravado masks real feelings; sometimes it does not. How can you tell what a student *really* feels about something? Perhaps we should recall another cliche: "Actions speak louder than words."

Teaching Self-Control Procedures

The ultimate goal of good behavior management is to help students learn to control their own behavior in self-enhancing ways. As we discuss in Chapter 4, teaching self-control is intimately connected to talking with students about their behavior. It is a way of getting them actively involved, cognitively and affectively, in their own self-growth.

Teaching Social Skills

Some students acquire social skills easily. They do not seem to require explicit instruction in order to learn the patterns of social interaction we consider acceptable. Just as is the case for academic skills, however, some students do not learn the critical skills in the same environment that is sufficient for most. Students who need a more explicit instructional program for learning social skills must be helped to think through the demands of social situations and their own options for dealing with everyday interpersonal problems.[3] The teacher must help these students become cognitively aware of others' expectations, their choices in responding to those expectations, and the probable outcomes of making given choices.

Finally, we believe it is important that you try to understand the emotions your students feel about the conditions of their lives, both in school and out of school. Your knowing how a misbehaving student feels will not, in itself, change the student's behavior, nor will it necessarily enable you to resolve the behavior problem by other means. Understanding the student's feelings will, however, improve your chances of developing a helpful relationship with the student. A helpful relationship is one in which the student is open to positive influence through your listening, talking, and providing consequences. A student is more likely to be open to positive influence by a teacher whose behavior indicates awareness of the student's feelings.

Our belief is that students' cognitive and affective change generally follow their behavioral change, although thoughts and feelings sometimes determine how a student behaves. Attempts to change students' feelings and patterns of thinking in the hope that these changes alone will be followed by behavioral improvement are, in our judgment, not very likely to be successful. Thus our prediction is that your best bet for helping students understand and feel better about themselves will be to put your primary effort into helping them change their behavior for the better, with secondary emphasis on affective and cognitive changes related to their behavior. Of course, the goal of teaching is to accomplish improvements in both behavioral and cognitive-affective domains. The questions for teachers are: Where do I begin? Where do I put my greatest emphasis? How do I view the relationship between what students do and how they think and feel about what they do?

Building helpful relationships with students requires both technical skills in using the operations of a behavioral approach and the ability to see events through the eyes and minds of pupils. Understanding the rage, loneliness, self-congratulation, suspicion, sadness, joy, or other emotions of the individual student is desirable in itself because it enables you to relate to that student as another human being. More important for you as a teacher, perhaps, such understanding might help you be able to predict, and thus make better choices about, the way you talk to the student and the way you construct expectations and consequences in the classroom.

Is my approach positive and supportive of appropriate behavior?

In any attempt to modify behavior you should reflect on the extent to which your approach emphasizes positive consequences for appropriate behavior. Negative reinforcement, extinction, and perhaps even punishment (within guidelines we have suggested) may be justified as part of a management scheme. However, unless your approach is overwhelmingly positive and supportive of appropriate behavior, we feel it is professionally and ethically questionable. Teachers need to ask themselves questions about their own behavior in the classroom and take action accordingly.

- How frequently do I offer praise or other positive evaluations (e.g., smiles, pats, approval) of my students' appropriate behavior? Most teachers overestimate their positive interactions with students. You may want to keep a tally of your positive and negative responses to students during specified periods for several days to see just what your ratio of positive to negative is. Yes, it is possible to overdo praise statements, but few teachers are in any danger of doing so. No, it is *not* enough just to make many positive statements and show approval to students; your positive attention must be *contingent* on the type of behavior you want your students to exhibit. You must make sure that inappropriate behavior receives no rewarding consequences from you.

- Do I ignore most minor misbehavior? One of the most difficult behavior management strategies for most teachers to learn is putting minor misbehavior on extinction–simply ignoring it and focusing attention on desirable behavior. It is very easy to fall into the trap of giving negative attention to minor misbehavior, which results in inadvertent reinforcement of it. Attention–even negative attention in the form of reprimands–can be a positive reinforcer, particularly when a student seldom receives positive attention. Some misbehavior cannot be ignored because it is dangerous or too disruptive to allow it to continue. But most of the minor disruptions and irritating behavior we see in classrooms is best treated as if it didn't happen. No one can give you an exact formula for when and what to ignore and when and what *not* to ignore. Becoming a good judge of exactly what and when to ignore is an important aspect of becoming a master teacher.

- Do I emphasize positive outcomes of desirable behavior rather than avoidance of negative consequences for inadequate performance? The distinction between positive and negative reinforcement is subtle but important. Positive reinforcement induces approach behavior; negative reinforcement is based on avoidance. To the greatest extent possible, your behavior management strategies should be based on motivation to obtain rewarding consequences, not avoid unpleasantness.

- Am I able to avoid getting drawn into power struggles and other forms of negative interactions with students? Some students with behavior problems are masters at drawing adults into arguments and verbal power struggles that they typically win. Whatever you say, they will question. Before you know it, you are engaged in an argument, usually about something that in retrospect seems silly, and feeling emotionally upset. Becoming aware immediately that you are being drawn in and terminating the interaction before it turns into a power struggle is an important skill for dealing with difficult students. In part, avoiding power struggles involves the recognition that you are responsible for your choices as a teacher and students are responsible for theirs.

- Do students like being in my classroom? One important test of whether your behavior management strategies are appropriate is whether students have generally positive feelings about your classroom. Certainly, you should not expect that students will *never* express unhappiness with you or the demands you make of them. Good teachers care about much more than their popularity with students. Nevertheless, if over a reasonable period of time students obviously do not like being in your classroom you are probably not meeting their needs in a professionally defensible way.

- Are my students learning academic and social skills at a level commensurate with their abilities? For the competent teacher, students' good feelings are not enough. Students must make progress in acquiring the academic and social skills that are self-enhancing and give them increased options in important areas of their lives.

Summary

Today's teachers have available to them a wide variety of behavior management suggestions, including "packaged" techniques. We urge teachers to use a reflective, self-questioning approach that makes creative use of basic principles. Before implementing elaborate or sophisticated management strategies, we suggest that teachers try the simplest, most obvious professionally defensible procedures. These include using instructions, showing and describing examples, and providing choices to students. When implemented very skillfully, these and other simple approaches are often sufficient to resolve behavior problems. In selecting other options for behavior management, teachers must weigh them in the light of best professional practices, personal experience and that of colleagues, available technical assistance, and reliable empirical research. Research in behavioral psychology and social learning applied to classroom problems provides, in our opinion, a sound basis for devising behavior management strategies. The five operations of a behavioral approach—positive reinforcement, negative reinforcement, extinction, response cost punishment, and punishment by presenting aversives—are based on the principle that consequences (events immediately following a behavior) can be altered to change behavior. Positive and negative reinforcement are ways of increasing the strength or probability of behavior; extinction and punishment are ways of decreasing or weakening it. The key to good behavior management is emphasizing positive reinforcement of appropriate behavior; the other four operations should play a secondary role. Teachers who use behavioral operations successfully must capitalize on the cognitive and affective aspects of behavior change. Students' thoughts and feelings must be considered when teachers talk with students, choose consequences for students' behavior, and teach self-management techniques and social skills. Understanding students' thoughts and feelings is important in building helpful relationships. Behavior management should be positive and supportive of appropriate behavior so that students receive frequent teacher approval, the focus is on motivation to obtain rewarding consequences, and students like being in the classroom and learn important academic and social skills.

References and Resources for Further Study

The following references provided the basis for many of our statements in this chapter. You may wish to consult selected references for additional information. Our reference notes for this chapter refer to sources in this list.

Goldstein, A. P. (1988). *The Prepare Curriculum: Teaching Prosocial Competencies*. Champaign, IL: Research Press.

Grossman, H. (1990). *Trouble-Free Teaching: Solutions To Behavior Problems In The Classroom*. Mountain View, CA: Mayfield Publishing Co.

Kazdin, A. E. (1984). *Behavior Modification in Applied Settings* (3rd ed.). Homewood, IL: Dorsey Press.

Kerr, M. M. and Nelson, C. M. (1989). *Strategies for Managing Behavior Problems in the Classroom* (2nd ed). Columbus, OH: Merrill/Macmillan.

Kerr, M. M. and Nelson, C. M., and Lambert, D. L. (1987). *Helping Adolescents with Learning and Behavior Problems.* Columbus, OH: Merrill/Macmillan.

Kratochwill, T. R. and Morris, R. J. (Eds.) (1991). *The Practice of Child Therapy* (2nd ed.). New York: Pergamon.

Macht, J. (1990). *Managing Classroom Behavior: An Ecological Approach to Academic and Social Learning.* New York: Longman.

Morgan, D. P. and Jenson, W. R. (1988). *Teaching Behaviorally Disordered Students.* Columbus, OH: Merrill/Macmillan.

Morris, R. J. (1985). *Behavior Modification with Exceptional Children.* Glenview, IL: Scott, Foresman.

Nelson, C. M. (1981). Classroom Management. In J. M. Kauffman and D. P. Hallahan (Eds.), *Handbook Of Special Education* (pp. 663-687). Englewood Cliffs, NJ: Prentice-Hall.

Stoner, G., Shinn, M.R. and Walker, H. M. (Eds.). (1991). *Interventions for Achievement and Behavior Problems.* Silver Spring, MD: National Association of School Psychologists.

Smith, D. D. (1984). *Effective Discipline: A Positive Approach to Discipline for Educators in al Settings.* Austin, TX: Pro-Ed.

Walker, H. M. (1979). *The Acting Out Child: Coping with Classroom Disruption.* Boston: Allyn and Bacon.

Webber, J. and Scheuermann, B. (1991). Managing behavior problems: Accentuate the positive . . . eliminate the negative! *Teaching Exceptional Children, 24* (1), 13-19.

Wielkiewica, R. M. (1986). *Behavior Management in the Schools: Principles and Procedures.* New York: Pergamon.

Reference Notes

1. Among the most widely used packaged disipline programs are the following:

Albert, L. (1989). *A Teacher's Guide to Cooperative Discipline: How to Manage Your Classroom and Promote Self-Esteem.* Circle Pines, MN: American Guidance Service.

Canter, L. and Canter, M. (1976). *Assertive Discipline: A Take-Charge Approach for Today's Educator.* Santa Monica, CA: Lee Canter and Associates.

Curwin, R.L. and Mendler, A.N. (1988). *Discipline with Dignity.* Alerandria, CA: Association for Supervision and Curriculum Developmet.

Nelson, J. (1987). *Positive Discipline.* New York: Ballantine.

Sprick, R. (1981). *The Solution Book: A Guide to Classroom Discipline.* Chicago: Science Research Associates.

Each has strengths and weaknesses that have been reviewed in the following article:

Chare, D., Smith, S. and Sugai, G. (1992). Packaged discipline programs: A consumer's guide. In J. Marr and G. Tindal (Ed.), *The Oregon Conference Monograph,* 1992 (pp. 19–26). Eugene, OR: University of Oregon, College of Education, Division of Teacher Education.

2. For further explanation of basic behavior principles, see Kazdin (1984), Kerr and Nelson (1989), and Nelson (1981).

3. See especially Goldstein (1988) and Walker (1979).

$$Chapter \quad 4$$

Talking with Students

Questions for Reflection

How does the classroom setting influence how I talk with students about their behavior?

How does talking with students about their behavior impact my teaching goals?

How will my approach to classroom management affect my communication with students about their behavior?

How can I prepare myself for talking with students about their behavior?

How can talking with students about their behavior teach personal responsibility?

What prerequisites for verbal and non-verbal communication must I model and teach?

What are the benefits of positive and negative talk with students about their behavior?

Are there appropriate ways of talking with angry or aggressive students about their behavior?

Do I talk with students who display less serious behaviors in the same way as I communicate with angry or aggressive students?

How can I use questioning to get the information I need from students about their behavior?

How do I talk with students when delivering consequences for their inappropriate behavior?

How can I teach students behavioral self-control.

Talk is cheap—some of the time. It can also be very costly. Some of the things teachers and students say are not terribly important, but both student talk and teacher talk are critical aspects of learning. Talk is also among the primary means of behavior management and causes of classroom conflict, as the vignette on page 62 illustrates.

Sarah: I was prepared for a lot of things in my first year. I'd even paid attention to some professors who had reminded me to think through how I was going to set up my class routine, the rules I wanted to impose, and what to do if certain unacceptable student behaviors popped up.

Looking back, though, having my own class has taught me far more than I ever imagined about talking with my students. I assumed that I was prepared for communicating with them. After all, I had been able to talk to people all my life! Boy, was I wrong! David taught me the most. He was so unpredictable and very good at getting me hooked into verbal sparring matches. I remember one time where he really pushed all my buttons. We were doing math, and I had instructed David to begin the written work I had assigned. He turned his face to the wall and that was that. I talked to him, but without eye contact I knew I wasn't getting anywhere. I tried everything from pleading and cajoling to shouting and yelling. Nothing. Not even a murmur. Then, as I walked away, he turned and said, quite deliberately: "You can't make me do anything I don't want to do!"

Well, that's all I needed. As I returned to his desk, I told him in no uncertain terms (I guess my voice *was* a little shaky though) that I was the boss, and that he'd toe the line or else. I still haven't figured out exactly why we ended up in the principal's office with David getting suspended, but in looking back I probably gave David exactly what he wanted.

Questions for Reflection

Talking with students is a complicated issue that permeates every level of behavioral assessment, the formulation of behavioral interventions, and the execution of behavioral plans. If you are constantly aware of and able to practice effective communication skills, you are more likely to accomplish your goals than if you forge ahead without careful reflection. As you approach the behavioral issues in your classroom, consider at least the following questions:

1. How does the classroom setting influence how I talk with students about their behavior?
2. How does talking with students about their behavior impact my teaching goals?
3. How will my approach to classroom management affect my communication with students about their behavior?
4. How can I prepare myself for talking with students about their behavior?
5. How can talking with students about their behavior teach personal responsibility?
6. What prerequisites for verbal and nonverbal communication must I model and teach?
7. What are the benefits of positive and negative talk with students about their behavior?
8. Are there appropriate ways of talking with angry or aggressive students about their behavior?

9. Do I talk with students who display less serious behaviors in the same way as I communicate with angry or aggressive students?
10. How can I use questioning to get the information I need from students about their behavior?
11. How do I talk with students when delivering consequences for their inappropriate behavior?
12. How can I teach students behavioral self-control?

How does the classroom setting influence how I talk with students about their behavior?

Classrooms are multidimensional spaces that allow many events and tasks to occur concurrently in a small, crowded space.[1] Conversational behaviors continually interact in a complicated, self-perpetuating cycle. At any given moment, some students may be talking to each other while others may be talking with the teacher, and so on. Classroom conversational events and tasks also occur at a very rapid rate throughout the day. There are constant demands and transitions that are expected of the student if you are to accomplish your teaching goals. One way that students and teachers negotiate their way through this layered environment is to agree on standards of behavior to accomplish smooth social interaction and learning. Classroom conversational events are often unpredictable. Sudden changes in your line of questioning, the pace of classroom conversation, or interruptions from other talkers contribute to instability. In addition, classrooms are conversationally very public places. Teachers and students operate with a conscious knowledge and awareness of what other people are saying. Student and teacher talk becomes knowledge shared by the whole class. Classrooms also make their own conversational history because classroom members accumulate personal and shared talking experiences over the course of time. This historical factor helps create attitudes and social connections with a strong influence on behavior.

It is important that students learn to match appropriate academic and social talking behaviors to different classroom situations. In order to achieve this, they must learn how to tell the difference between appropriate and inappropriate behaviors, how to take responsibility for their actions, and how to develop internal control over their behavioral choices. They must practice communicating in appropriate ways with their peers and the teacher while building behavioral skills that will support them in a variety of situations.

How does talking with students about their behavior impact my teaching goals?

There appears to be a link between appropriate student behaviors and learning. Generally, the more appropriate the behavior of the student, the greater chance there is of the teacher maintaining order in the classroom, and the greater the opportunity for on-task learning. Therefore, talking with students about their behavior is not only important for increasing their interactive social skills, but also for acquiring academic competence.

How will my approach to classroom management affect my communications with students about their behavior?

Many aspects of classroom management will help you in talking with students about their behavior. By structuring the classroom setting you will improve your ability to talk with students in a meaningful way about their behavior. First, it is likely that a well thought-out classroom structure will reduce the amount of time spent on unnecessary dialogue about behavior, such as repetitive conversations about rules, consequences, or classroom routines. Second, you will have more time to talk with students about their behavior when there is a real need for intervention or interaction. Finally, a structured classroom will help you model effective talking.

If possible, ignore minor, fleeting rule infractions or misbehavior when talking with a student will be more disruptive than the behavior you are addressing. Your level of tolerance for rule infractions will be directly related to your personal view of classroom management and your beliefs about appropriate behavior. Should sustained misbehavior require your talking with a student, try to do so without disrupting the activity of the rest of the class.[2]

Try to keep transitions between activities as smooth as possible in order to maintain the momentum of daily routine. Lessons and activities that pass too quickly or too slowly or disrupting activities in favor of others and then switching back tends to work against effective management of the classroom as a whole.

It is likely that monitoring the entire class regularly and often will increase your management efficacy. The more aware you are of your surroundings, the more likely you will be to anticipate or see potential problems. Talking with students about their behavior before their actions escalate to a major disruption is often effective. This "with-it-ness" will allow you to constantly assess the behavioral status of the classroom.[3]

How can I prepare myself for talking with students about their behavior?

Talking with students about their behavior will depend, to some extent, on how you choose to run your classroom. While many talking skills are almost always effective, some communication skills may need to be modified depending on your personal choice of a classroom model. For instance, if you choose a strictly behavioral approach, this will mean a different emphasis in talking with students than if a psychoeducational or ecological model is used.

Sometimes students who are angry or upset become verbally abusive. It is easy to take these remarks personally. Students know that teachers are vulnerable to personal attacks and some seem to have an uncanny sense for knowing what will be especially hurtful and offensive to you. Working hard at not taking student remarks to heart will help you avoid power struggles and keep you from becoming angry or hurt. Feeling personally affronted by every negative student comment will distract you from the real work of teaching and will signal to students that you are a victim rather than a professional. While it is impossible to be without emotions it is equally important to model restraint and not be sidetracked from your professional responsibilities. This is not to suggest that effective teachers are unfeeling robots who simply grind away at getting through the curriculum. There are times when expressing frustration with a student in a controlled, appropriately responsible way can be extremely effective. Such a strategy, however, should be used sparingly and under ideal circumstances.

How can talking with students about their behavior teach personal responsibility?

A major function of talking with students about their behavior is to teach them to assume responsibility for their actions and choices in social interactions and in their work.[4]

During schoolwork, teachers teach students personal responsibility, for example, by getting them to remain on task, to complete their work on time, and to work on assignments independently or in groups. Teachers encourage interpersonal responsibility and social interaction by teaching students skills such as how to share resources and how to behave in a socially appropriate way. Evidence of this responsibility may be directly visible through observable behavior or indirectly apparent through assessing student attitude and motivation.

Many students act irresponsibly. They may not accept responsibility for their own behavior, instead blaming their actions on others (usually parents, the teacher, or peers), bad luck, a lack of ability, or the difficulty of the task. These externally controlled students are often unable to accurately gauge whether, in reality, they have control of the outcome of their behavior or not. Consequently, they tend to believe that their personal efforts make little difference and they give up trying to improve their behavior. The less they try to improve their behavior, the lower their motivation and willingness to attempt any significant behavioral changes. Students who have more internal control, on the other hand, attribute their behavior to their own personal efforts (or lack thereof) and are more likely to take responsibility for the way they act. They are also more likely to be self-motivated and goal-directed than students who blame their behavior on external causes.

In talking with students about their behavior teachers must encourage them to assume personal responsibility for their choice of behaviors. In this way, student self-control and delay of immediate gratification are enhanced.

What prerequisites for verbal and nonverbal communication must I model and teach?

There are several prerequisites for communication which teachers can model and teach. Students may need to be taught that in talking with others, people take turns, allowing one speaker to speak at a time. It may also be necessary to teach students how not to interrupt while someone else is talking. Students may need to learn how to maintain a focus on discussing their behavior without wandering. They should also be encouraged to increase their awareness of how much to say about their behavior without being repetitive or evasive. Finally, students may need to be taught how to avoid ambiguity or vagueness while at the same time being polite and considerate.

There are also nonverbal prerequisites for talking with students about their behavior. Students may need to be taught how to remain engaged in talking with you, for example, by maintaining eye contact during the conversation. They may need to be taught how to listen to what you are saying, and how to use appropriate facial expressions and body language to maintain social connection.

Personal proximity is important when talking with students about their behavior, especially seeing that some students have poorly defined personal boundaries. Being too far from a student while talking may be misinterpreted as meaning you are disinterested, whereas getting too close may be threatening. Maintain a comfortable distance of approximately an arm's length, although you may find that some students appear to need more personal space than others. Angry and aggressive students probably need more space than calmer or compliant pupils.[5]

Body language and posture convey a sense of interest or lack thereof. Slouching or leaning back is more likely to communicate disinterest than leaning slightly forward and being attentive. However, try not to be physically rigid or "posed" either. You want to appear confident, in control, and assured, but not arrogant. Body movement and gestures can be either encouraging or negative during a conversation, so be aware of any personal gestures that may interfere in talking with a student.

Eye contact conveys a sense of interest and friendliness. Focused vision also adds to your credibility. However, staring without any break should be avoided.[6] Try to maintain eye contact for a few moments after the end of the conversation. Sometimes, if the student avoids looking at you, a touch on the shoulder or a gentle verbal cue such as "Look at me" may prompt eye contact. If a student refuses eye contact, maintain your gaze and continue talking.

Facial expressions will convey what you are thinking during your conversation. It is important to listen carefully to what the student is saying so that you will not be caught unawares, perhaps responding to a shocking comment with an inappropriate or exaggerated expression. In addition, extended disapproving expressions can be very distracting. It is more appropriate to match your expression carefully to the conversational content.

Talking with students involves a careful use of language that conveys very definite and clear messages about your demands. Think through what you intend to say before talking with a student about his or her behavior. Taking a moment to consider how you will phrase a question or comment or being aware of your body language can save a great deal of energy which might otherwise be spent on explaining ambiguity or vagueness. It is helpful to put yourself in the student's place and see if you can answer your question or respond to your comment as if you were the student.

Your choice of language when talking with students about their behavior will be either descriptive or judgmental. Judgmental language evaluates a situation or behavior subjectively according to your own personal bias of whether the behavior is appropriate or not. Applying such a label to student behavior may damage the climate of cooperation between teacher and student. It also tends to reinforce unnecessary labeling of students as smart, slow, or as behavior problems.

Descriptive language is preferable when talking with students about their behavior.[7] Descriptive language portrays a given situation or behavior by describing what is happening without attaching subjective judgment. Descriptive language does not label behavior with an emotional overlay that can cause communication problems. It is also richer in factual information about the current situation. The more factual the language, the more precise your feedback to the student about his or her behavior, and the greater the opportunity for you to remain neutral rather than angry or upset. Furthermore, descriptive language is less likely to provoke an escalation of the misbehavior.

Select your vocabulary carefully to reflect what is happening as neutrally as possible. Familiar words and brief statements are preferable to involved and vague wanderings. Ensure that the language you use is appropriate for the occasion and applies specifically to the behavior and its context. It also helps, where appropriate, to use vivid language in the form of metaphors or similes.[8] However, repeating the obvious or saying the same thing in different ways when the student clearly understands does not help the student maintain a conversational focus.

How you use your voice will tell students a great deal about your expectations and emotional state. Students are extremely sensitive to changes in vocal tone and pitch. At least in some instances, your success in talking with students about their behavior may be more dependent on how you talk rather than what you actually say.

Your voice should be loud enough so that students can hear you clearly, although being overloud is just as detrimental to conversation as speaking too softly. While excessive volume tends to distort words, a quieter than usual voice is sometimes effective in getting a student's attention. Speaking at one volume level, however, will mean that nothing you say will stand out from among your other comments. Varying the volume of your voice will stimulate interest and help the student maintain focus on what you are saying. Varying your voice pitch will convey different messages to students. A shrillness or monotone will decrease your ability to hold student attention and is often a good indicator of your emotional state.

The pace at which you converse is also important. There is a good chance that when you are talking with a student about his or her behavior, you may be extremely excited, frustrated, or angry. These emotions will tend to make you speak more quickly. Speak slowly enough so that your words are not garbled or incompletely formed. On the other hand, do not speak too slowly or hesitantly, as this may communicate that you are unsure of yourself and not in control of the exchange.

You can also use verbal cues that will enhance conversations about behavior. For example, using silence effectively can encourage students to reflect upon their behavior or to expand on their explanations about their behavior. However, overlong silences create "dead space" which is of little benefit to either the student or the teacher.

You may prompt students by using recognition statements which simply acknowledge that you have heard what they have said to you (e.g., "I see, . . . yes . . . "). Another way to prompt students is to use reflective statements which mirror what the student has said (e.g., if the student says "I hate Sally," you can say something like "So you hate Sally . . . ").

You may wish to interject brief intermittent summaries of what the student has been saying. Summarizing student talk will reflect back to the student what has been said, and will also provide a point of reference which the student can use for further discussion. Reframing what a student is communicating by asking for confirmation may also help (e.g., "Let me see if I understand what you are trying to say. Did you mean that . . . ?"). That is, you may wish to repeat the views of the student without attempting to evaluate the student's feelings or nonverbal impressions.[9]

Teaching students to be responsible for their own behavior may be a difficult task, so avoid using language that makes others responsible for the students' personal conduct (e.g., "It seems like Sally's behavior has made you very angry"). Instead, describe the situation in language that emphasizes personal decisions and responsibility for one's actions (e.g., "So, you got really angry when Sally . . . "). Try not to become sidetracked by student attempts to avoid being held accountable for their actions. Many students are provocative or hostile as a means of reinforcing their external control and low self-esteem. For example, if a student can engage you in talking about how others are to blame for his or her behavior, it is likely that you will spend valuable time attempting to convince the student otherwise. By this time the student will be in control of the conversation and an opportunity for teaching will have been lost.

In order to maintain control of the conversation for the purposes of teaching responsibility, you can respond to the student in one of two ways. First, you may use a directive response with students who have limited problem-solving skills. Offer the student one of two choices (e.g., "You must stop misbehaving or you may go to time out") and allow him or her to decide which will occur. Second, with students who are more internally controlled and who can therefore consider a wider range of alternative behaviors, you can present the student with a number of appropriate behavioral alternatives. Discuss each alternative with the student and negotiate which one will be chosen. This process encourages the student think through each possible solution and to weigh different solutions for behavior change.

Whichever approach you use, you can choose a level of talk appropriate to the behavioral ability level of each individual student. First, you can address the literal meaning of the misbehavior and make no attempt to deepen the implications or considerations of the student's actions. Discuss why the behavior is inappropriate and the steps that are necessary to change it. Once the student is aware of the acceptable alternative, the discussion ends. It is at this level that most talking with students about their behavior occurs.[10] This approach has the advantage of immediately and directly addressing the inappropriate behavior with corrective feedback. A major drawback here, however, is that there may not be enough emphasis on getting the student to reflect on what can be done differently in the future and may not allow the student enough time to contemplate alternative solutions. Also, the student may simply tell you what he or she thinks you want to hear, thereby not taking the discussion seriously enough to ensure appropriate behavior in the future.

Second, you may address the thoughts that motivated the student's behavior to increase the student's intellectual understanding and insight into the problem. The idea here is to give the student an opportunity to practice "thinking before acting," that is, to rehearse contemplating alternative, appropriate behaviors before acting on impulse. This activity is often very helpful to students who may not be aware that their behavior is inappropriate. However, if the student is unable to make the connection between the misbehavior and the motivation that caused it in the first place, he or she may become confused and frustrated.

Third, you may address the underlying feelings of the student which may have caused the misbehavior. Here you try to determine the emotional component that may have motivated the misbehavior. This approach can be useful if you suspect that the student can articulate his or her feelings and can describe any links between behavior and emotion. However, you run the risk of "playing psychotherapist." You may also get deflected into dealing with the student's emotions rather than the behavior.

Talking with a student about his or her behavior in this manner increases awareness of the misbehavior, the consequences of the misbehavior, and the availability of appropriate, alternative solutions.

Active listening is another important prerequisite when talking with students about their behavior so as to differentiate between the emotional and intellectual content of what the student is saying. To accomplish this, it is necessary for you to give the student your full attention by blocking out other distractions. Pay close attention to the verbal and nonverbal actions of the student and try to decide which parts of what the student is saying are facts and which are emotional messages. In this way you can attempt to consciously gauge student feelings and reactions in discussing their behavior. Listen to what the student is saying long enough to evaluate his or her behavioral status. In addition, because active listening is an intensely individual activity, remember that your personal feelings toward the student will influence the unspoken messages you hear.

Active listening provides the student with an opportunity to deal with inappropriate behavior and frustration. Utilizing good listening skills will also convey a sense of empathy to the student and support the possibility of behavioral improvement.

What are the benefits of positive and negative talk with students about their behavior?

Talking with students about their behavior is not limited to discussing inappropriate actions. When appropriate behavior occurs, recognize it and insure that students know that it is appreciated, especially if they have accomplished a difficult task. For some students, being able to choose appropriate behaviors and to increase their personal responsibility for actions is a great achievement.

Some teachers believe that copious praise of appropriate behavior is necessary. Others believe that "catching them being good" applies for every appropriate behavior, and that failing to praise students unceasingly is cause for at least some student misbehavior. Experienced teachers, however, know that the amount of praise is not nearly as important as whether the praise you give is dependent on the student demonstrating desired appropriate behavior. Praise and positive reinforcement applied without careful consideration can be counterproductive or even misleading.[11] Praise that is not contingent on appropriate behavior may also damage your credibility as the teacher.[12]

It is important to avoid using praise as a means of shielding students from the consequences of their actions. If you praise students indiscriminately, you may convey an unrealistic sense of accomplishment to them. Indiscriminate praise may also embarrass a student in that he or she may feel singled out from the rest of the class. You further risk teaching students that their internal motivation is totally dependent on external praise for what they do. If this happens, students will have difficulty in situations where praise is not given but where certain behaviors are expected. Furthermore, while praise is a powerful reinforcer, overuse will lessen its effect. Make sure, too, that your praise reinforces exactly what you want it to, and not another associated unacceptable behavior. For example, if a student with a history of aggressive behavior finally refrains from hitting another child, but curses instead, do not give the message that inappropriate verbal behavior is acceptable—concentrate instead on the increased control in not hitting.

It is equally true, though, that praise should be used more than negative or aversive comments.[13] To be effective, praise should be genuine and for a justifiable, earned reason. When you praise a student, it's best not to be overly dramatic, as some students interpret this as a sign of insincerity. Instead, deliver praise in a calm, natural voice. Praise should be spontaneous and should not be disruptive either to the recipient or the rest of the class. Students may be embarrassed by public praise from a teacher and by ridicule from peers for receiving it.[14] For some students, it is preferable to praise effort in private, although many students enjoy recognition in front of their peers for a job well done. How you deal with this issue relies on your knowledge of each individual student.

Use praise in relation to a specific student behavior which acknowledges a task especially well done. It also helps if you avoid using ambiguous statements that do not directly address the behavior being praised.[15] Praise should be used with all students, not only those who mostly provide desirable behaviors. In fact, students who have the most problems with behavior may be the very students who benefit most from praise.

Try not to use praise as a way of interpreting your own expectations and attitudes. Instead, use it to guide students towards more self-determination, self-control, and learning (e.g., instead of saying "Good, when you do that it makes me feel great," you might want to say "Good, you made a great choice about how to do that.") Using praise in this way encourages internal control in the student because it calls attention to personal student accomplishments rather than compliance with the desires of the teacher, which fosters external control.

Negative teacher talk is detrimental to appropriate student behavior and achievement. Constant negativity or belittling talk is unlikely to convince a student to improve behavior. It may, however, easily have the opposite effect. There is little point in embarrassing a student when talking about his or her behavior, especially in front of the rest of the class. Resorting to language that causes shame is a personal attack on the student's self-esteem. Your objective should be to address the student's behavior and ways of improving responsible actions. Sarcasm, insults, and offensive language should be avoided. Polite, courteous language is not only professional—it also provides a model for students to learn from throughout the year. If possible, addressing issues in private is preferable, although this will not always be practical. When you talk to students about their behavior in front of their peers, confine conversation to the behavior itself. If it becomes necessary to confront a student, allow for an opportunity for the student to save face. A partial solution to this problem may be to talk to the student close by and in a soft voice. In this way you will reduce the chances of other students overhearing what you are saying. Doing this also teaches the rest of the class that they may expect the same dignified treatment.

You can structure interactions with students by talking in such a way that you reduce the number of negative messages and increase the number of positive messages. Increased use of positive messages will increase the chances of favorable behaviors recurring. For example, even critical feedback can be worded without being attacking or personally offensive. Using "I" messages that take responsibility for your feelings are helpful (e.g., "I feel that throwing the book on the floor was a poor choice of behavior"). In this way you are able to express disapproval without attacking the character of the student. It does not follow, however, that the more positive the teacher talk, the better student behavior and achievement will be. A neutral and businesslike approach in talking with students is at least as effective as an overly positive approach. Most successful teachers maintain a supportive but controlled attitude in their classrooms.[16] Less successful teachers tend to engage in talk that is either excessively positive or excessively authoritarian and harsh.[17] Also, teachers who are more internally controlled take responsibility for their talk and the progress of their classes and are more effective than teachers who blame the way they talk with students on circumstances or their students.

Are there appropriate ways of talking with angry or aggressive students about their behavior?

It is likely that most teachers do not have carefully prepared and rehearsed responses to angry or aggressive students. Sometimes teachers fail to prepare for this eventuality because such situations are usually few and far between. It is also difficult to prepare for every possible situation because the circumstances of each encounter are unique. You can, however, prepare yourself in a general way. First, define for yourself which behaviors you will tolerate and which are unacceptable. Generally, completely unacceptable behaviors involve situations in which one or more students display behaviors that either lead to, or may lead to, serious classroom disruption or physical/property damage. Such situations may involve fighting, self-injury, destruction of property or attacks on the teacher. Second, once you have a clear set of limits, think through as many problem situations as possible, envisioning how you will act. Work out a "prepackaged" strategy for dealing with each situation and rehearse the physical and verbal steps that will be necessary to regain control of the communication. Third, practice speaking in a calm tone and rehearse giving firm directions and commands. This kind of "imaging" will not prepare you for every eventuality, but it will provide enough support "on the spot" so that you have time to think of other solutions or, if necessary, to get assistance.

Ideally, preventative talking strategies are preferable to reactive interventions. There is much more to be gained by nipping a problem in the bud by a simple comment than in trying to deal with a full-blown crisis, where talking with a student tends to become less and less effective as the crisis escalates. It is important, however, that while you do not let a situation get out of control, you do not overreact, either. Overreaction sometimes causes major problems that can be avoided by ignoring minor infringements in the first place. Judging what to ignore and what to attend to will increase with experience, but your decisions will be helped by constant vigilance and your clear understanding of what you are prepared to tolerate in your classroom.

If you are forced to deal reactively with a suddenly out-of-control situation, the first prerequisite is to prevent any harm to anyone in the room and to de-escalate the emotionally charged situation as quickly as possible. In this situation, talking with a student is rarely effective. For example, if two students are fighting, telling them to stop is not likely to work. Physical intervention may be required.

Assuming there is no physical danger, talk in a firm yet nonthreatening manner, conveying that you are in control and are not threatened or intimidated by the behavior. If an angry student perceives that you are afraid, there is always the chance of increased aggression. Speak calmly and in a natural voice. Simultaneously lower and relax your hands and arms to appear nonthreatening. Be alert, however, for any physical threat to yourself or other students. Avoid touching the student, as this may escalate their anger. Talk only about what is happening at that moment and avoid reciting past problems or transgressions. It is best, too, in spite of any personal feelings that you may have, to avoid having the last word. Do not, at all costs, taunt the student. Do not threaten or talk about how much you will punish the student. Instead, delay talking about consequences until later when tempers have cooled and you are sure to be in full control of the discussion.

Initially, try to buy some "breathing room." The object of buying time is to allow you to regroup and move into your "prepackaged" verbal strategies that will reduce the immediate problem. To buy time, you can command students to different parts of the room, instruct them to engage in a new or different classroom activity, or insist on silence among arguing or fighting students until the situation is calmer. Sometimes an angry student can be deflected by your suggestion of an alternative behavior or activity. This also provides an interim time for the student to regroup and to regain some control. Another useful intervention involves asking the students to comply with a small request rather than insisting on a total move from anger to compliance.

Do I talk with students who display less serious behaviors in the same way as I communicate with angry or aggressive students?

Not all behaviors require such structured verbal intervention. In many instances minor outbursts from a defiant or angry student can be handled differently. Punitive measures are not always necessary for the first outburst, but you should communicate that you are aware that the misbehavior has occurred and that continued misbehavior is unacceptable. You also want to let the student know that if he or she continues to misbehave, consequences will follow. In addition, some students may need to be reminded of appropriate forms of behavior. In these instances, talking with students about their behavior should be brief, to the point, and unattached to any other conversational content. It may be necessary to remind the rest of the class to keep on working, thereby communicating that you will not let the outburst detract from on task behavior. Later, you should reflect on what caused the misbehavior, and, if necessary, adjust the classroom climate to avoid further problems.

How can I use questioning to get the information I need from students about their behavior?

Most teachers see questioning as part of teaching the curriculum rather than a critical part of talking with students about their behavior. However, the way questions are used and the employment of different questioning techniques may mean the difference between effective communication or understanding and alienation or disruption. Questions may be used to motivate students, to help them think about their behavior, and to provide them with information for more appropriate behavior. Questions also allow you to assess a student's behavioral state of mind.

Questioning students about their behavior usually takes the form of either open or closed questions. Closed questions are more restricting because they ask for either very specific information or a yes/no response. It is best to avoid excessive use of yes/no questions except as a warm-up for other questions (e.g., "Did you tear the page?" would be a warm-up question for addressing alternative behaviors for refraining from tearing pages). There are several disadvantages in using closed questions. First, closed questions allow only a simple choice between two alternatives. This means that the student is forced to pick one answer over another, effectively preventing discussion or reflection on more appropriate behavior. Second, closed questions do not give the teacher much information about what the student is thinking. Third, unless closed questions are used sparingly, teachers often end up asking one yes/no question after another—a practice that is ineffective and frustrating for both teacher and student.

On the other hand, open questions are less restricting because they allow students to formulate their own answers. Students who have to think of their own answers must engage in internal self-talk to select from a variety of responses to your question. For example, instead of saying "Did you tear the book?" (closed question) you may make more progress by asking an open question such as "What can you tell me about the torn book?"

Bear in mind that questions should contain natural, everyday language (i.e., as opposed to textbook language) and should be simply worded at a level appropriate to the age and ability of the child. Many students are easily confused by questions containing unfamiliar words. Make questions brief, because briefer questions are usually clearer than longer ones. Make sure that you ask one question at a time. Some students find it difficult to remember long or multiple-part questions. Questions should be purposeful and address exactly the behavior you wish to discuss. At the same time, however, make the question demanding so that the student will need to carefully consider before answering.[18]

There is little point in asking trick questions as they only convey a sense of powerlessness to the student. Trick questions will also increase student reluctance to answer questions in the future. Avoid using elliptical questions, where the question is asked in the form of an incomplete sentence (e.g., "The reason you can't behave is . . . ?"). The only person who knows exactly what the completed question (and therefore the answer) is will be you. Elliptical questions force children to guess. Tugging questions, where students are repeatedly prompted for an answer, should also be avoided ("Well, ... C'mon . . .). Students may perceive tugging questions as a form of nagging or bullying. It is also less helpful to ask questions where students have to guess the answer (e.g., "What will your parents think about your misbehavior?"). Leading questions (e.g., "Don't you agree that you should behave better?") are equally ineffective.

Wait-time in conversation is especially important when questioning students about their behavior. Wait-time communicates that an answer is expected and simultaneously allows the student sufficient time to think about a response.[19] Most researchers recommend that 3 to 4 seconds is appropriate when waiting for a student response. Many teachers do not allow enough time for students to formulate answers before prompting answers or asking another question. Not waiting for a student response may communicate to the student a feeling of being rushed or pressured to answer.

How do I talk with students when delivering consequences for their inappropriate behavior?

When talking with students, insist on appropriate behavior. Be consistent in reminding students of rules, consequences, and the limits you have set. Consistency in your conversations about behavior will convey a sense of predictability that students can use to judge their future behavior.[20] State your case firmly and when you are not angry. On the other hand, trying to enforce your demands apologetically may indicate that you can be intimidated out of applying consequences. Rules and consequences should be stated clearly and briefly without "lecturing." Do not resort to asking questions about obvious misbehavior or make unnecessary threats or appeals to higher authority. Try to keep it simple: This is the violation, this is the rule, this is the consequence.

In spite of your best efforts, there will probably be times when you impose consequences which, as soon as you have imposed them, seem unreasonable or impractical. In these instance it may be appropriate to withdraw the consequence and tell the student why (e.g., Sarah, I told you that you would need to stay in at recess every day for the next month. I said this when I was frustrated and upset, and now it seems an inappropriate consequence. I will think of a fairer consequence and tell you about it before the end of school today"). Of course, if you do this repeatedly, students will come to understand that you are either not serious about what you say or that you are unable to control their inappropriate behavior in consistent ways.

A similar approach is probably best when giving students directions. Make sure that you are clear in your mind as to what you want done. Giving students directions that are then changed because you are not clear about what you expect will be confusing and frustrating. It's best to be sure that the student is listening before proceeding in a firm clear voice.

Often when you follow this direct communication pattern, students may attempt to make excuses or whine in order to avoid consequences of their actions. Do not accept these behaviors if you are sure that rules have been broken. The simplest solution is to repeat the consequence and ignore the ploy to entrap you in a protracted conversation about the legitimacy of your classroom rules. If whining continues to the point of becoming disruptive, an appropriate intervention such as time out may be considered.

Coping with students' excuses about their behavior can be especially troublesome. Don't be fooled by denial, the blaming of others, or self-deprecating excuses, which often make teachers think that the student is taking responsibility for the misbehavior. First, it is usually unproductive to ask the student why the misbehavior happened. Invariably, the answer is "I don't know." The "why" question serves no purpose in either changing the behavior or in teaching the student behavioral responsibility. Second, moralizing about the misbehavior only tells the students what they already know, namely, that they have transgressed in some way. The information the student needs is how to improve his or her behavior the next time around. Third, it may be best not to accept statements of good intentions. While students are usually sincere, promising to "be good" in the future may have little meaning because they have learned that promising good intentions is often expected by adults. Furthermore, children often forget their good intentions shortly after fervently insisting that the misbehavior will never happen again. Instead, talk with the student to define the problem, talk about a possible range of alternative solutions, select an appropriate solution, and then obtain a commitment from the student to carry through with the selected solution the next time a similar situation arises.

Stating consequences in the manner described above will lessen the likelihood of getting into a power struggle with a student over inappropriate behaviors. Most power struggles with students revolve around refusal to comply with your classroom limits and work demands. Engaging in a power struggle may result in an escalating conflict—hardly a way to teach appropriate behavior. You are more likely to avoid power struggles if you are not angry and if you ignore the student's attempts to engage you in the struggle. If the student persists in trying to draw you into an argument or conflict, you may be able to remain unengaged by simply acknowledging the student's feelings. Another solution may be to acknowledge privately to the student that you are aware of the ploy to engage you in the power struggle and that you refuse to be part of it. Power struggles can further be avoided by knowing the unique perceptions of your students and by being sensitive to when intervention is necessary, or when you would be better served in the long run by waiting for another time for confrontation.

How can I teach students behavioral self-control?

Self-control and the autonomous selection of appropriate behaviors are prime goals in dealing with students with mild disabilities.[21] Talking with students about their behavior is a first step towards getting students to assume control over their actions. Some students consistently show only small gains in transferring what they learn about their behavior in specific situations to more generalized social skills. A major aim of talking with students, therefore, must be focused on assisting students to monitor, evaluate, and modify their behavior on their own. In this way your role in taking responsibility for student behavior will be lessened over time as the student assumes greater control.

A student's self-assessment of his or her behavior is the initial step toward self-control. First, help the student decide if his or her behavior is appropriate. In order to make this decision, the student must carefully compare personal actions to the standard set by the classroom rules of conduct, learning, and peer social interaction. If the behavior is inappropriate, encourage the student to modify the misbehavior by considering several possible solutions to the problem. Discuss each option with the student and be supportive of the process of selecting a more appropriate behavior. Reinforce the student for choosing an appropriate behavior to be used in the future.

Encouraging self assessment depends largely on the willingness of the student to change his or her behavior to more acceptable alternatives and the ability to understand why the behavior change is necessary. Negotiation of the new behavior will be shaped by the expectations of both the teacher and the student. Negotiation is effective because there is little point in using teacher-imposed expectations that students are unable or unwilling to attain.

Second, when the replacement behavior has been agreed upon, devise a self-recording system so that the student can accurately note how often the new, appropriate behavior occurs and how well it was implemented. The recording system provides a measure of the student's ability to consciously be aware of the behavior change. Self-recording of the replacement behavior encourages the student to use self-talk. Further, it helps the student keep a record of the degree of control he or she has over the change in behavior. Self-recording also helps the student internalize control of the new behavior. In turn, the more internal control the student can exercise over his or her new behavior, the greater the likelihood that what is learned in one specific behavioral situation will generalize to other behaviors and situations. Once self-recording has begun, you can talk with the student about his or her progress. Be sure to reinforce increases in appropriate behavior. As the new behavior emerges, the student can evaluate the success of the replacement of the old misbehavior. It is important that you keep a tally of the appearance of the new behavior. When you talk with the student about how well the behavior has been implemented, you can compare your tallies to those kept by the student. Such a comparison will help refine the accuracy of the self-recording and will be a "reality check" for unrealistic expectations held by the student or teacher.[22]

Third, students begin administering their own reinforcement for increased appearance of the new appropriate behavior. At this point the student can be instructed to rehearse the steps necessary for maintaining an appropriate behavior, either by internal dialogue or by whispering. Self-talk helps the student improve behavior by talking through the steps necessary to assess, and, if necessary, modify behaviors.

Summary

Talking with students about their behavior cuts across almost all classroom situations. Teachers rely heavily on talking with students as a way of modifying behavior and for teaching appropriate decision-making skills that will result in students being able to control their behavior internally.

Communicating with students about their behavior encompasses much more than casual conversation. The complex setting of the classroom affects how you talk with students. Your skill in talking with students can also have an impact on your instructional goals for individual students and the class as a whole. While there are many talking skills which are equally effective in most situations, your choice of a classroom management model may influence some aspects of talking with students about their behavior. Communication with students about their behavior begins before you become engaged in conversation. Be sure about the purpose you wish to accomplish in talking with the student. A major function of talking with students about their behavior is to foster personal responsibility and for making appropriate behavioral choices. Conversing with students about their behavior involves both verbal and nonverbal strategies which you must model and teach in your interactions with students. It is important to maintain a balanced, business-like approach rather than indulging in excessive praise. On the other hand, negative talk is almost always unproductive and can provoke student anger and stress. Talking strategies differ when you are dealing with angry, aggressive students or students with less serious behaviors. One of the most important skills in talking with students about their behavior is your use of questions. Use direct, clear talking strategies when delivering consequences to students. Remember that a prime aim of talking with students about their behavior is to move them towards independent, internalized responsibility for their actions.

References and Resources for Further Study

The following references provided the basis for many of our statements in this chapter. You may wish to consult selected references for additional information. Our reference notes in this chapter refer to sources in this list.

Brophy, J. (1983). Classroom organization and management. *The Elementary School Journal, 83,* 265-285.

Brophy, J. and Good, T. L. (1986). Teacher behavior and student achievement. In M. C. Wittrock (Ed.), *Handbook of Research on Teaching* (3rd ed.) (pp. 328-375). New York: Macmillan.

Burke, R. R. (1984). *Communicating with Students in Schools.* New York: University Press of America.

Cazden, C. B. (1986). Classroom discourse. In M. C. Wittrock (Ed.), *Handbook of Research on Teaching* (3rd ed.) (pp. 432-463). New York: Macmillan.

Cooper, J. M. (Ed.). (1986). *Classroom Teaching Skills*, (3rd ed.). Lexington, MA: Heath.

Doyle, W. (1986). Classroom organization and management. In M. C. Wittrock (Ed.), *Handbook of Research on Teaching*. New York: Macmillan.

Emmer, E. T., Evertson, C. M., Sanford, J. P., Clements, B. S., and Worsham, M. E. (1989). *Classroom Management for Secondary Teachers*. Englewood Cliffs, NJ: Prentice Hall.

Good, T. L. and Brophy, J. E. (1987). *Looking in Classrooms* (4th ed.). New York: Harper and Row.

Jones, V. F. and Jones, L. S. (1986). *Comprehensive Classroom Management*. Boston: Allyn and Bacon.

Kerr, M. M. and Nelson, C. M. (1989). *Strategies for Managing Tehavior Problems in the Cassroom* (2nd ed.). Columbus, OH: Merrill/Macmillan.

Korinek, L. (1987). Questioning strategies in special education: Links to teacher efficacy research in general education. *Journal of Research and Development in Education, 21*(1), 16-22.

Kounin, J. S. (1970). *Discipline and Group Management in Classrooms*. New York: Holt, Rinehart, and Winston.

Lemire, D., Bailey-Robertson, Y., and Fetsco, T. (1986). Nonverbal communication in middle schools: The importance of teacher and student body language. *Techniques: A Journal for Remedial Education and Counseling, 2*, 167-172.

Levine, H. G. and Mann, K. (1985). The nature and functions of teacher talk in a classroom for mentally retarded learners. *Elementary School Journal, 86*, 185-198.

Macht, J. (1990). *Managing Classroom Behavior*. New York: Longman.

Seiler, W. J., Schuelke, L. D., and Lieb-Brilhart, B. (1984). *Communication for the Contemporary Classroom*. New York: Holt, Reinhart, and Winston.

Selman, R. L. and Demarest, A. P. (1984). Observing troubled children's interpersonal negotiation strategies: Implications of and for a developmental model. *Child Development, 55*, 288-304.

Steere, B. F. (1988). Becoming an Effective Classroom Manager: A Resource for Teachers. Albany: State University of New York Press.

Weber, W. A., Crawford, J., Roff, L. A., and Robinson, C. (1983). *Classroom Management: Reviews of the Teacher Education and Research Literature* [Monograph]. Princeton, NJ: Educational Testing Service.

Webster, R. E. (1986). Use of the process interaction model for therapeutic intervention with behaviorally disordered adolescents. *Techniques: A Journal for Remedial Education and Counseling, 2*, 156–166.

Webster, R. E., and Johnson, M. M. (1987). Teacher-student verbal communication patterns in regular and special classrooms. *Psychology in the Schools, 24*, 174–179.

Wood, F. H. (Ed.). (1990). When we talk with children: The life space interview. *Behavioral Disorders,* [Special Section], *15*, 110–126.

Wood, M. M., and Long, N. J. (1991). *Life Space Intervention: Talking with Children and Youth in Crisis*. Austin, TX: Pro–Ed.

Zigmond, N., Sansone, J., Miller, S. E., Donohoe, K. A., and Kohnke, R. (1986). Teaching learning disabled at the secondary level: What research says to teachers. *Learning Disabilities Focus, 1*, 108–115.

Reference Notes

1. See Doyle (1986) for further description of classrooms.
2. See Good and Brophy (1987) for discussion.
3. See Kounin (1970) for discussion of "with-it-ness."
4. See Macht (1990), Wood (1990), and Wood and Long (1991).
5. See Steere (1988) for discussion of the effects of space on students.
6. See Emmer et al. (1989) for discussion of eye contact.
7. See Jones and Jones (1986).
8. See Burke (1984) for discussion of the use of metaphors and similes.
9. See Emmer et al. (1989).
10. See Webster and Johnson (1987).
11. See Macht (1990).
12. See Good and Brophy (1987), Jones and Jones (1986), and Kerr and Nelson (1989) for discussion of effective praise.
13. See Good and Brophy (1987), Jones and Jones (1986), and Kerr and Nelson (1989) for discussion of reprimands and other aversive comments.
14. See Good and Brophy (1987).
15. See Good and Brophy (1987), Kerr and Nelson (1989), and Macht (1990) for discussion of specific praise statements.
16. See Zigmond et al. (1986) for elaboration.
17. See Brophy and Good (1986).
18. See Good and Brophy (1987) for further discussion of questioning.
19. See Good and Brophy (1987) for further discussion of wait time.
20. See Kerr and Nelson (1989) and Macht (1990) for discussion of consistency.
21. See Kerr and Nelson for discussion regarding students with disabilities.
22. See Kerr and Nelson for further discussion of self-recording.

Chapter 5

Using Peer Influence

Questions for Reflection

How might I use observational learning and vicarious consequences to affect the behavior of my students' peers?

What type of group contingency might I use to create desirable peer pressure?

How might I engage classroom peers as confederates?

How might I use peer tutors as a classroom resource?

What options should I consider in teaching social skills?

We usually assume that the most important things students learn in school are the things they learn from their teachers. Our assumption may or may not be correct. We know that students learn a great deal from each other. Our hope is that what they learn from each other improves their conduct and achievement, but we know that this is often not the case. Students learn much by observing each other, and their observations sometimes lead to conflicts or withdrawal. Frequent serious conflicts with peers or minimal interactions with peers are indications that a student is likely to have long-term personal problems, as we noted in Chapter 1.

Teaching requires the management of groups to foster positive and satisfying peer relations. Teachers must recognize the pervasive influence of peer groups in nearly every person's life. Our peer group is a relentless influence on our behavior, regardless of our age or societal role. As adults—more specifically, as teachers—we are concerned about what our peers think of us. Moreover, our colleagues' behavior influences our perceptions of important events, many of our decisions, and significant aspects of our professional relationships.

As responsible adults, we are aware of peer influences. We may consciously choose certain friends and control our relationships with our peers to enhance our professional skills, ethical conduct, and personal satisfaction. Many of our students, however, are not so aware of peer influence nor so astute in choosing their associations. Teachers have an obligation to do what they can to make positive peer influence an important aspect of their students' lives in the classroom and to help students learn to make wise

Sally: Kevin, as I said, was a real problem because he didn't comply with my requests or commands. That's the reason I made up little compliance lessons in which I had him practice doing what I told him. My first thought was to teach him individually, but then two things occurred to me. First of all, he didn't interact much with any of the other kids in my class. He was a very, very strange little boy in many ways and didn't seem to pay much attention to his classmates. Most of the time he seemed "spaced out" and not in touch with what was going on around him. Second, I had another child in my class, Derrick, who was a lot more compliant than Kevin but still needed a little improvement. I thought it'd be a good idea to teach Kevin and Derrick together in my compliance lessons. Derrick could serve as a model for Kevin because he would usually do what I asked. My strategy early in the lessons was to get an appropriate response from Derrick to one of my instructions, reinforce him, then ask Kevin to do the same thing. I also alternated instructions so that Derrick wasn't always the first to respond. This approach worked really well because Derrick was, at first, a good model for Kevin. But I also found that Kevin started interacting with Derrick at other times during the day.

Chris: Ned was considered a "nerd" by his classmates. I even heard some of them say things like "Oh, God, it's Ned the nerd!" to his face or call him "Dopey" or "Sleepy." The teasing he took from some of the less thoughtful kids was awful. He was an easy target because he was so painfully shy and got terribly flustered if anybody asked him anything. He almost never talked to anyone in school, peers or adults. I found out that he spent most of his time at home in his room. The kids in the neighborhood that he had anything to do with were 8- and 10-year-olds, and he was 14. The school counselor and I noticed that Ned had just about zero social skills. He didn't look people in the eye when he talked to them, he didn't have any idea how to start up a conversation with his peers, and he didn't know how to respond when someone tried to start a conversation with him. We developed some lessons in conversational skills for Ned, including how to initiate conversations, how to respond to others' initial comments, how to show interest and emotional responses, and how to handle eye contact during conversations. The counselor taught these basic skills in one-to-one sessions with Ned at first. She would discuss the importance of the skill, model it, and then have Ned rehearse using it with her. Ned not only learned the social skills we taught him in these sessions, but he learned how to use them with his peers. In fact, he started asking classmates to visit him at home, began dating, and even tried out for a school team.

"Chris" is based on Franco, D. P., Christoff, K. A., Crimmins, D. B., and Kelly, J. A. (1983). Social skills training for an extremely shy young adolescent: An empirical case study. *Behavior Therapy*, *14*, pp. 568–575.

choices about peer relationships. The vignettes "Sally" and "Chris" illustrate some of the issues teachers face in helping students get along with and learn appropriate behavior from their peers.

Peer pressure will be at work in the classroom whether the teacher harnesses it or not. Social pressure from peers is more obvious in some classrooms than in others. In some classrooms it obviously affects every student, while in others it is seen most clearly in an "in group." In some classrooms the pressure of the in group is for academic achievement, but in many classrooms there is pressure to resist academic learning and to be disruptive. Some classrooms are characterized by feelings of belonging or togetherness of all the students, while others are characterized by tension, divisiveness, scapegoating, exclusive cliques, and destructive competition.

Experienced teachers know that every group, like every individual student, is different from every other. Some groups are easy and some are difficult to manage. The group's character seems to depend on the mix of individuals comprising it and the circumstances that bring it together. The differences in peer relations that we observe in different classrooms are not due only to differences in teachers' skill in managing groups. Still, there are enough common or predictable features of groups and peer interactions that we can offer suggestions about strategies that are likely to be useful in accomplishing specific goals. Important questions teachers need to ask themselves about managing peer influence include these:

- How can I harness peer pressure as an effective force for improving my students' behavior and achievement?
- How can I encourage cooperation and caring for each other among my students?
- How can I help students on the social fringes of the class become better accepted among their peers?

Questions for Reflection

As you contemplate what you might do to foster good peer relations among your students and how you might use group pressure effectively and humanely, you will need to keep in mind the basic psychological processes involved in social groups. For example, people in groups learn much by observing each other, especially by noticing the positive and negative consequences others experience. Watching what happens to others not only reveals how to obtain consequences, it also allows the observer to experience those consequences *vicariously*—as a substitute for one's own experience. Finally, individuals in groups are loosely or tightly bound together by structures that are imposed by group leaders or by an outside authority. The way individuals relate to each other as group members depends partly on the rules for sharing in each others' success and failure. We suggest that you ask yourself at least the following questions about specific strategies:

1. How might I use observational learning and vicarious consequences to affect the behavior of my students' peers?
2. What type of group contingency might I use to create desirable peer pressure?
3. How might I engage classroom peers as confederates?
4. How might I use peer tutors as a classroom resource?
5. What options should I consider in teaching social skills?

How might I use observational learning and vicarious consequences to affect the behavior of my students' peers?

Teachers must always be aware that they are serving as models for their students. Youngsters learn a lot about teaching, parenting, relating to peers, and other aspects of socialization by watching adults. We need to be particularly concerned about whether we are practicing what we preach, as our students probably will learn at least as much from what they see as they do from what they hear. One question always in our minds should be whether our students would be behaving appropriately if they imitated us. We recognize that adults have prerogatives that children and adolescents do not have. Yet, we do not want to lose sight of the importance of adults providing good models for younger generations.

Children and adolescents are also keen observers of each other. Perceptive teachers use students' tendency to watch and imitate their peers as a means of improving the conduct of those who exhibit inappropriate behavior. They do this by having students whose conduct is desirable serve as models for others who are misbehaving or having difficulty learning. The inappropriate conduct that may be improved through peer modeling includes a wide range of problems such as inattentive, aggressive, or socially withdrawn behavior; it may also include lack of study skills or specific academic difficulties.

Using observational learning successfully requires careful selection of the model whom you hope will be imitated. You also must reward the model and the student(s) you want to imitate the model in ways that do not discourage the observers. When you use procedures that are intended to enhance observational learning, it is likely that most or all students in the classroom will experience vicarious effects. That is, when any student receives reinforcing or punishing consequences, those who are watching probably will be affected indirectly through their vicarious experience of the reward or punishment.[1]

Models Who Are Likely to Be Imitated

Some individuals are much more likely than others to be imitated by their peers. This means that when you use an observational learning strategy you must attempt to choose a model whose behavior probably will be most influential with the target student. Research does not indicate precisely the type of model who is most likely to be imitated in every circumstance, but we can offer some general guidelines. Usually, you would be wise to choose a model whom the target student sees as attractive, competent, and similar to himself or herself in important ways (e.g., someone of the same sex and close to the same general ability level). If the behavior you hope the target student will imitate is one that he or she has had considerable difficulty learning, then a *coping* model is likely best—a model whom the target student can see overcoming difficulties on the way to mastery, not one who has already mastered the behavior and performs it effortlessly and flawlessly. For example, if you are looking for a model to help a target student overcome a serious fear of talking in class, the best classmate to serve as a model will not be one who enjoys public speaking. Rather, it will be one who has some hesitation about speaking up but manages to overcome his or her anxiety about it. Watching someone who shares your anxiety or difficulty overcome it and perform successfully tends to make you feel that you can do the same; observing someone who apparently never shared your struggle isn't nearly as encouraging.

There are two principles to keep in mind: First, the model must be personally attractive to the observer, or imitation is not likely to occur. We tend to imitate people we admire, not those whom we see as offensive, obtuse, or undesirable. We tend to see people as attractive models if we perceive them as sharing some of our characteristics but as somewhat "better" than ourselves along certain dimensions. Second, the model must exhibit behavior that the observer believes he or she can imitate successfully. We often imitate people we admire, even if we perceive that they are very different from us in most respects, but what we imitate may have little or nothing to do with the primary reason we find them attractive. For example, people often imitate the dress or mannerisms of popular musicians but have no intention of imitating—and no ability to imitate—their musicianship. If someone is just learning to play a musical instrument or learn another skill, the best model is someone who can demonstrate a level of skill just above his or hers. Virtuosic performances may provide inspiration to continue learning, but beginners who are expected to imitate a master are likely to get discouraged and give up. Teachers sometimes make the mistake of choosing models who are too "good" or too competent to be encouraging of imitation by the target student.

Rewarding the Model and Target Student

Sometimes models are imitated even though the imitators are not directly rewarded. However, the target student is much more likely to imitate the model you have chosen if he or she sees the model receiving reinforcement for appropriate behavior. Thus it is important to provide the reinforcement for the model when the target student is watching. In some cases, if the target student is unaware that the model is to be imitated, you may need to prompt the target student by telling him or her to watch the way the model behaves (or solves a problem). Then you must be sure to reinforce the target student immediately when his or her behavior approximates that of the model. If the target student observes that others receive rewards for a given behavior, but that he or she is not rewarded for the same behavior, the result may be demoralization or inappropriate behavior. The model's behavior should demonstrate the kind of behavior or performance you expect; your response to the model should demonstrate that such behavior will be rewarded; and the target student's attempts to imitate the model should be rewarded.

In the typical classroom, a lot of things are going on simultaneously. Individual students' behavior is sometimes good, sometimes not so good. You will be more likely to encourage good behavior in the group if you call attention to the specific conduct of well-behaved students. Make your social reinforcement of desirable conduct as specific as possible, so that the behavior you want to encourage in observing students is not only demonstrated by the model but described. "John, I like the way you waited to be called on" is better than "Thank you, John, for being polite" because it is a more specific description of the behavior you want observers to imitate.

Limits of Vicarious Effects

Teachers who are excellent behavior managers often make good use of vicarious effects to encourage good conduct. For example, when they observe minor misbehavior they ignore it and show obvious approval for appropriate behavior of another student, usually someone in close proximity to the one who is misbehaving. In this way they offer a vicarious prompt to the misbehaving student; they are saying, in effect, "Behave in this way (like the appropriately behaved student), because then you will get my attention and approval." They focus on desirable conduct, knowing that the observing students may not only be prompted to behave appropriately but experience vicarious gratification when they behave in the same way as those who are being rewarded.

Rewarding models in the hope that observers will imitate desirable behavior can backfire if you are not prepared for at least two possible complications. First, you must be careful not to rely on a single model or a small group. If only one or a small group of students is constantly featured as fulfilling your expectations, then the rest of the class is likely to see you as playing favorites or having "pets." This will quickly destroy the effectiveness of the models and undermine your use of rewarding consequences. Make sure that you catch the good behavior of as many different students as possible and call attention to it. Second, in some groups—and this tends to be a particular problem among adolescents—"teacher pleasing" behavior is an anathema—taboo, something that carries a stigma. You must be prepared for groups in which typical statements of praise or approval are *not* rewarding and may, in fact, be punishing. This does not mean that you cannot use vicarious consequences or that you must become punitive. It means that you must be very shrewd in rewarding the behavior you want to encourage. You may need to keep your praise and approval minimal and emphasize—matter-of-factly—rewarding consequences that are meaningful to the group. These consequences may be activities or privileges that members of the group see as desirable.

We caution further that few people, if any, can live by vicarious effects alone. We may be able to share to some extent in the joy and pain we see others experiencing directly, but others' lives can not become a substitute for our own direct experience. Compared to direct experience of consequences, vicarious effects are weak. Furthermore, vicarious approaches typically work well with groups that are generally well-behaved; they are not likely to work with groups that are highly disruptive or out of control. For very poorly behaved groups, frequent direct rewards for individuals who are behaving appropriately are typically necessary.

We offer an additional caution about the limitations of vicarious effects. If an individual observes others receiving consequences for certain behavior but receives no consequences for the same behavior, the effect is likely to be the opposite vicarious consequence. For example, if a student in your class sees others receiving rewarding consequences for certain behavior, yet he or she seldom or never is rewarded for behaving similarly, then the effect will in all likelihood be vicarious punishment—he or she will feel, by comparison to others who are being rewarded, punished. Alternatively, if a student sees others being punished for certain behavior, yet he or she is not punished for similar behavior, then the effect will be vicarious reinforcement—he or she will feel rewarded. This principle suggests that favoritism or bias in a teacher's consequences will compound behavior problems. Students who observe their classmates receiving rewarding or punishing consequences for a specific kind of behavior should receive the same treatment. If they do not receive at least similar treatment, then the effect on their behavior is likely to be the *opposite* of that for those who are receiving direct consequences.

What type of group contingency might I use to create desirable peer pressure?

The contingencies of reinforcement teachers use often apply to individuals without any reference to the peer group. However, contingencies can also be arranged for groups in a variety of ways, some of which produce considerable peer pressure on individuals to behave in ways that earn rewards or avoid punishment.

The phenomenon of group pressure is well-known to all of us, and it is a pervasive feature of social groups. Consider the group pressure that is part of political parties, unions, professional organizations, fraternities and sororities, and religious groups. All of these rely on peer pressure as one means of controlling the behavior of members and furthering their collective aims. We cannot conclude that group pressure is undesirable, although we can think of examples in which groups have destructive aims or use excessive and cruel peer pressure. As teachers, our task is to encourage peer pressure for appropriate behavior and keep it from becoming excessive or inhumane.

Any contingency oriented toward a group will create some level of peer pressure. Group-oriented contingencies include those in which the same rules apply to all individuals independently, those in which consequences for the entire group depend on the behavior of one member, and those in which the consequences for the entire group are interdependent—all members of the group obtain the same consequences based on the combined behavior of its members. Each type of contingency has certain advantages and disadvantages in the classroom. Combinations of group and individual contingencies are possible, and you may want to consider how you could combine contingencies to structure the most effective learning environment for specific individuals and groups.

Independent Group Contingencies

Independent group contingencies are those that apply uniformly to each student, regardless of the performance of the group. For example, you might establish the following contingency for students in your classroom: If you turn in acceptably completed homework, you are allowed to participate in a 5-minute period of free time for talking with friends. This is a group contingency, in that it applies to the entire class; it is independent, in that one student's behavior does not affect any other student's consequences (the possible exception being a conversation partner).

Independent group contingencies have the advantage of focusing on individual responsibility. Their disadvantage in managing a group is that they do not generate much peer pressure. About the only pressure from peers will be that already present in the form of friendship ties and the relatively weak and indirect influences of modeling and vicarious consequences.

Dependent Group Contingencies

Dependent group contingencies are those under which rewards are available for all group members only when requirements are met by one member or a small subset of the group. An example of a dependent group contingency is the "hero procedure" used by Gerald Patterson and his colleagues.[2] They made class "heroes" of hyperactive, disruptive students by setting a contingency under which these students earned rewards for the entire class by paying attention and behaving appropriately.

An advantage of dependent group contingencies can be positive peer pressure—peers may "root for" the target student and do whatever they can to encourage him or her to behave appropriately because they have something to gain by doing so. Another possible advantage is that the social status of the target student may be improved if his or her behavior becomes a source of rewards for peers. A disadvantage is that the misbehaving student can become a target for peer harassment and the other members of the class can feel that they are being denied an "entitlement" when they do not receive a reward. The way the dependent group contingency is presented, as well as the nature of the group to which it is applied, may determine whether the advantages outweigh the disadvantages or vice versa. The reward earned for the entire group by the target student must be an extra—an add-on to the rewarding consequences routinely available to the group—or there is too much risk of negative peer reactions when the reward is not earned.

Interdependent Group Contingencies

Interdependent group contingencies are those in which a specific requirement for a reward applies to all members of the group but the reward depends on the combined or total performance of the group, as well as the behavior of individuals. That is, the group's combined performance is the criterion for anyone's receiving reinforcement, and all share equally in the reward. For example, a teacher might allow the class to participate in a special activity after each member of the class completes an assignment successfully. Team sports are, basically, interdependent group contingencies—individuals contribute to the team's success, but it is the team, not an individual, that wins.

The "Good Behavior Game" is an interdependent group contingency that has been used in a variety of forms by teachers.[3] The essential features of the game are these: (1) the teacher states certain rules that apply to all members of the class, (2) all members of the class can earn points for the class (or their "team," a subgroup of the class) by behaving according to the rules, and (3) the class (or team) earns rewards, depending on the total number of points earned by the group's members. In some variations on the game, the class or team has earned a reward for accumulating *less* than a certain number of points given for specific misbehavior (i.e., the rules of the game were reversed, with low misbehavior points "winning").

Interdependent group contingencies typically create peer pressure; whether it is primarily positive or negative pressure depends a lot on the composition of the "teams." One member can sabotage the team, creating considerable hostility among other team members. Teams that are clearly unequal in ability quickly create problems. Overemphasis on competition can cause scapegoating and other negative peer interactions. Our suggestion is that you consider using interdependent group contingencies, as they are powerful devices for harnessing peer pressure, but that you use them with considerable caution.

Cooperative Learning

Nearly every teacher has at least heard the term "cooperative learning," if not read about or been instructed in cooperative learning procedures. Many variations on the theme of cooperative learning are possible, but they all have in common the combined use of independent and interdependent group contingencies. Pairs or larger teams of students work under contingencies in which their combined performance, as well as their individual improvement, is evaluated and rewarded. Some variants of cooperative learning deemphasize individual achievement and concentrate on group performance and reward. Cooperative learning procedures hold great promise as a means of fostering positive peer interactions. We encourage the use of cooperative learning strategies with the cautions we offer for all group contingencies.

Cautions about Group Contingencies

Group contingencies of the types we have described can encourage positive peer pressure, but they can also backfire and result in negative pressure and coercion if they are not carefully managed. We offer five suggestions for avoiding the common problems of threats, criticism, and harassment from peers when a student does not perform as his or her peers would like. If, in spite of your following our cautions, a group you are managing is putting negative pressure on certain of its members, we recommend that you revise or eliminate the contingency.

First, be certain that the performance standard you set is not too high. You must begin with a criterion for reward that the target student or group can meet easily, then gradually increase the requirement for reward. If you set the standard too high in the beginning, everyone may be disappointed; if you expect gradual improvement over time, however, the target student or group is more likely to win approval from the rest of the class. Early success in achieving the reward should be virtually guaranteed in the beginning by setting a requirement that represents slight improvement over current behavior.

Second, emphasize reward for appropriate performance rather than punishment for undesirable behavior. Whenever possible, state the contingency positively and reward the group for good behavior (e.g., "We'll all take a 10-minute break when everyone has finished this math assignment" is preferable to "Nobody can take a break until everyone has finished this work"). The alternative–stating rules not to be broken and giving points for misbehavior–means that one or a few students can easily sabotage their peers' efforts by deliberate misbehavior. These "spoilers" may encounter a lot of hostility and threats from their classmates, and this may set the stage for escalating coercive interactions.

Third, keep the competition fair. If you divide the class into teams, make certain that the teams have about equal chances to "win." Whenever possible, allow everyone to earn a reward for good performance and the "winners" to earn a little extra.

Fourth, when using interdependent group contingencies, encourage everyone to participate, but do not require it. Forced participation will almost certainly set up the group for failure. Group contingencies will not work for all students in all circumstances. Use the group only for students who are willing "players." Let those who do not want to be team members "sit out."

Fifth, make allowances for those who do not work well as part of any group you can construct. In spite of your best efforts, some students may repeatedly or purposely torpedo their group's efforts. Do not merely exclude these students from participation in groups. Set up individual contingencies for them, and keep open the possibility of their rejoining a group when they are willing to work cooperatively with their peers. Removing one or a few individuals from the group contingency is often better than abandoning it for the majority. For those who are removed, however, you must have individual expectations and provide rewarding consequences for appropriate behavior.

How might I engage classroom peers as confederates?

Students are a potential classroom resource as teachers' confederates—accomplices, allies, or assistants of the teacher in specific interventions. Sometimes a peer confederate is able to extend the teacher's reach by carrying out specific intervention procedures that the teacher can not implement because of a lack of time or because the object of the intervention is to enhance peer relations which only another student can initiate directly. When a peer is serving as the teacher's confederate, the confederate's role may be explained to the target student, but this is not always the case. Depending on the specific role of the confederate and the nature of the target student's behavior, you may need to obtain parental permission and administrative approval before implementing the intervention procedures. You must exercise careful professional judgment in deciding whether the interactions between confederate and target will be such that parents or school administrators might question their appropriateness. If in doubt, discuss the role you propose for the confederate with your supervisor or principal before proceeding.

Peers are particularly useful as models and tutors for specific skills, as we discuss elsewhere in this chapter. Students may also learn to deliver social reinforcers very effectively in naturally occurring peer interactions. In addition, peers may be very helpful as confederates in initiating social interactions with students who are socially isolated or withdrawn. Confederates must be carefully chosen and trained. The teacher must know precisely the role the student is to play in the intervention, model that role for the confederate, and provide feedback as the confederate rehearses precisely what to do. Moreover, the teacher must monitor the confederate's performance to make sure he or she is implementing the procedures as intended.

Not all students are capable of serving as confederates, and any student who does so will require careful training and supervision. Peer confederates must be reliable in several respects: school attendance (so that you are able to depend on their availability), generally positive in their interactions with peers, able to avoid negative interactions with peers under nearly any circumstance, and able to follow your instructions. You should not select as peer confederates a student who is not liked by the target child; the confederate should be socially attractive to the target student, or at least socially neutral.

Some interventions may be appropriate if implemented by the teacher but not if they are implemented by a peer confederate. Using a peer confederate to assist in punishment is not, in our opinion, justifiable (with the possible exception of some peer-implemented conflict resolution procedures). Peer confederates are best used to provide good models, tutor or coach fellow students in specific skills, initiate positive social interactions with target classmates, and deliver positive reinforcement for specific desirable behavior as determined by the teacher.

Conflict resolution by trained peers is a strategy that has been implemented in some schools and classrooms. Students serve as counselors or mediators who try to help their peers resolve disputes in nonviolent ways. They are trained in specific negotiation procedures to resolve minor problems, the goal being to catch conflicts before they escalate into major struggles. Some conflicts clearly are too much for peers to manage, and proper training will help students recognize problems that need to be dealt with by an adult. However, many students at all grade levels can learn to help their peers step back from minor confrontations, to ask questions that clarify each party's goals and point of contention, and to negotiate a nonviolent solution that is satisfactory to both parties. In some schools, mediation or conflict resolution has been made a part of the social studies curriculum. We note that not every attempt to train and use peer mediators has been successful. Training takes time and special expertise on the part of teachers, and peer mediators need time and a private place in which to resolve disputes. The resources required for successful peer mediation are not always available.

How might I use peer tutors as a classroom resource?

Peer tutoring has become an extremely popular idea in the 1990s. No teacher should plunge into peer tutoring, however, without a clear idea of what the tutoring is to accomplish. The skills to be acquired by the tutees must be stated explicitly. Also important are the objectives for the tutors. Using a classroom peer as a tutor solely to save the teacher's time and effort is highly questionable. Tutors should be learning valuable skills themselves during the process of tutoring, and the teacher should be able to state exactly what that skill is. Some studies have shown that tutors' academic performance or social behavior has improved, but such improvement cannot be taken for granted. Before launching a peer tutoring intervention you should be able to answer these questions:

- What specific skills do I expect the tutee to acquire from this tutoring?
- What specific benefits do I expect for the tutor?
- Is peer tutoring the most effective and efficient way I can attain my goals for the tutee and tutor?

Choosing and Training Tutors
Ordinarily, teachers assume that when they enlist peers as tutors they are making better use of their time and operating a more efficient and effective instructional program. Before assuming that peer tutoring makes better use of your resources, however, you

must consider how much time and effort will be required to train and supervise the tutor(s). Some teachers have implemented relatively unstructured and unsupervised tutoring. The teacher has merely told students to work in small groups and help each other learn academic tasks, such as spelling words. Other teachers have given tutors very explicit and relatively extensive training in how to teach specific skills. This kind of training has sometimes involved modeling by the teacher, rehearsal by the tutor under the guidance of the teacher, and frequent feedback on performance. Obviously, the specific objectives for the tutor and the tutee as well as the abilities of the tutors and tutees will determine how much training and supervision are required and, therefore, how much of the teacher's time, if any, is saved.

Class wide peer tutoring has been implemented by some teachers, while others have involved only a few of their students. Sometimes same-age peers have been used; sometimes tutors have been substantially different from their tutees in age. In spite of the popularity of peer tutoring as an academic intervention, research does not yet indicate clearly the characteristics of the optimum tutor-tutee match. In any case, you should consider how a variety of characteristics of the students involved as tutors or tutees might contribute to the success or failure of peer tutoring: relative ages, gender, social class, ethnicity, and skill development, for example. Also critically important are behavioral characteristics, especially the tendency to be punitive toward others, the ability to give contingent praise and other rewards, and susceptibility to peer influence. The specific tutoring arrangements you choose must be based on your knowledge of the individual students involved and your estimate of how they will interact, given the specific tasks you have set for them.

Limitations of Peer Tutoring

Effective teachers and aides are not easily recruited, trained, and evaluated. We doubt that untrained and unmonitored peer tutors will provide instruction equal in effectiveness to that of most classroom teachers and aides. Although we recognize its potential benefits, we believe the simplicity and cost effectiveness of peer tutoring are exaggerated in some reports of its use. Peers can and often do help each other, but they do not always do so and they are not likely to do so without careful planning, monitoring, and training.

Peer tutoring might create more behavior problems than it resolves if it is not carefully implemented. Depending on the match of tutor and tutee, the specific skills being tutored, and the training, supervision, and reinforcement for the students involved, peer tutoring can have remarkably positive or negative outcomes. Some disruptive, unmotivated students will learn a great deal and become more tractable when they serve as a tutor for a peer or when they are tutored by another student. Students who are socially withdrawn and unresponsive in a larger group may develop close relationships and learn critical social skills when involved in a peer tutoring arrangement. Others, however, will carry their behavioral difficulties into the tutoring interactions. Some students may engage their tutees or tutors in coercive interactions or fail to use their assigned time together in the manner intended by their teachers. You must be aware that peer tutoring has the potential for negative outcomes and be ready to modify or terminate tutoring arrangements in which coercion or inappropriate use of time allocated for tutoring is a problem.

What options should I consider in teaching social skills?

Within the past decade, teachers and researchers have begun to recognize the fact that social skills are perhaps as important as academic skills in determining students' futures. Without good social skills, students' academic progress is likely to be less than optimal, their future educational opportunities are likely to be restricted, and they are less likely to make a successful transition to adulthood and employment. Consequently, most educators now place more emphasis on the social learning that occurs in the classroom.

Social skills are taught by parents, families, peer groups, and teachers. To a large extent, the social skills training children receive is informal and incidental—we might even say haphazard. We are now beginning to realize that many students fail to learn social skills under these conditions, just as they fail to learn academic skills when instruction is haphazard. As is true in the case of academic instruction, most teachers have neither the time nor the expertise to develop their own curriculum and instructional materials for teaching social skills. Fortunately, social skills training programs, including specific materials and lessons, have been developed for students at both the elementary and secondary levels. We urge you to consider using one of the social skills training programs listed in our references and resources at the end of this chapter if you teach students with apparent social skill deficits. Regardless what program you adopt or what social skills training activities you plan for your students, you will need to ask yourself the following questions:

- What are the particular social skills that my students need to learn? Careful observation and reflection may help you understand exactly what it is about the social behavior of particular students that is problematic (e.g., inappropriate eye contact during interactions, lack of response to social initiations from others, maladaptive responses to instructions from authority, giving or responding to criticism inappropriately, impulsive or aggressive responses that provoke social conflict, inability to demonstrate appropriate affect). Understanding the demands of positive social interactions and relationships is critically important in describing the social skills one needs. Try to describe precisely what your students need to learn to do, as well as what they need to learn not to do, if they are to become more successful in their relationships with others.
- Do my teaching strategies promote social competence? Some teachers employ instructional approaches that minimize social interaction, providing almost no opportunity to learn social skills. These teaching strategies, which focus almost exclusively on independent work and individual responses, demand so little interpersonal competence that social skills become relatively trivial.
- Do I teach social skills explicitly? Most teaching activities should encourage social interaction. However, providing opportunities for social interaction is not enough for many students. Explicit instruction is often necessary. A social skills curriculum

must focus on helping students acquire and use an acceptable level of specific social skills. Talking about social skills is not enough. Rehearsing and practicing them with feedback on performance are necessary.

- Am I able to generalize training in social skills from simulated to actual social situations? It is one thing to be able to exhibit social skills in a familiar and friendly environment; it is quite another to exhibit the same skills in the presence of unfamiliar and unresponsive or antagonistic individuals. Your curriculum and instructional strategies for social skills must take into account the importance of helping students extend their skills beyond the training sessions in which you teach them.

- Is my approach to social skills training consistent with the needs of students with mild disabilities, and students at risk? Students with disabilities—especially mild mental retardation, learning disabilities and emotional or behavioral disorders—may need social skills training that most students do not. Likewise, students at risk (i.e., seemingly headed for academic or social failure but not yet identified as handicapped) may not respond like most students to particular social situations. Students with disabilities and at-risk students may need more explicit and directive instruction in social skills than the more typical student.

Summary

Teaching requires managing the behavior of groups. Peer pressure is always present in groups, whether harnessed by the teacher or not. The teacher must attempt to foster positive and humane peer pressure that encourages a sense of togetherness or belonging among members of the class, cooperation and caring of students for each other, and better acceptance of those who are at the social fringes of the group. Students are keen observers of each other, as well as of adults. Teachers often use observational learning and the tendency to imitate certain peers and adults as a means of improving behavior. Effective observational learning procedures highlight the appropriate behavior of attractive models, and that includes rewarding consequences for both the model and those who imitate the model. The vicarious experience of consequences by those who witness models being reinforced for desirable conduct may influence the observers' behavior. Vicarious effects are relatively weak, however, and direct consequences are necessary for managing serious behavior problems. Group contingencies create peer pressure and can be used in a variety of forms, including independent, dependent, and interdependent contingencies. Cooperative learning procedures involve a combination of individual and group contingencies. Care is needed to avoid possible negative peer pressure when group contingencies are used. With proper selection and training, many students can serve as effective confederates of the teacher in implementing positive behavior management procedures. With proper selection and training, most students can also serve as effective tutors for their peers. Teaching social skills necessarily involves group learning and a curriculum designed to teach appropriate interpersonal responses.

References and Resources for Further Study

The following references provided the basis for many of our statements in this chapter. You may wish to consult selected references for additional information on specific topics. Our reference notes for this chapter refer to sources in this list.

Observational Learning

Bandura, A. (1977). *Social Learning Theory*. Englewood Cliffs, NJ: Prentice Hall.

Birnbrauer, J. S., Hopkins, N., and Kauffman, J. M. (1981). The effects of vicarious prompting on attentive behavior of children with behavior disorders. *Child Behavior Therapy, 3*, 27-41.

Kazdin, A. E. (1973). The effect of vicarious reinforcement on attentive behavior in the classroom. *Journal of Applied Behavior Analysis, 6*, 71-78.

Ollendick, T. H., Dailey, D., and Shapiro, E. S. (1983). Vicarious reinforcement: Expected and unexpected effects. *Journal of Applied Behavior Analysis, 16*, 485-491.

Sharpley, C. F. (1991). Two strategies for reducing the aversive effects of implicit rewards. *Behavior Modification, 15*, 156-172.

Peer Tutoring

Cooke, N. L., Heron, T. G., and Heward, W. L. (1983). *Peer Tutoring*. Columbus, OH: Charles E. Merrill.

Gerber, M. M. and Kauffman, J. M. (1981). Peer tutoring in academic settings. In P. S. Strain (Ed.), *The Utilization of Classroom Peers as Behavior Change Agents* (pp. 155-187). New York: Plenum.

Greenwood, C. R., Carta, J. J., and Maheady, L. (1991). Peer tutoring programs in the regular classroom. In G. Stoner, M. R. Shinn, and H. M. Walker (Eds.), *Interventions for Achievement and Behavior Problems* (pp. 179-200). Silver Spring, MD: National Association of School Psychologists.

Jenkins, J. R. and Jenkins, L. M. (1987). Making peer tutoring work. *Educational Leadership, 44* (6), 64-68.

Osguthorpe, R. T. and Scruggs, T. E. (1986). Special education students as tutors: A review and analysis. *Remedial and Special Education, 7*(4), 15-25.

Scruggs, T. E., and Richter, L. (1986). Tutoring learning disabled students: A critical review. *Learning Disability Quarterly, 9*, 2-14.

Group Contingencies and Peer Confederates

Barrish, H. H., Saunders, M., and Wolf, M. M. (1968). Good behavior game: Effects of individual contingencies for group consequences on disruptive behavior in a classroom. *Journal of Applied Behavior Analysis, 2*, 119-124.

Fishbein, J. E. and Wasik, B. H. (1981). Effect of the good behavior game on disruptive library behavior. *Journal of Applied Behavior Analysis, 14*, 89-93.

Greenwood, C. R. and Hops, H. (1981). Group-oriented contingencies and peer behavior change. In P. S. Strain (Ed.), *The Utilization of Classroom Peers as Behavior Change Agents* (pp. 189-259). New York: Plenum.

Patterson, G. R. (1965). An application of conditioning techniques to the control of a hyperactive child. In L. P. Ullmann and L. Krasner (Eds.), *Case Studies in Behavior Modification*. New York: Holt, Rinehart, and Winston.

Patterson, G. R., Shaw, D. A., and Ebner, M. J., (1974). Teachers, peers, and parents as agents of change in the classroom. In F. A. M. Benson (Ed.), *Modifying Deviant Social Behaviors in Various Classroom Settings*. Eugene, OR: University of Oregon, Department of Special Education.

Smith, L. K. C. and Fowler, S. A. (1984). Positive peer pressure: The effects of peer monitoring on children's disruptive behavior. *Journal of Applied Behavior Analysis, 17*, 213-227.

Strain, P. S., Kerr, M. M., and Ragland, E. U. (1981). The use of peer social initiations in the treatment of social withdrawal. In P. S. Strain (Ed.), *The Utilization of Classroom Peers as Behavior Change Agents* (pp. 101-128). New York: Plenum.

Social Skills Programs

Berler, E. S., Gross, A. M., and Drabman, R. S. (1982). Social skills training with children: Proceed with caution. *Journal of Applied Behavior Analysis, 15*, 41-54.

Hazel, J.S., Schumaker, J. B., Sherman, J. A., and Sheldon-Wildgen, J. (1981). *ASSET: A Social Skills Program for Adolescents*. Champaign, IL: Research Press.

McGinnis and Goldstein (1984). *Skillstreaming the Elementary School Child*. Champaign, IL: Research Press. [also available: Goldstein et al. (1980), *Skillstreaming the Adolescent*.]

Sabornie, E. J. (1991). Measuring and teaching social skills in the mainstream. In G. Stoner, M. R. Shinn, and H. M. Walker (Eds.), *Interventions for Achievement and Behavior Problems* (pp. 161-177). Silver Spring, MD: National Association of School Psychologists.

Stephens (1978). *Social Skills in the Classroom*. Columbus, OH: Cedars Press.

Walker et al. (1983). *The Walker Social Skills Curriculum*. Austin, TX: Pro-Ed.

Cooperative Learning

Johnson, D. W. and Johnson, R. (1986). Mainstreaming and cooperative learning strategies. *Exceptional Children, 52*, 553-561.

Slavin, R. E. (1983). *Cooperative Learning*. New York: Longman.

Slavin, R. E. (1984). Students motivating students to excel: Cooperative incentives, cooperative tasks, and student achievement. *Elementary School Journal, 85*, 53-63.

Slavin, R. E. (1984). Team assisted individualization: Cooperative learning and individualized instruction in the mainstreamed classroom. *Remedial and Special Education, 5* (6), 33-42.

Slavin, R. E. (1986). *Using Student Team Learning* (3rd ed.). Baltimore: Johns Hopkins University Center for Research on Elementary and Middle Schools.

Slavin, R. E. (1988). Cooperative learning and student achievement. *Educational Leadership, 46*(2), 31-33.

Conflict Resolution[4]

Edleson, J. L. (1981). Teaching children to resolve conflict: A group approach. *Social Work, 26*, 488-493.

Harvard Graduate School of Education. (1989). Talking it out: Students mediate disputes. *The Harvard Education Letter, 5*(1), 4-5.

Medland, M. B. (1990). *Self-Management Strategies: Theory, Curriculum, and Teaching Procedures*. New York: Praeger.

Reference Notes

1. See Bandura (1977), Kazdin (1973), and Ollendick et al. (1983) for further information on modeling and vicarious effects.

2. See Patterson (1965) for an early description of the "hero" procedure.

3. See Barrish et al. (1968) for description of the "Good Behavior Game."

4. For further information you may want to contact one of the following: National Association for Mediation in Education, 425 Amity Street, Amherst, MA 01002; School Mediation Associates, 702 Green St., no. 8, Cambridge, MA 02139.

$Chapter$ **6**

===

Working with Other Educators

Questions for Reflection

When do I need to seek assistance from colleagues?

How might I work with others to solve problems?

What specific procedures should be followed, and to what extent should I participate?

How can administrators, parents, and students help me in the collaborative problem solving process?

How do team members monitor and evaluate the effectiveness of interventions?

What are some cautions on collaborating with others?

Many have said that teaching is a lonely profession. Perhaps this is so because most teachers rarely have the opportunity to work with others or to help each other problem-solve in a systematic, long-term manner. Except for those few opportunities provided to discuss problems informally in the faculty lounge or on bus duty, teachers have little unencumbered time to discuss problems and challenges that they face daily. Lack of time for collaboration makes it difficult to analyze problems cooperatively and develop possible solutions. This is unfortunate, because teachers possess an untapped storehouse of knowledge on what might work and what probably won't. For every problem a particular teacher encounters in the classroom, there is perhaps another who has experienced a similar problem and has developed a strategy to deal with it effectively. Hence, as evidenced by the following example, teachers need greater access to one another's expertise in dealing with problems they encounter (see vignette, page 98).

Many times, it is possible to handle behavior problems alone. In fact, if you use the problem-solving and analysis strategies we provide in Chapters 1 through 5 you will develop skills in approaching problems independently. Sometimes, however, as evidenced in Cindi's case, help from outside sources—perhaps from professionals like yourself who may have experienced a similar problem—may be quite beneficial. In fact, we suggest that when you are faced with difficult problems you routinely ask yourself, Do I have to go it alone?

Cindi: This year, I have an unbelievable fifth-period history class and I feel that I am in no way prepared to deal with the problems I face each and every day I walk into my room. There are 16 of these kids, and all but four have some type of problem that requires special education. One was shot in the head accidently three years ago and is severely brain-damaged. Another was in an automobile accident when he was 18 months old. He, too, suffered irreversible brain damage and is physically disabled. He understands most of the information we cover in class, but he can't write anything. I have to either assign someone to take notes for him or I have to copy the notes for him myself. In addition to his disabilities, this student is extremely immature. Consequently he becomes the brunt of many jokes during class time and he constantly throws temper tantrums when the other students tease him.

Sometimes it's like a three-ring circus in this class! Sometimes I feel so frustrated. If I try giving my two severe students the attention they need, the others get restless and start to misbehave. On a test day, if I spend too much time reading the questions or dictating answers for these two students, the other students have an absolute field day trying to cheat. Sometimes I have to leave them, knowing that they haven't understood a single word that I've said and can't possibly complete a written assignment.

In addition to these students, there are others who can't sit still for five minutes. Some of them are on medication for hyperactivity. Some really need to be, but their parents are bitterly against using medication in this way. If I'm not careful, some will look out the window and daydream. Some of them are extremely disorganized. Once, though, they all brought their textbooks to class on the same day. I nearly died! It was a miracle! Unfortunately, it was one of those short-lived miracles that lasted all of two days.

Finally, in addition to these problems, I have to deal with students who are experiencing many family difficulties. Some of them are abused by their parents. Carlton's parents threw him out and he is now living in a tent. I even have students in this class who sleep in garages, live in cheap hotels totally on their own, and work 40 hours a week to support themselves. As a result of all of these problems, sometimes I just don't know what to do or where to turn. Some need social skills, some know nothing about taking notes and being organized, some are reading at the third-grade level, and some can't even spell or write a complete sentence.

Don't get me wrong. I enjoy these students, and I think they're some of the greatest kids I've ever taught. Sometimes, one of them will come by to see me or I'll see one of them at the mall and they'll run over and talk with me. But I'm constantly so frustrated because they have so many needs that I just can't meet by myself.

Questions for Reflection

In seeking assistance from others, it is important to note that carefully planned strategies resulting from systematic problem-solving procedures may be what you need to tackle the learning and behavior problems your students exhibit. You also need to work with individuals who are able to examine the nature of the problem objectively and provide suggestions in a nonthreatening, nonsupervisory capacity. Also, those who work with you to solve problems must remember that, in the final analysis, you are probably going to be the one who must implement the interventions. If you are not comfortable with the intervention—for example, if you feel that the procedure may be unfair to other students or may require too much time—it may be of little use to seek outside help. In addition, these are questions you need to ask yourself when you wish to consult with colleagues about problems you are experiencing in your classroom:

1. When do I need to seek assistance from colleagues?
2. How might I work with others to solve problems?
3. What specific procedures should be followed, and to what extent should I participate?
4. How can administrators, parents, and students help me in the collaborative problem-solving process?
5. How do team members monitor and evaluate the effectiveness of interventions?
6. What are some cautions on collaborating with others?

When do I need to seek assistance from colleagues?

Many times, you may follow the steps we have presented in the first five chapters of this book and still find that you are unable to handle behavior problems to your satisfaction. For example, you may have analyzed the problem, used behavior modification strategies such as positive reinforcement and extinction, used contracts, or made modifications in instruction designed to accommodate some disability that might cause a student to act out. We can see from Cindi's example that she tried some problem-solving approaches. She has made modifications in the way she gives tests and requires students to take notes, but these modifications have only resulted in problems with other students in the classroom. Even though she is extremely frustrated with her class, Cindi is very empathic toward her students and desires to help them through some very difficult situations. Though she has not developed procedures that allow her to get the results she desires, she still has not developed feelings of hostility toward her students.

These factors indicate that the time is ripe for Cindi to seek assistance from her colleagues. You might suspect that she has only limited teaching experience or, perhaps, that she has only worked with above-average and gifted students and has a very low tolerance for the behaviors that her new group of students displays. Perhaps she has too many difficult cases in her class and needs support from other teachers as well as administrative support. Perhaps she has never been trained to analyze behavior problems and provide students with the compensatory skills that they need to be more organized, more attentive, and more compliant. These and other factors may be indicative of a need to seek the help of others.

Several different models of collegial support are in use in schools across the country. If more than one model is provided in your school, you must select the one that is most suitable to your personality, instructional style, and teaching responsibilities.

How might I work with others to solve problems?

Working effectively with others to solve problems requires more than deciding it's a good idea and finding someone with whom to discuss problems and alternatives. The way teachers approach each other or ask for assistance from someone else—and the specific roles and working relationships that are worked out—are matters that need considerable forethought. We describe three general plans or models that have been tried: consultants, teacher consultant teams, and collaborative teaching.

Consultants

Consultants assigned to work with teachers who are experiencing problems in their classrooms provide opportunity for partnership and growth. When a cooperative approach is used, the consultant (e.g., another teacher, a school psychologist, a guidance counselor) comes to the situation with the idea that he or she will not have all the expertise in the situation but will provide support to a colleague who is experiencing problems. Beginning with an iterative process (restating the problem until it is clear), the consultant helps in planning interventions to the extent desired by the teacher who is seeking assistance.[1]

The consultant and the consultee will need to meet to monitor and modify the behavioral interventions that are implemented. The result should be resolution of the problem or the realization that other steps need to be taken to handle the problem adequately (e.g., direct administrative involvement). Also, the process is designed to improve the skills and the problem-solving repertoire of the consultee so that he or she may use the strategies in the future when similar problems arise with other students.

Teacher Consultation Teams

Teacher consultation teams (TCTs), sometimes called prereferral teams (PRTs) or child study teams (CSTs), are comprised of teachers who function as problem-solving units that provide ongoing assistance to referring teachers.[2] In most cases, these teams do not fulfill any requirements set forth by federal and state mandates to provide special education services to students who qualify. The basic assumptions underlying the establishment of these teams include the following:

- Teachers rarely have the opportunity to share with one another.
- The teams will help teachers remember skills and strategies that they sometimes forget or cease using.
- Teachers can work together to solve problems; they do not always have to seek the advice of an expert.[3]

Collaborative Teaching

In collaborative teaching, teams divide responsibilities according to the strengths and weaknesses of individual teachers. In many cases, pairs are created so that regular classroom teachers can work cooperatively with special education teachers. In this way, the teachers plan and teach the academic curriculum to all students within the classroom.[4]

Each of the three models represents strategies used to help teachers of students with learning and behavior problems develop interventions that will allow these students to be maintained in regular classrooms to the greatest extent possible. In addition, program developers believe that collaborative approaches will reduce the rate of unwarranted referrals for special education, allow all educators to share knowledge and learn from one another, improve attitudes of regular educators about students with disabilities, and improve communication between regular and special education teachers.

For students, program developers believe that these models and interventions will reduce the stigma attached to being pulled out of the regular classroom and labeled, lessen the disruption of instruction caused by leaving one setting to receive services in another, provide students with disabilities with positive role models, and promote independence among students with disabilities.[5]

What specific procedures should be followed, and to what extent should I participate?

In each of the models we have described, cooperation and collaboration are essential to success. In addition to availability, the type of model you decide to use should be based on your willingness to seek the assistance of a problem-solving team and your willingness to team up with another teacher.

Working with Consultants

Much research has indicated that consulting teacher models, TCTs, and collaborative teaching models work best when teachers are encouraged to use them on a voluntary basis.[6] In working with consultants, you will ordinarily be the one who initiates a request for assistance. You and the consultant will need to work together to determine the best way to approach the behavior problem resulting in your request for assistance. The consultant will need certain information from you. For example, he or she may ask you questions regarding what you feel are the skills that your students need to possess to be successful in your classroom and what behavior you simply will not tolerate. Both you and the consultant can then use this information to compare your teaching style and operating procedures with what is known about the learning styles and behavior of the student or students experiencing problems.

After preliminary discussion of your classroom environment, you and the consultant should discuss how you will proceed. Depending on your knowledge and orientation to behavior management, you may take one of several approaches. In the following paragraphs we describe how you might work with a consultant if you adopt a behavioral approach.

In a behavioral approach, your first task will be to devise a way to measure the identified target behaviors more precisely and reliably. If the problem is instructional, the consultant may request that you complete checklists prepared in a developmental, sequential manner so that holes and gaps in the student's learning may be detected (e.g., checklists in handwriting, math, or spelling). In addition, the two of you will need to develop systems to monitor and record the frequencies of the inappropriate behaviors. Such procedures may include classroom observations, review of cumulative and confidential folders, and contacting parents to obtain information regarding their perception of the problem. These data collection procedures should establish an adequate baseline so that comparisons in behavior can be made after implementation of the intervention.

After identification and assessment of frequency of the target behavior, it will be necessary to develop a specific plan of action. During this time, it is critical that you take a vital role in the development of interventions to be implemented in your classroom. You must feel comfortable with these interventions and feel that you will have the time to follow through with the chosen procedures. Also, you must be sure that the implementation of the procedures will not disrupt your relationships with students who are not posing problems.

During the meeting and planning phase, you and the consultant should review the information obtained as a result of your assessment, prioritize the behaviors according to their urgency, identify one or two target behaviors to address initially, reach a consensus about the nature of the problem, specify in objective and measurable terms the target behaviors you decide to focus on initially, and develop interventions to deal with the problem. In addition, it will be necessary to identify those persons (e.g., teachers, administrators, parents, students) who will be involved with the implementation of the intervention and outline their responsibilities. For example, the consultant may come into your classroom to model appropriate implementation of an intervention. This information should be documented, disseminated, and explained to all participants, including the student(s) involved. Finally, you and the consultant should develop a system to monitor your implementation of the intervention and evaluate its effectiveness, including a schedule for meeting to take stock of progress and problems.

After the assessment and planning phases, it will be time for the two of you to implement your intervention. Direct and daily measurement should be collected based on tools such as systematic recording, daily progress reports, mainstream checklists, and work samples.[7]

Operational Guidelines for Teacher Consultation Teams

In general, the TCT operates much like the consultant model we have described. The primary difference is that in the TCT a larger number of people are involved in the problem-solving process. The teachers involved usually represent different levels of experience, grades, and instructional styles. The team is managed by a coordinator, a role that is sometimes rotated from member to member. The coordinator assumes the responsibility of completing necessary paper work and serves as the contact person for the group. The first two steps in this process, then, are identical to the process used in the consulting teacher model. In step three—the specify and plan phase—all members of the team, along with the coordinator and the referring teacher, meet to problem-solve. Prior to this meeting, the members may be asked to observe in your classroom, read cumulative and confidential folders (if permitted), and make note of general suggestions that may be presented at the meeting. Again, at this point, the meeting follows a format similar to that in meetings of consultant and teacher. More specifically, you might expect the following:

- The coordinator will share information obtained during the assessment period.
- Team members, along with the referring teacher, will engage in a systematic problem-solving strategy to reach consensus about the nature of the problem.
- All persons present will rank the target behaviors in order of importance.
- The selection of behaviors and interventions will be recorded.
- The group will identify responsibilities for those who will assist with implementation.
- A follow-up plan for continued support and evaluation will be developed.[8]

In most cases, during the implementation phase a consultation intervention plan (CIP) is initiated, measurement of the target behavior from the serving teachers is collected, and parents are contacted if they are included in the intervention. Once again, during this period different people may be called in to help with the intervention. For example, if a student earned a certain number of points, his or her reward may be to eat lunch with the principal, spend time with a particular teacher or friend, assist the custodian . . . The possibilities for designing interventions are unlimited. Appropriate behavior and its reinforcement may be monitored by both school personnel and the parents. Another teacher or staff member may be used to teach a targeted social skill. The TCT process should encourage many persons to become involved in helping the student be successful in school. Also, as the referring teacher you will be comforted to have the support of other adults who are available to assist you.

Working as a Collaborative Teacher

Collaborative teaching can be implemented based on at least three different arrangements—team teaching, complementary teaching, and supportive learning activities. These arrangements may be used individually or in combination to teach a given lesson. The division of responsibilities we present is the one seen most frequently, but individual teams will divide responsibilities according to the strengths and weaknesses of the teachers involved.

Team teaching occurs when the general and special educators alternate their presentation of segments of a lesson, with the nonteaching educator monitoring student performance or behavior. Complementary instruction allows the regular educator to maintain the primary responsibility for teaching the academic curriculum, while the special educator teaches the organizational and study skills necessary for students to master the material. Supportive learning activities are devised by the special educator to provide students with practice activities based on the skills presented by the regular educator.[9]

How can administrators, parents, and students participate in the collaborative problem-solving process?

In addition to active participation in any of the models we have described, administrative support for management and planning is crucial to program success. The organizational structure of the models depends upon administrative support for implementation. The administration should be responsible for establishing classes, selecting teachers to participate in the programs, scheduling of common planning periods, supporting the use of strategies by ensuring availability of resource materials, and providing information to the school and to the community about the significance of the programs.

Parents and the targeted student may also be involved directly with the development of an intervention developed in conjunction with a consultant, a teacher consultation team, or a team of collaborative teachers. One way to include parents and students in the consultative/collaborative process is to develop a consultation contract outlining the responsibilities of all the individuals involved. For example, in Cindi's class, one of her students (Jarvis) is failing to complete homework assignments because of poor organization and inability to monitor his behavior. Jarvis is 17, but extremely impulsive and immature for his age. He is also diagnosed as having a learning disability in reading and is enrolled in the resource program for one period per day. In most cases, Jarvis completes his assignments in class but rarely, if ever, completes his homework assignments. After a meeting with the TCT, Cindi notified Jarvis's parents and asked them to attend another meeting with the group to develop a consultative contract. Because team members decided that Jarvis would need a great deal of structure and monitoring, the following consultative contract was developed:

To help Jarvis complete more of his homework assignments in U.S. History, the following consultative contract will take effect on _____ . *The responsibilities of all involved parties are outlined. All involved parties will meet once every three weeks to monitor progress.*
The Resource teacher will:
1. *Develop an assignment pad for Jarvis to use on a daily basis to copy his assignments for U.S. History.*
2. *Monitor Jarvis's use of the assignment pad.*
3. *Teach the study skills of a) copying homework assignments, b) gathering appropriate materials to take home, and c) following instructions during the resource period.*

The U.S. History teacher will:
1. *Write homework assignments in a designated area on the chalkboard each day.*
2. *Check with Jarvis each day to be sure that he has copied the assignment on his assignment pads.*
3. *Initial Jarvis's assignment entries each day.*

Jarvis will:
1. *Carry the necessary materials to U.S. History class each day.*
2. *Carry his assignment pad to class each day.*
3. *Write down his assignment each day and have his history teacher initial his assignment pad.*
4. *Carry the needed material home each day.*
5. *Complete his homework assignment.*

6. *Have his parents initial his assignment pad, acknowledging that they have reviewed his work.*
7. *Bring the completed assignment to class each day.*

Jarvis's parents will:
1. *Review Jarvis's assignment in U.S. History with him each night to make sure he understands it.*
2. *Initial the assignment pad to indicate that the assignment has been completed.*

Consequences
1. *If Jarvis completes at least 85% of his homework assignments with an average grade of "C" or better on a weekly basis, he will be allowed to drive the car to an outing on either Friday or Saturday night each week.*
2. *If Jarvis does not comply with the specified terms of the contract, he will be grounded for the entire weekend.*

Student signature _____

Parent signature _____

Teacher signature _____

Teacher signature _____

If each person involved, including Jarvis, lives up to his or her responsibility, then a change in Jarvis's behavior should be forthcoming. Assigning roles and responsibilities in writing and establishing times to meet and assess progress creates a sense of team effort which may motivate the student to comply with the instructional demands of school.

How do team members monitor and evaluate the effectiveness of interventions?

In evaluating the effectiveness of interventions developed through collaboration, it is essential to remember that problems will not disappear overnight, and in some cases they will become more intensified before getting better. Those who are working collaboratively may need to modify the intervention plan periodically if it is the general agreement that such a modification may move the student closer to displaying the appropriate behaviors.

Also, in monitoring and evaluating interventions, it is important to judge performance based on the circumstances and the setting. No prereferral or consultative model should be used to deny students services in special education programs. Additionally, TCTs and collaborative teaching programs should not be used to maintain students with disabilities in regular classrooms when such placements are inappropriate.

The special education service delivery model is designed to provide a comprehensive continuum of services for students with disabilities. This continuum of alternative placements includes the full range of public school options: total placement in the regular classroom; indirect services within the regular classroom (e.g., consultants and TCTs); direct services and instruction within the regular classroom (e.g., collaborative teaching); resource room services; self-contained classes; and special alternative schools.

Theoretically, within each option children with disabilities are placed according to their particular needs. As their needs are met and as students make progress, they are moved along the continuum to an alternative setting that will more appropriately meet their new educational needs. As the student moves from a self-contained setting to regular classroom placement, the interactions between special educators and regular educators should increase. There should be more planning, more coordination whereby personnel can work together to modify curriculum and develop coping strategies, learning strategies, social skill competencies—generally, to help the child make the necessary transitions and find success in the new setting. While these skills should be a part of the curriculum in more restrictive settings, in order to promote internalization and transfer of skills both special and regular educators who work with students with disabilities must be aware of the strategies and techniques used to teach and reinforce these skills. In focusing on monitoring and evaluation of consultative interventions, then, we must remember that there are several models along the continuum that have been successful with some students, but that no one option has been used successfully with all students with disabilities.

When consultation intervention plans, consultative contracts, and collaborative teaching plans are developed, the evaluation component should be specified in writing and criteria for judging program effectiveness should be specified. For students with disabilities who are served in regular education classrooms, failure of an intervention to instigate improved performance may be indicative of a need for placement in a resource or self-contained special education placement. For students who are nondisabled, failure of an intervention to bring about desired change after modifications and adjustments are made may signify that the student needs to be referred to a child study team for assessment and to determine whether special education services are warranted.

What are some cautions on collaborating with others?

To identify the problems that arise when implementing consultative interventions, we now return to Cindi after she has gone through the process. Cindi's perspective has now changed. After working through the TCT at her school, she came to the conclusion that some of the behavior problems that she experienced were related to her instructional style and the incongruence of such style with her students' skill levels, learning styles, and disabilities. As a result of her work with the TCT, Karen, a teacher of children with learning disabilities, was assigned to work with her on a regular basis for this class period (see page 107). The special education supervisor brought to the

Cindi: Since Karen has started to work with me, things are so much better! I can actually see a light at the end of the tunnel. I have learned so much about modifying instruction from Karen. She has shown me how to develop study guides with the page numbers and key words listed to help students find answers quickly. On tests, I now divide the matching questions into several sections so that the students will not be so overwhelmed. Boy, I used to be famous for my two-page matching sections! I've seen a difference in performance since Karen introduced me to this simple modification.

I guess the most important thing about the team teaching is that students get more attention now. This really cuts down on inattentiveness and other behavior problems. Just the other day, we were doing a writing assignment and the difference was like night and day. Karen worked with half of the class and I worked with the other. We were able to get around to all the students, and I was feeling great at the end of the period. Last semester, the one time I tried this, I was ready for a straight jacket by the end of the period!

If I had to say anything negative about the program, it would be that we just don't have enough time to plan what we want to do. Sometimes I'll call Karen at home or she'll call me. This is really unfair because, you know, there **is** life after sixth period. I hope that the situation will improve if we continue with the program next year.

Karen: Working in Cindi's class is really great! Even though she does most of the core teaching, I am beginning to teach some of the content, and I'm really enjoying it. Last week Cindi had laryngitis and I had to teach almost the entire period. I realized that I'm learning a great deal of history and I'll be really prepared if I have to do this again next year.

I also do a lot with modifying the instruction and teaching study skills and organization. We do a notebook check every Friday, and the students have really gotten into this. They know it's an easy grade, and they're almost always prepared. I'm helping the kids with mindmapping, and we do a lot with mnemonic devices and other memory strategies to help the students retain information. I guess that another one of the important aspects of the program is that not just students with learning disabilities are being helped. I'm able to share these "LD" skills with all of the students in the class. If Cindi continues to reinforce the skills as she is now doing, I'm sure that student performance will continue to improve.

Overall, I think this model has really enhanced our resource model, even though most of our kids are on consultation. For those who see us in the team-taught class and also see us in resource, we are able to give them a double dose. For me, I'm more aware of what's going on now because I'm in there with the kids. I don't have to rely on their telling me what they did in class and what the next assignment is. Half the time, they gave me the incorrect information. Now, I get it firsthand, and· it's so much better this way.

We still have some bugs to work out of the system, but all in all, I think we have a pretty good program going on here. We need to look more closely at our high functioning kids who could possibly make it in higher level classes. And we need to pull some kids back into resource and self-contained classes because even with the consultation and teaming they aren't being successful. We need to look at the scheduling and planning issues, and we need to encourage our administrators to be more supportive of the program. Nevertheless, I really think what we are developing here is helping regular educators become more aware of different learning styles and different techniques that can be used to modify their teaching styles. And who knows, maybe on day I'll be able to fill in a U.S. map with all the states and capitals!

principal's attention the fact that when so many students with disabilities are placed in a regular classroom the regular support of a special educator is necessary. Cindi and Karen evaluated the effectiveness of their collaborative teaching experiences. In analyzing their working relationship, we can identify four problems:

Lack of Time to Plan Together

> *Cindi:* Probably one of the biggest problems with collaborative models is that we don't have as much time to work together as I would like to. We're lucky, in that we have the same planning period, but that doesn't always mean a lot because we don't always have the period to plan together.

Cindi identifies one of the major problems involved in implementing a collaborative model. With bus duty, hall duty, and other meetings to attend, it is sometimes extremely difficult to meet and develop plans that are well thought out and structured in a way that would yield optimal results.

Lack of Support from Administrators

> *Cindi:* To tell you the truth, I didn't realize my principal had a role in the program. We get no feedback from him. He's never once asked me anything about what we do when we meet and come up with those plans that are helping so many teachers. Frankly, I think that there should be more positive advertising and mentioning of us at the faculty meetings. This should be a part of Mr. T.'s "Whatever" memos. He should ask us to talk about what we do during our faculty meetings. Sometimes I wonder if he even cares.

Cindi has just identified a crucial element that could make or break the effectiveness of a collaborative program. Motivating participants and encouraging others to become involved is a major responsibility that fits nicely into the role of the building level administrator. Even though teachers sell good programs by word-of-mouth and personal testimony, encouragement and recognition from the principal will quite possibly strengthen support for the program.

The principal should also be aware of the needs of the participants. As we mentioned previously, this person can influence program effectiveness by providing the necessary materials and resources available for teachers to use. Also, the principal must be instrumental in developing ways to circumvent the problems that arise when there is no time for meeting and planning. In such instances, the principal should work with his staff to develop creative scheduling system that will allow more teachers to collaborate. If the principal is not responsive to these needs, consultative programs will not be very successful. In some cases, they will fail.

Lack of Positive Relationships and Identification of Roles

Cindi: A consultant or special educator who teams with a regular classroom teacher must know the students with disabilities inside and out—what works, what doesn't work. I think these people must be incredibly creative and flexible. They must be good listeners, motivated to learn about the subject matter of the regular classroom teacher, and know how to incorporate the teaching of compensatory skills like study skills, social skills, and learning strategies into the content that I must teach in my class.

Karen: Many of the teachers that I consult or team with teach remedial level classes, and they want my help. A regular classroom teacher has to really want you there. You can't just go in and say, "OK, I'm going to work with you this year and we're going to get these kids through history" unless they really want you there.

Cindi and Karen make it quite clear that the ability to work with one another is critical to establishing effective consultative relationships. The regular educator must be willing to accept support, use feedback constructively, and share teaching responsibilities if teaming will take place. In addition, the roles of all individuals who will work together collaboratively must be clearly outlined and understood by all participants. Failure to adhere to these usually simple but sometimes complicated rules will result in haphazard implementation.

Accessibility of Consultants and Collaborative Teachers

Cindi: Karen tells me that as the year progresses, and as I learn to use the special techniques and strategies that she is teaching me, she will have to stop working with me directly and move on to another teacher who needs her help. I think that this would be a great disadvantage to all the kids in my class, not just the ones with disabilities. All these kids need a great deal of attention, and half way through the year they will continue to need that attention. That's not going to change. I will know the skills, but I can't be on both sides of the classroom at the same time.

Because of time constraints, consultants and collaborative teachers are sometimes unable to provide the direct services that are needed to help regular educators implement an intervention optimally. If ample time is not available for modeling, coaching, and providing feedback, interventions may not be as effective as they might be. Also, if a majority of the students experience extreme behavior and learning problems, a team teacher may need to be provided during the entire year.

Summary

Teachers possess expertise and knowledge that make them well-suited to work collaboratively with one another to solve problems they encounter in the classroom. However, before teachers refer problems to consulting teachers, teacher consultation teams, or agree to work as a team teacher, they should be familiar with the operational process associated with each model. If more than one option is available, teachers should select the program that best coincides with their personalities and teaching styles. In addition, it is extremely important for teachers to seek collegial support after they have unsuccessfully attempted to change behavior, but before they develop feelings of resentment and hostility toward targeted students.

In working with consultants, consultation teams, and team teachers, both consultant and consultee should establish and follow a systematic approach to problem-solving. The problem should be sufficiently defined and measured, consensus regarding the nature of the problem should be established, and a system to monitor, modify, and evaluate the intervention should be developed. During the intervention development stage, the referring teacher should make certain the he or she is comfortable with implementing and taking ownership of the plan. When working as a team teacher, team members should engage in planning that will result in identification of their individual strengths and weaknesses. Based on such planning, roles and responsibilities should be established in an equitable manner. Within each model, care must be taken to include administrators, parents, and students in the development and implementation of the intervention stage. None of the models should be used as administrative structures created to deny special services to students who are disabled. Finally, teachers, consultants, and administrators must realize that, to a large degree, program effectiveness will depend on the amount of time allocated for planning, the support given by administrators, the proper identification of responsibilities and roles, and the accessibility of consultants and collaborative teachers.

References and Resources for Further Study

The following references provided the basis for many of our statements in this chapter. You may wish to consult selected references for additional information on specific topics. Our reference notes for this chapter refer to sources in this list.

Consultation Models

Idol, L., Paolucci–Whitcomb, P., and Nevin, A. (1986). *Collaborative Consultation*. Rockville, MD: Aspen Systems.

Idol, L., and West, J. F. (1987). Consultation in special education (Part II): Training and practice. *Journal of Learning Disabilities, 20*, 474–493.

Paolucci–Whitcomb, P., and Nevin, A. (1985). Preparing consulting teachers through a collaborative approach between university faculty and field–based consulting teachers. *Teacher Education and Special Education, 8*(3), 132–143.

Tindal, G., Walz, L., and Germann, G. (1987). Mainstream consultation in secondary settings: The Pine County Model. *The Journal of Special Education, 21*(3), 94–106.

West, J. F., and Cannon, G. S. (1988). Essential collaborative consultation competencies for regular and special educators. *Journal of Learning Disabilities, 21*, 56–63, 28.

Teacher Consultation/Prereferral Teams

Carter, J. and Sugai, G. (1989). Survey on prereferral practices: Responses from state departments of education. *Exceptional Children, 55,* 298–302.

Chalfant, J. C., Pysh, M. V., and Moultrie, R. (1979). Teacher assistance teams: A model for within-building problem-solving. *Learning Disability Quarterly, 2,* 85–96.

Evans, R. (1990). Making mainstreaming work through prereferral consultation. *Educational Leadership, 48*(1), 73–77.

Graden, J. L. (1989). Redefining "prereferral" intervention as intervention assistance: Collaboration between general and special education. *Exceptional Children, 56,* 227–31.

Graden, J. L., Casey, A., and Christenson, S. L. (1985). Implementing a prereferral intervention system. Part I: The model. *Exceptional Children, 51,* 377–384.

Collaborative Teaching Models

Bauwens, J., Hourcade, J. J., and Friend, M., (1989). Cooperative Teaching: A model for general and special education integration. *Remedial and Special Education, 10*(2), 17–22.

Harris, K. C., Harvey, P., Garcia L., Innes, D., Lynn P., Munoz, D., Sexton, K., and Stoica, R. (1987). Meeting the needs of special high school students in regular education classrooms. *Teacher Education and Special Education, 10*(4), 143–152.

Kirk, S. A. (1986). Redesigning delivery systems for learning disabled students. *Learning Disabilities Focus, 2*(1), 4–6.

Reed, J. C. (1987). Using a team approach when mainstreaming special needs students. *Business Education Forum, 41*(7), 3–4.

Robinson, E. B. (1984). Hamilton P.S.: An alternative that's working. *Perspectives for Teachers of the Hearing Impaired, 3*(1), 11–12.

Issues and Problems Related to Collaborative and Consultative Models

Bradford, R. H. (1976). How to fail in mainstreaming without really trying. In P. A. O'Donnell and R. H. Bradford (Eds.), *Mainstreaming: Controversy and Consensus.* Rafael, CA: Academic Therapy Publications.

Idol-Maestas, L. and Ritter, S. (1985). A follow–up study of resource/consulting teachers: Factors that facilitate and inhibit teacher consultation. *Teacher Education and Special Education, 8*(3), 121–131.

Kunzweiler, C. (1982). Mainstreaming will fail unless there is a change in professional attitude and institutional structure. *Education, 102*(3), 284–288.

Lloyd, J. W., Crowley, E. P., Kohler, F. W., and Strain, P. S. (1988). Redefining the applied research agenda: Cooperative learning, prereferral, teacher consultation, and peer-mediated interventions. *Journal of Learning Disabilities, 21,* 43–52.

McLoughlin, J. A. and Kelly, D. (1982). Issues facing the resource teacher. *Learning Disability Quarterly, 5,* 58–64.

Sapon–Shevin, M. (1988). Working towards merger together: Seeing beyond distrust and fear. *Teacher Education and Special Education, 11*(3), 103–110.

Reference Notes

1. See Idol et al. (1986) for a description of consultation.
2. See Graden et al. (1985) for discussion of prereferral intervention strategies.

3. See Chalfant et al. (1979) for a description of general education teachers working together.

4. See Bauwens et al. (1989).

5. See Paolucci-Whitcomb and Nevin (1985).

6. See Chalfant et al. (1979).

7. See Idol et al., (1986).

8. See Chalfant et al. (1979).

9. See Bauwens et al. (1989) for elaboration on collaborative teaching.

$$C \quad h \quad a \quad p \quad t \quad e \quad r \qquad 7$$

Working with Parents

Questions for Reflection
Why should I involve parents?
Why is it so hard to involve parents?
When should I involve parents?
Should I expect all parents to be involved?
How should I communicate with parents?
In what ways can I involve parents?

Understanding the role of teacher in relation to the role of parent is not easy. The role of teacher has frequently been designated in legal language as "en loco parentis," meaning in place of parents. And, unfortunately, some teachers take this legal phrase all too literally, seeing themselves as substitute parents. The teachers who adopt this role seem to believe that the actual parent is superfluous to the educational process—a third party to be tolerated and mollified with bits and pieces of information twice a year at dreaded parent-teacher conferences. Only when they encounter a student with serious behavior problems do these teachers consider the importance of parents, and then typically to blame parents for the problems.

Fortunately, most teachers do not try to usurp the role of their students' parents. Still, as teachers it is tempting to allocate credit and blame in a way that puts ourselves in the most flattering light. When our students are well-behaved and learning quickly, we like to attribute success to our instructional and behavior management skills. On the other hand, when students present serious behavior problems and have learning difficulties, we are often too quick to place exaggerated emphasis on the influence of parents. We then may come to see parents as the enemy—the pernicious influence to be conquered before we can hope to improve the child's behavior.

Many experienced teachers are able to steer a middle course in defining their role and form positive, productive relationships with parents. They are able to draw on parents for strength and help when they run into difficulty in teaching or managing a child's behavior. Rather than seeing parents as adversaries, these teachers view parents as invaluable allies.

To become a truly effective manager of behavior in your classroom it is imperative that you cultivate your skills in working with parents. Although skills in communicating and collaborating with parents may not be sufficient to make someone an effective teacher, these skills most definitely are necessary. Far too many teachers have an excellent knowledge of behavioral principles and their application in the classroom but, nevertheless, lack effectiveness because of their naivete and ineptitude in working with parents. They seem to take the attitude, perhaps acquired or strengthened in their teacher education programs, that teaching only encompasses what goes on within the four walls of their classroom.

Unfortunately, many teachers learn the hard way just how important parents are to children's learning and behavior. Only after unpleasant encounters with parents do they discover that parents cannot be ignored. Some teachers learn from these encounters and harness the influence of parents. Others are so threatened by the confrontations with angry parents that they are forever leery of talking with them, and even more wary of working with them. Still others are startled by reactions of parents that they see—sometimes correctly—as inappropriate or something with which they are not equipped to deal. Consider the experiences of Sadie and Marie in the following vignettes.

Sadie: Mrs. Hecht had three boys, all of them kids with mild mental retardation and every one of them a serious behavior problem in school. Roger, the youngest, was in my class. I was pretty successful in dealing with his behavior in my classroom, and I didn't feel a particular need to get his mother involved, other than through the usual notes home and an occasional phone contact. I knew she herself had had serious problems in school, and my guess was that she had about the same level of intellectual ability as her sons. She was a single parent, and very hard working. When I arranged to meet her in my classroom at 7:45 one morning (the only time she could come to the school because of her work) so that she could sign Roger's IEP, I had no idea what I was in for. As soon as I put the IEP in front of her, she started sobbing uncontrollably. This took me completely by surprise, and I had no idea what she was crying

about until, after a few minutes, she pulled herself together enough to say between sobs, "I just don't know what I've done, I just don't know how I've hurt my boys so. They're all so messed up, and I know it's my fault, but I just don't know what I've done . . ." She really went on and on about how guilty she felt for having three boys with such terrible problems—not able to get along with other kids, failing in school, driving her crazy at home, and so on. I ended up feeling terribly sorry for her, crying along with her, and trying to reassure her that it wasn't her fault. But I really didn't think it was fair for me to have to deal with this. I mean, I'm not a psychologist or a counselor, I'm just her kid's teacher! Besides, I don't know how she might have actually contributed to her boys' problems. Maybe reassurance wasn't what I should have offered. I don't know. It was really an upsetting experience for me.

Marie: Rusty Farmer was one of the most violent young students I've seen in my 15 years of teaching. At age 8, he exhibited very serious aggression in my classroom. He hit other children, he hit me, he threw things—I was concerned about other children in the class being seriously hurt by him. Since the beginning of the school year, I had dealt with his taunting his classmates until they hit him and he then pummelled them in return; his attacking me with his fists and feet; his sweeping everything off other children's desk and throwing such items as books and pencil boxes; his overturning desks and throwing chairs. Fortunately, my principal, Betty Vogel, was very supportive, and we worked out a plan for simply removing him from the class as calmly as possible and taking him home whenever one of these violent episodes occurred. By November, Betty had taken Rusty home several times, but she had never been able to engage Rusty's mother in a serious conversation about his behavior, partly because Mrs. Farmer seemed to have a sullen disposition and partly because she cared for several neighbors' young children and didn't seem to have time to talk. Eventually, of course, it was my turn to take Rusty home. Mrs. Farmer, who was 24, seemed quite approachable to me and to be seriously concerned about Rusty's behavior, although we couldn't really talk because of the pandemonium created by six young kids in the house. She did seem surprised, though, at my bringing Rusty home and said, "He don't give me no problems like that at home." I thought I'd have a good chance of getting her help in dealing with Rusty's aggression. When I called her later and explained my concern about Rusty's violence toward adults and other children, her exact words to me were, "I don't know why you folks let him do that to you at school. He don't try none of that kind of stuff with me no more. Don't you let him rear up like that on you, no ma'am! I don't put up with none of that at home, and I don't want you to put up with it at school neither. You just knock him on his ass. That's what I do with him, I just haul off and knock him right on his ass if I see him doublin' up his fist or somethin'. He deserves it when he acts like that!" What could I say? I was dumbfounded. And what was I to do now? Taking him home seemed to us a nonviolent and effective way of dealing with his aggression in the classroom. But I was appalled at Mrs. Farmer's attitude, and I certainly didn't want to increase the chances that Rusty would be abused.

In reflecting on how you might improve your relationships with parents, questions like the following will undoubtedly come to mind:

- What is my ethical responsibility for keeping parents informed about their child's behavior?
- How can I avoid undermining parents or seeing them as adversaries when their way of managing their child is unacceptable to me?
- When is it appropriate for me to side-step encounters with parents and try to avoid contact?
- Under what conditions should I try to serve as a sounding board for parents who are frustrated with their child?

- What are my options when I need parental support but I simply cannot get a response from the child's parent?
- Under what circumstances should I give up the idea of working cooperatively with a parent?
- How can I avoid allowing the child to play the parents against me and vice versa?

Parents are as varied a group as students, and the circumstances under which you may find yourself working with parents may present you with unusual challenges. Nevertheless, it is important to keep in mind that most parents are truly concerned about their child's behavior and academic progress and are likely to respond positively to your desire to work with them. We focus, therefore, on the questions most often encountered by teachers in working with parents of students whose behavior is a problem in the classroom.

Questions for Reflection

Clearly, you might consider a wide variety of questions regarding the most appropriate roles of parents and teachers and various strategies for working productively with parents. We have organized our discussion in the remainder of this chapter around six essential questions:

1. Why should I involve parents?
2. Why is it so hard to involve parents?
3. When should I involve parents?
4. Should I expect all parents to be involved?
5. How should I communicate with parents?
6. In what ways can I involve parents?

Why should I involve parents?

Expert teachers recognize that, even though they spend a great deal of time with students and wield a great deal of influence over them, only in rare instances do they really supplant parents. A child's teacher changes from year to year. Except in cases of divorce or death and remarriage, parents do not change. A child's teacher sees hundreds of new students every year and probably teaches at least 20. Even in large families, the adult-child ratio is considerably smaller. A child's teacher holds only a limited number and variety of reinforcers for the student. Parents have a large number and variety of reinforcers they can employ with their children. And most important, the emotional ties between parents and children are immeasurably more binding than between teachers and students.

Another reason for involving parents is to minimize the chances that the child will be able to play them against you—or you against them. To be most effective in managing behavior, teacher and parent need to be united in their expectations and discipline, just as parents need to present a consistent, united front. The only way to avoid the problem of children manipulating differences between adults is to maintain close communication between home and school. Close communication does not guarantee that the child will be unable to play adults against each other, but it does make such manipulation more difficult.

Reciprocity of Parent-Child Interaction

Expert teachers also realize that parents of students with behavior problems are not always the cause of their child's problems. Researchers in recent years have confirmed what many parents have contended for a long time: Some children are born with temperaments that make them more difficult to parent and teach. Many parents of more than one child will tell you that almost from the moment of birth they noticed distinct differences between their children. For example, one baby was happy and easy to soothe, the other was irritable and hard to please. Research has now shown that different temperaments can have a powerful influence on how parents deal with their babies and children. Difficult babies can place a great deal of stress on parents. For many years, the dominant child development theorists viewed child-parent interaction as a one way street running from parent to child. We now know that the relationship is reciprocal. Parents can and do influence children. But it is also the case that children can and do influence parents.

That parent-child interaction is reciprocal has important implications for how teachers view parents, especially parents of children with behavior problems. Keep two things in mind. First, parents of children with behavior problems are not necessarily to blame for their children's behavior. Second, even if you witness poor parenting of children with behavior problems, it may not be entirely the parents' fault. Some of the most intelligent and well-intentioned parents can easily get caught up in an interactive pattern that results in their exhibiting inappropriate parenting behaviors. It is instructive to keep in mind your own interactions with intractable students. Given that on occasion you have found it difficult to maintain your professional composure with particularly nasty and ill-mannered students, think of having to contend with such behavior daily over the course of several years.

At the same time as you should not be quick to blame parents, neither should you deny that they can at times be culpable. Poor parenting, especially abusive parenting, can directly cause behavior problems in children. And some parents indirectly contribute to the behavior problems of their children by consistently responding in a maladaptive manner to their children's misbehavior. We caution here that you should not assume that parents do not care about their children if they are poor parents. Nearly all parents are concerned for the welfare of their children, even if they abuse them. Parents who have poor parenting skills may want to be good parents, but they may simply not have the knowledge of alternative ways of rearing children or not learned the self-control required to discipline their children humanely.

Why is it so hard to involve parents?

The seeming contradiction—that parents hold a great deal of influence over their children but should not be automatically blamed for the behavior problems of their children—is what perhaps makes it so very difficult for novice teachers to work constructively with parents, especially parents of students who misbehave. You need to maintain a very delicate balance between recognizing that parents are important to the educational process and not immediately pointing the finger at them when their children misbehave.

Shared Responsibility

Another reason why teachers and parents are sometimes at odds is that, even though they share responsibility for looking out for the best interests of the child, there are usually no formal mechanisms in the public schools for working together. Unless one or the other party initiates it, there is virtually no opportunity for the two parties to collaborate. Given parents, who have the right and responsibility to want the best for their children, and teachers, who have similar rights and responsibilities, coupled with little means for working together, it is little wonder that so much parent-teacher conflict occurs. Below is a case wherein the parents and teacher square off, both perceiving the other as a threat, each side believing the other does not know what is best for the child.

Karen: I knew before I accepted this fifth-grade teaching assignment that the students were a particularly difficult group to manage. Last year's teacher requested and was granted a midyear transfer because she encountered so much difficulty with discipline. Before the first six weeks were over, I had managed to get most of the students settled and into routines. Five of these students, however, continued to be a real challenge. They fought with each other and disrupted class frequently despite the self-monitoring and reward system I used. During a recent assembly, I had to remove two of them for spitting on each other. Their aggressiveness toward each other was so unpredictable and persistent that the thought of them going with the class on an upcoming field trip to the state fair was unsettling.

I approached the principal about my concerns, and she agreed that the five were not demonstrating the self-control necessary for us to assume responsibility for them on the field trip. She arranged a meeting with the five students and informed them that they would not be allowed to make the trip unless each had a parent to accompany him. Although she was careful to substantiate her rationale, the students were angry and upset. When they returned to the classroom, they sulked for the rest of the afternoon.

I suppose both the principal and I were wrong in assuming that all of the parents of the students would agree with our decision. It didn't occur to either one of us to garner their support before we delivered this ruling.

As it happened, all except two of the students' parents agreed that their child would remain in school the day of the trip. One mother decided to go with her son. I was pleased about this because I felt that she was showing her support of both her son and me. If only Gordon Johnson's mother had been so cooperative!

The evening of the principal's announcement to the students, the telephone rang during my dinner. It was Gordon's mother. She told me that she felt that her son was being punished for something he had not yet done, and that he had cried when he got home. Ms. Johnson sounded angry and defensive. I tried to assure her that I understood Gordon's disappointment, but I also explained the decision the principal and I had made. I tried to tell her about the things I was doing in class to help Gordon with his behavior. I wanted her to understand that I was not trying to be mean to her son.

She was not to be swayed. In fact, she seemed to become more aloof and contentious. As my dinner grew cold, she began to make thinly veiled threats. First she said, "You know, Ms. Martin, what goes around comes around." I was so shocked with this seemingly out of context remark that all I could manage to voice was a faint, "What . . . ?" While my mind raced, she followed my reply with a directive. "I want it put in writing that my son is not allowed to go on this field trip." She was vehement about this. It occurred to me that she was hinting at taking legal action. I reiterated that she was welcome to accom-

pany him. She shot back that she had to work and couldn't go along.

By this time, I could feel my initial panic turning to anger. Were both her husband and she so consumed with their work that one of them could not get away for a single day? No, they would rather the school take on all of the work of helping their son learn some self-control. Why, I supposed they were not concerned about Gordon's behavior so long as they didn't have to contend with it. That's probably his problem, I thought. They give in to him the moment he raises the least protest. I was determined to stand firm. "Yes," I heard myself reply. "I'll have the principal put it in writing." I excused myself by telling Ms. Johnson that I would have the principal contact her tomorrow. We both managed a stiff "goodbye," and I hung up the telephone too upset to resume my meal.

Thus, parents and teachers can perceive one another as a threat. Teachers worry that parents will call their behavior management practices into question or make unreasonable demands. Parents, especially ones who themselves had unpleasant school experiences, are fearful of their children having similarly devastating experiences. Yet, despite the tension which may develop, parents and teachers need each other. And, because the teacher is the professional, it is incumbent that he or she make deliberate efforts to develop productive relationships with parents.

When should I involve parents?

To be as effective as possible, it is important that teachers attempt to build solid relationships with parents from the start of class. It helps to have already established some contact with as many of the parents in your class as possible so that should the need arise for more intense involvement you have already developed some rapport upon which to build. Parents often complain, especially those who have a child with behavior problems, that the only time they hear from the schools is after their child has done something wrong. Likewise, when instituting a procedure that involves parents it is imperative that you approach them first and obtain their cooperation. Karen Martin and her principal assumed too much in believing that parents would agree with their actions and rationale. Had they taken the time to contact the parents in advance, they may have been able to work with those who expressed dissent. Perhaps together they could have exchanged information and ideas that might have led to a satisfying solution for everyone. At the very least, they would have become aware of the potential disagreement and have been more prepared to handle it constructively.

Given the demands placed on teachers, of course, it is not possible for you to establish close relationships with all of the parents. What you might want to do is prepare a brief letter of introduction to the parents of each of the students in your class, acquainting them with your goals for their children over the course of the year and inviting any of them to make individual appointments with you if they desire.

As the year progresses, should a behavior management problem arise with a student, you then need to consider whether it warrants contacting the parents. Relatively minor offenses (e.g., talking back) of a short duration do not require your notifying parents. More serious offenses (e.g., fighting, stealing, consistently late homework), however, do signal the need to contact parents.

Should I expect all parents to be involved?

One of the most important findings to emerge from recent research on families is that not all parents wish to be very involved in the education of their children. Some parents view teachers as the experts and do not wish to be bothered with what goes on in the school.[1]

Some parents may want to be more involved but find it nearly impossible to do so. Demographic changes in our society are undoubtedly responsible for some of this. The two-parent family with only the father employed is no longer the norm. Demographers predict that by the year 1995 over three-quarters of the parents of school-age children will have a mother in the work force, and one out of five families with children is headed by a single parent. Furthermore, poverty is on the rise, with one out of every five children now living in poverty. Parents from some of these circumstances may have neither the time nor the resources to be very involved. For example, work shifts may make it impossible for them to attend parent-teacher conferences during typical hours or oversee their child's homework.

Regardless of the reasons parents have for not being involved, it is important that teachers respect their wishes. You should not come on too strongly with parents, assuming that they will want to be involved in the education of their children and be able to be involved. Their reasons may be good or bad according to your values, but in either case it is useless to try to coerce parents into more involvement.

How should I communicate with parents?

Several people have come up with ingenious and elaborate ways of keeping in touch with parents.[2] For example, some teachers use a recording on their home telephone answering device to keep parents up to date on the general progress of the class. And some teachers go to the trouble of sending home periodic newsletters for the same purpose. All of these ideas are good, but they lack the specificity needed for talking with parents about students who are exhibiting behavior management problems. They might help establish rapport, which will help in communicating directly with a particular student's parents about misbehavior, but they fall far short of helping in the delicate task of talking with parents about the inappropriate behavior of their child.

Parent Conferences

The three most common ways of communicating with parents about their child's problems are by letter, telephone call, or conference. We recommend a combination of the three, with the emphasis on the conference. A letter is usually too formal and should be avoided unless the parents have no phone. A telephone call, by itself, is problematic because it is difficult to establish rapport over the phone. You should avoid this option unless you already have a good relationship with the parents or you need to talk with them immediately. We prefer an initial telephone call in which you briefly indicate your desire to have a conference, followed by a letter that reiterates the time and place of the meeting.

Before making the call, make sure you have your emotions under control. Calling while you are still angry about a student's behavior makes it difficult to think clearly about what it is you want to say. Another helpful tactic is to imagine yourself in the parent's place. It is only natural to be on the defensive when someone calls you about the conduct of your child. In the case of children with behavior problems, the parents may already have had their fill of unpleasant conversations with angry school personnel. In the telephone call it is not necessary unless really pressed to go into great detail about the nature of the student's conduct. After some preliminary remarks to establish rapport, your part of the conversation might go something like the following:

> *Ms. McNergney, the reason I'm calling is that I'd like to set up a time when you and I can chat about Bobby. He's a really creative and energetic student, and in most respects he's doing fine. But lately I've had somewhat of a problem keeping him on task, and I'm concerned that we find a way to handle this so that it doesn't become a big problem. I don't think there's need to be too alarmed, but I'm getting concerned about his attitude in class lately. For the past few weeks I've found it really hard to get him to stay at his desk and cooperate. When I've tried to talk with him about it, he's been really negative and lippy with me. And today it was all I could do to keep him from keeping out of some of the other kids' desks. I don't think it's anything to get too terribly alarmed about, but I thought you and I could talk about it. Maybe the two of us can come up with some ways to approach this. I've got some ideas about what we might do, but I wanted to see what you think of them. I know you're busy, but I've found that it really helps sometimes to talk with parents about some of the things going on with their kids.*

Most experienced teachers agree that the key to conducting a successful parent-teacher conference is planning. Ann and Rudd Turnbull, from the University of Kansas, have written extensively about the need to plan ahead for meetings with parents.[3] Based on the work of the Turnbulls, Table 7–1 contains some questions you should ask yourself about the mechanics of conducting parent-teacher conferences. In addition to these questions, you should also keep the following in mind before you have your meeting.

TABLE 7–1 Questions for Teachers to Ask Themselves Regarding Parent-Teacher Conferences

Preconference Preparation

Notifying Families
— Did I, or the school, provide parents with written notification of the conference?
— Did I provide a means of determining that the parents knew the date and time?

Preparing for the Conference
— Did I review the student's cumulative records?
— Did I assess the student's behavior and pinpoint areas of concern?
— Did I make notes of the student's misbehavior to show to parents?
— Did I consult with other relevant professionals about the student's behavior?
— Did I mentally rehearse and review what I was going to say at the conference?

Preparing the Physical Environment
— Did the setting provide enough privacy?
— Did the setting provide enough comfort?

Conference Activities

Developing Rapport
— Did I allow time to talk informally before the start of the meeting?
— Did I express appreciation for the parents' coming to the meeting?

Obtaining Information from Parents
— Did I ask enough open-ended questions?
— Did my body language indicate interest in what parents were saying? (Did I maintain eye contact and look attentive?)
— Did I ask for clarification on points I didn't understand?

Providing Information to Parents
— Did I speak as positively as possible about the student?
— Did I use jargon-free language?
— Did I use specific examples to clarify my points?

Summarizing and Follow-up
— Did I review the main points to determine next steps?
— Did I restate who was responsible for completing the next steps and by when?
— Did I end the meeting on a positive note?
— Did I thank the parents for their interest in attending.

Postconference Follow-Up

— Did I consider reviewing the meeting with the student?
— Did I share the results with the appropriate other professionals who work with the student?
— Did I make a record of the conference proceedings?

Source: Adapted from A. P. Turnbull and H. R. Turnbull (1990). *Families, Professionals, and Exceptionality: A Special Partnership* (2nd ed.). Columbus, OH: Merrill/Macmillan.

- Am I able to avoid blaming parents? One of the least helpful things a teacher can do is lay the blame on parents for the misbehavior of their children. Parents will already be on the defensive because you have called them to have this meeting. Weigh your words carefully so as not to give the impression that you think they are the culprits. Even if you are convinced that they are the cause of their children's problems, you should avoid accusations. If they are at fault, it is better to let them arrive at that judgment on their own.

- Am I willing to admit it when I'm wrong? Some teachers, especially those who are relatively inexperienced, feel that it is a sign of weakness to acknowledge to parents that they have made mistakes. We don't think you need to see the meeting as an opportunity to reveal all of your shortcomings, but if you have doubts about how you have handled the student it is a good idea to concede this point.

- Am I willing to admit it when I don't know the answer to parents' questions? Again, be careful not to fall into the trap of feeling that you need to have answers to every question posed by the parents. Confident teachers are more than willing to say that they are not all-knowing. In fact, teachers should view the parent-teacher conference as an opportunity to learn more about the child from the parents.

- Can I accept the family as it is? Some teachers view parent-teacher conferences as quasitherapy sessions in which they should try to influence family dynamics. Your focus should be on what the student is doing in your classroom. To be sure, you will want to talk about how the child behaves at home, and you may want to suggest that parents carry out certain procedures in the home to back up what you are doing at school, but you should not see yourself as a family therapist.

- Am I attuned to cultural differences between myself and the parents? It is important that you respect the cultural backgrounds of parents and not misinterpret their behavior or offend them because their customs vary from yours.

- Can I find something positive to say about the child and something positive about the parent that I can support? It is very important that you try to find something positive and supportive to say about the child and the parent in every parent contact. Sometimes this may be difficult. Nevertheless, if all the parent receives is negative information, you are not likely to get very far in resolving the problem. Dishonesty about your feelings and perceptions is not helpful. Going out of your way to find something—anything, regardless how small—that you can be positive about or support will make your attempts to work cooperatively with a parent more likely to be successful.

Meeting with parents about a student's misbehavior demands a delicate balance between providing an objective account of the misbehavior and demonstrating that you are an advocate for the child. Even though you need to be sensitive to the possibility that the parents are going to be unreceptive to what you have to say, it is important that they hear what you have to say about their child's problem behavior. At times it is tempting to spare parents the anxiety caused by information which will likely prove disheartening. Conveying only good news skews their perspective, however, just as much as conveying only negative information. If a serious incident arises, they have no sense of background or warning. Filling them in at this point may lead them to conclude that the teacher is withholding information and provoke a sense of mistrust. When telling parents unpleasant information, it helps not only to be as objective as possible, but also state the case in a way that clearly conveys your advocacy of the student. When it is obvious to the parents that the teacher is angry or upset with their child, parents become apprehensive about the treatment the child may receive. A common response to this sense of dread is a defensiveness which polarizes parent-teacher relationships.

Parents need to know how their children are progressing. This is how they know we are doing our job as teachers. Highlighting students' progress motivates students as well as parents. Although this sounds like conventional wisdom, following through often gets pushed aside as the demands of the school day obscure the importance of doing so. Take the case of Karen Martin mentioned earlier. Work on her behavior management program had actually resulted in her students making considerable progress. Even Gordon and his more intractable classmates had shown improvement, although their behavior remained far from acceptable. Had Ms. Johnson been aware of her son's progress, she would most likely have been able to draw on a sense of context when evaluating the situation. As the year progressed, Karen made efforts to convey to Gordon's parents her sincere desire to help him learn self-control. By consistently and objectively reporting his progress as well as his occasional lapses in a supportive manner, she succeeded in building a very cooperative relationship with his parents. Although she initially resented Ms. Johnson's negative attitude, she realized that it would be a serious mistake if she did not take the initiative to turn the situation around. She correctly reasoned that Ms. Johnson cared a great deal about her son, despite the fact that Gordon's mother did not show it by agreeing to accompany him on the trip. It made sense to build, on this foundation, some common ground between Ms. Johnson and herself.

In what ways can I involve parents?

Simply meeting with the parents may be enough to resolve the problems you are having with a student. Often, such meetings are enough to let the student know that his or her behavior has stepped over the bounds of what one should be expected to tolerate in the way of unruly behavior. It sends a message that you are more than mildly annoyed about the behavior. Alerting the parents to a problem is often enough, too, because they can then exert pressure on the student at home.

In behavioral terms, parents have control over a number of very powerful reinforcers, e.g., privileges related to dating, driving, television, telephone. And knowing the child as they do, they are in an excellent position to know which reinforcers are likely to be the most effective.[4] In many ways, parents are in a much better position to apply behavioral consequences than are teachers. In fact, should a meeting not be enough to change the student's behavior for the better, you might wish to take advantage of parental reinforcement in a more systematic fashion through the use of a home-note program.

Home-note Programs

Home-note programs, sometimes referred to as home contingency programs, are probably the best and simplest way to involve parents directly and systematically in changing the inappropriate behavior of students in your classroom.[5] With a home-note program, you evaluate the student's behavior, but the parents deliver the consequences. The teacher fills out a brief report on the student's behavior, the student takes it home, and the parents deliver the reinforcement. We also recommend that you have the parent sign it and send it back with the child the next day. Figure 7–1 is an example of a note that might be used in such a program. This note is designed for children in approximately grades 2 through 5. Versions for younger children might contain fewer categories and happy and sad faces. Versions for older students might contain places for the evaluations and signatures of multiple teachers.

There are several things to keep in mind in setting up a home-note program. Most important, of course, is that you meet with the parents to work out the features of the program. In this meeting, you should leave as many choices as possible up to the parents, especially with regard to the types and amount of reinforcers as well as the schedule of reinforcement (i.e., how many "good" notes it takes to receive a reinforcer). The more they feel they are working with you in the development of the home-note program, the more likely parents are to want to carry it out consistently. You should also consider the possibility of including the student in on the planning at some point. It is usually best to meet with the parents first and then decide whether to include the student in another meeting.

There are two areas in which you will want to be directive. First, you must discourage parents from using punishment. Although it is theoretically possible for parents to use punishment with a home-note system, most researchers recommend against it.[6] Therefore, teachers should suggest to parents that they only consider positive reinforcers as possible consequences. You may find that some parents are highly punitive with their children and perceive even an absence of a perfect report as evidence that they should punish the child. Recall Marie's description of Rusty's mother in the vignette near the beginning of this chapter. In this case, Marie should use extreme caution in setting up any home contingency for Rusty, given his mother's obvious reliance on harsh punishment. In some cases, teachers must simply avoid getting parents involved in management of their child based on communication from the school. Second, you must also specify what the behaviors are that you are going to be evaluating. It should be clear to the parents as well as the student what it is you will be monitoring. You should also stipulate that lost notes will be treated as a negative report.

Although you should be as precise as possible in defining the criteria you will use in judging the occurrence or nonoccurrence of behaviors, the note home to parents need not be detailed. In other words, the feedback to parents need not be lengthy or complicated. Unless they request it, all you need do is inform them that the child has or has not engaged in the desired behavior. As depicted in Figure 7–1, you might wish to leave space for teacher or parent comments, but you might use this option only occasionally.

Most researchers suggest that teachers begin by using the home-note system on a daily basis. Once it has been working successfully for a couple of weeks, you can begin

Day _____   Date _____

Social Behavior Acceptable	YES	NO	NA
Homework Completed	YES	NO	NA
Homework Accurate	YES	NO	NA
In-Class Academic Work Completed	YES	NO	NA
In-Class Academic Work Accurate	YES	NO	NA

Teacher Comments:

Tonight's Homework Assignments:

Parent Comments:

_____   _____
Teacher's Signature   Parent's Signature

FIGURE 7–1   Example of a Home Note For Use With Students in Approximately Grades 2 through 5.

TABLE 7–2   Checklist of Variables That Influence the Effectiveness of a School-Home Note Program

School-Home Note Program Checklist

Target behaviors
1. _____ Target behaviors are defined in a specific manner.
2. _____ Target behaviors occur frequently and are potentially sensitive to change.
3. _____ The behaviors are judged as important by the teacher, parents, and student.
4. _____ Target behavior definitions are understood by the parents, teacher, and student.
5. _____ Target behaviors are easy for the teacher to monitor
6. _____ Target behaviors are worded positively.
7. _____ Target behaviors are evaluated by the teacher in all relevant situations.

Evaluation criteria and performance goals
1. _____ The evaluation anchors (e.g., happy vs. sad face) are well defined.
2. _____ The parent, teacher, and student understand what behaviors warrant positive versus negative evaluations.
3. _____ The child clearly understands what must be done to earn rewards.
4. _____ The parent, teacher, and student agree that the required level of performance is fair and within the student's current ability to achieve.
5. _____ Improvements in the student's performance result in improved global evaluations by parents and teacher.

The note
1. _____ The actual school-home note is uncluttered, organized, and easy to complete.
2. _____ The note is pleasing to the child and developmentally appropriate with regard to wording and performance criteria.
3. _____ Data derived from the note are easy to summarize.

Administration
1. _____ Parent, teacher, and student responsibilities are clear to all involved (e.g., it is understood who provides the blank note daily).
2. _____ Each teacher completes the note daily and provides meaningful comments to the student and parent.
3. _____ The note is minimally intrusive for the student and teacher.
4. _____ The child is not ridiculed or excessively questioned by other students about the note.
5. _____ Each teacher completes the note in a friendly, facilitative manner and avoids making hostile, embarrassing, or excessively critical statements to the child.
6. _____ Parents provide feedback to the teacher about home consequences and ask questions when they arise.
7. _____ Both the parents and teacher use the note as a communication tool rather than a weapon, and take time to acknowledge improvement and each other's problem-solving efforts.
8. _____ The note is used for at least a few weeks after behavior is quite acceptable and then faded systematically (or reintroduced if performance diminishes).

Feedback and consequences
1. _____ The target behavior goals and consequences for goal achievement are clear and written in a contract.
2. _____ The child earns both daily and weekly rewards.
3. _____ The child participates in generating the rewards for goal achievement.
4. _____ Rewards are important and truly rewarding to the child.
5. _____ Teacher provides feedback about performance and goal achievement at regular intervals throughout the day.
6. _____ Parents review the teacher's comments daily and promote improved performance through problem-solving with the child.
7. _____ Parents and teacher praise the child for goal achievement.

Source: Kelley, M. L. (1990). *School-home Notes: Promoting Children's Classroom Success.* New York: Guilford Press, pp. 105–106.

to wean the child from the system by going to a once-a-week note. In the early stages, especially, you should check frequently with parents. Even at later stages, you should make periodic checks with parents to see how they think the system is working. If from your point of view you are not seeing any changes in the behavior of the child, or if the parents perceive that it is not working effectively, there are two things to look for. First, try to determine if the parents are being consistent in the delivery of the reinforcement. Second, question whether the reinforcement is strong enough. Keep in mind that some ordinarily very effective rewards can lose their effectiveness after a period of time. Simply changing the reward can sometimes revitalize a reinforcement program that has started to become listless. Table 7–2 lists some more components of an effective home-note system.

Although home-note programs are far from a panacea, research indicates that they can be highly effective. They are palatable to most parents and students and require a minimum of teacher time. They also provide a means by which parents and teachers can work together in a constructive manner.

Summary

The ability to work with parents is often the critical difference that divides good teachers from those who are truly excellent. Possessing skills in instruction and behavior management in the classroom can serve teachers well with many students, but they are often not enough. In order to achieve excellence, teachers must be able to communicate effectively with parents. By so doing, they can enhance their behavior management techniques by leveraging the influence that some parents have over their children. Although working with parents does not come naturally to all teachers, those who take the time and effort to develop such skills will be rewarded handsomely.

References and Resources for Further Study

The following references provided the basis for many of our statements in this chapter. You may wish to consult selected references for additional information. Our reference notes for this chapter refer to sources in this list.

Davies, D. E. and McLaughlin, T. F. (1989). Effects of a daily report card on disruptive behaviour in primary students. *B. C. Journal of Special Education, 13,* 173-181.

Hutton, J. B. (1983). How to decrease problem behavior at school by rewarding desirable behavior at home. *The Pointer, 27*(4), 25-28.

Kelley, M. L. (1990). *School-home Notes: Promoting Children's Classroom Success.* New York: Guilford.

Kerr, M. M., and Nelson. C. M. (1989). *Strategies for Managing Behavior Problems in the Classroom.* (2nd ed.). Columbus, OH: Merrill/Macmillan.

Kroth, R. L. (1985). *Communicating with Parents of Exceptional Children: Improving Parent-Teacher Relationships.* (2nd ed.). Denver, CO: Love.

Lazarus, B. D. (1990). A cooperative home-school token economy. *Preventing School Failure, 34* (4), 37-40.

Morgan, D. P. and Jenson, W. R. (1988). *Teaching Behaviorally Disordered Students: Preferred Practices*. Columbus, OH: Merrill/Macmillan.

Patterson, G. R. and Forgatch, M. S. (1987). *Parents and Adolescents Living Together*. Eugene, OR: Castalia Publishing Co.

Swassing, C. S. (1984). Helping your child adjust to junior high school: A home-school contingency plan. *The Pointer, 29* (1), 4-7.

Taylor, V. L., Cornwell, D. D., and Riley, M. T. (1984). Home-based contingency management programs that teachers can use. *Psychology in the Schools, 21*(3), 368-374.

Trice, A. D., Parker, F. C., Furrow, F., and Iwata, M. M. (1983). An analysis of home contingencies to improve school behavior with disruptive adolescents. *Education and Treatment of Children, 6* (4), 389-399.

Turnbull, A. P. and Turnbull, H. R. (1990). *Families, Professionals, and Exceptionality: A Special Partnership*. (2nd ed.). Columbus, OH: Merrill/Macmillan.

Wielkiewicz, R. M. (1986). *Behavior Management in the Schools*. New York: Pergamon Press.

Reference Notes

1. See Turnbull and Turnbull (1990) for more on parents' perspectives on their involvement.

2. See Turnbull and Turnbull (1990) for further discussion.

3. See Turnbull and Turnbull (1990).

4. See Kroth (1985) and Patterson and Forgatch (1987).

5. See Davies and McLaughlin (1989), Kelley (1990), Swassing (1984), Taylor et al. (1984), and Wielkiewicz (19) for further description and examples.

6. See Kelly (1990) for discussion of the punishment issue.

$Part$ II

Cases For Analysis,
Discussion, and Reflection

What You Don't Know Can Hurt You!

JOHN MCCULLUM

When John thought about his seventh period class, his breathing became shallow and a radiating knot of anxiety formed in his stomach. This class, the only one which proved to be troublesome, consisted of fifteen eighth-grade students, seven very high-achieving students and eight who performed considerably lower academically. Of these eight, five talked, laughed, and attempted to dominate the class and him throughout the period. Although John had managed to cope with these problems on a more or less passable basis, doing so had taken a great deal of energy. John had a difficult time concentrating on his lesson delivery as he was constantly distracted by the students who seemed to want to set up a situation in which either he or they won control of the class. He braced himself daily to confront this group. He thought he was familiar with the problems and potential pitfalls in this class. But John was soon to learn that it is easier to fall prey to the dangers of the unexpected and that they often hold the most dire consequences. He was to learn this lesson from a usually quiet student in this seventh period class.

One afternoon, John planned to conduct a test review in the form of a quiz-show game. On this particular day, his clinical instructor (supervising teacher) was absent and a substitute teacher was in his place. The clinical instructor seldom if ever attended class, so this day was much like any other for John. He was accustomed to having complete freedom to plan for and instruct this class as he deemed best. Because he was given this autonomy, he chose to take a different approach with the class than the clinical instructor. The clinical instructor had usually given the students individual written assignments to complete and he used very little direct instruction or group work approaches with them. John felt that it was important to use a variety of instructional techniques for these students.

After directing the students to form groups of their choice, he began the game with the expectation that although the class would be "rowdy," the game would prove to be an enjoyable and effective review technique. Very little time had elapsed before John realized that the students had selected themselves into groups along racial and academic achievement lines. Six high-achieving white students formed two groups of three each. Only one black female was high achieving. Of the low-achieving students, seven were black and one was a white male. These remaining nine students formed three groups of three each. John knew that the white students also came from upper middle-class neighborhoods whereas the other students came from relatively poor homes. Although he was aware of these factors, he was yet to appreciate the potential volatility of the situation.

When an argument erupted between one of the students from a high-achieving group (Chris), and one of the low-achieving students (Richard), he immediately rose and stepped between them. Ignoring the obscenities being exchanged, John moved quickly to separate them because they had already begun pushing and shoving one another. After separating the students, he was able to recommence the game which continued more or less successfully until the end of the class period. As the class was dismissed, however, the two students resumed their hostile exchange at the door.

Again, John moved to intervene, calling both students back to the classroom. Only Chris complied. Richard ran down the corridor and turned the corner. Because Chris did not start the argument, and because John thought that it would have been fruitless to discuss the issue with only one of the students involved, he released Chris to go home.

In the empty classroom, John reflected on the incident. Despite Richard's academic difficulties, he had not been, up to this point, a behavioral problem in class. In fact, John knew very little about him beyond the fact that he was an academically weak student and had been retained several times. Consequently, Richard was much older and larger than his classmates. John felt that he should not allow Richard's flagrant disobedience to go unaddressed. He decided to go look for Richard. Finding Richard at the bike rack just outside the building, he approached him and said that he wanted to talk. Richard responded by jumping on his bike and stating, "I don't got time for this," as he rode away. John, stinging with indignation, immediately went to the office and submitted a disciplinary referral.

Upon Richard's arrival at school the following morning, John presented him with the referral notice and walked with him to the office for a conference with the vice-principal. On the way, John explained that the referral meant an automatically assigned afternoon detention period in his classroom for refusing to stop when he called.

Less than half an hour later, John went to the office to complete some copying and noticed Richard still waiting outside the office for his conference with the vice-principal. As he went about his chore, Richard began to make comments in a somewhat staged whisper to the student next to him. These comments amounted to threats directed toward John such as, "I'm going to break his jaw." At this point, John decided to ignore the remarks.

As he was leaving, he once again encountered Richard, who had gone to the hallway water fountain. John glanced at him as he walked by, and Richard retorted sharply, "Don't be looking at me, boy!" John was becoming increasingly angered by Richard's exhibition in front of another student. Although he thought it best to ignore the remarks, he wheeled around and faced Richard. Taking a deep breath to catch himself, he slowly hissed through clenched teeth, "Go in, sit down, and don't make anything worse on yourself. Just sit down and shut up and wait for Mr. Roberts to see you." After mumbling a few unintelligible remarks, Richard complied.

Although Mr. Roberts had agreed to keep Richard in the in-school suspension (ISS) rather than sending him to John's class that afternoon, Richard showed up in class. Obviously, Mr. Roberts had bungled the ISS schedule somehow, and now John had to deal with Richard in spite of the tensions created by the situation. Fortunately, Richard remained quiet and low-key throughout class.

When John reminded him of the detention that afternoon, Richard declared that he had to catch his bus or he would have no way home. Doubting that this was the case, John told Richard that he could go home so long as he made arrangements to stay the following day. He also warned him that failure to do so would result in a rereferral and possible suspension.

John's difficulty with Richard escalated the next day during the suspension period. Ironically, John had not seen Richard in class because he had been kept in ISS. He couldn't help feeling a little resentful that Mr. Roberts had failed to keep Richard the day before and then kept him when it no longer mattered. At least, he thought, they could give me a little support downstairs. How hard could it be, after all, to keep a simple ISS schedule straight?

Upon arrival for his afternoon detention, Richard announced, "The only reason I'm staying this detention is because Mr. Roberts said I had to." When John attempted to explain to him exactly why he was given detention, Richard's behavior became erratic. A sickening knot formed in John's stomach as he realized that he was losing control of the situation.

Because Richard refused to be seated, and walked around the room striking the computer, walls, desks, and other objects with a yardstick, John was forced to ask students who had remained after school to complete a project to go to the library. John told him several times to be seated and tried to explain to him why he had gotten the referral. Each time, Richard retorted, "How come Chris didn't get a referral?" John attempted to explain several more times that the referral was not given for fighting, but for running away and refusing to return. Several times during John's explanations, Richard covered his ears and began singing a rap tune. With each explanation, he repeated the same refrain, "How come Chris didn't get a referral?"

Soon, Richard began performing a rap song with graphic lyrics that detailed his plan to beat-up Chris. Several times he told John that he was going downstairs to tell the vice-principal that, "You were trying to beat me up, that you were trying to hit me with the yardstick, and that you were trying to slit my throat." He called John "stupid" and "peanut-head," declared that he hated him, and asked him why he didn't go back to the university. John began to sense that the differences in race and backgrounds had something to do with the animosity he was receiving from Richard.

At intervals, Richard pulled a small bottle from his jacket pocket and drank from it. The contents looked like water, but he called it his "beer" and "wine." Two times during this period, Richard wandered outside of the classroom. John followed him, reminding him that during detention, he must stay in the room. When Richard decided to return to the classroom, he preceded John inside, pulled the door closed, and held it so that he could not get in.

Once inside the classroom, John attempted to get some work done, but Richard's singing was too loud for him to concentrate. When John delivered a stern look in his direction, Richard leaped from his chair and confronted him. "You staring at me! Don't be looking at me! Have you got a *problem*?" Implicit in this confrontation was a physical threat. John sensed that Richard was soliciting a fight. His pulse quickened, and much to his chagrin, John found himself sizing-up Richard's physical bearing, comparing it to his own, inch by inch, pound by pound.

At that moment, John saw a student walking down the hall. Slipping out of the room, he asked the student to get the teacher next door. The teacher, who happened to be Richard's English teacher, was quick to grasp the situation. Stepping inside the classroom, she ordered him in a stern tone of voice to sit down. Richard retaliated with several sharp remarks. It was clear that he was ready to take her on as well. Realizing this, she went downstairs to the vice-principal, who told her to release Richard from detention.

Before he released Richard, John told him that he intended to report his behavior and to rerefer him. Initially, Richard refused to leave until he had completed his detention because he thought that John would not be able to rerefer him if he stayed for the duration of the period. Finally, John told him that he could stay if he wanted, but he would still get rereferred. Richard insisted upon remaining for the entire period.

John left school that afternoon with an abysmal sense of failure. He mentally reviewed the events leading up to this afternoon like a bad song that he could not get off his mind.

Two days later, during a discussion with the English teacher and a special education teacher, he discovered that Richard had been attending classes for students with behavior disorders for the past two years. Still, Richard had not been a problem before during this class, and John blamed his own ineptness for creating the situation. If only he hadn't . . .

Grandma's Boy

HELEN JAMISON

Part A

"I was totally unprepared to deal with those people." Helen Jamison took a sip from the apricot tea that Cindy, her roommate, had just brewed. "All I could think of was poor Justin and how awful it must be for him to live with such a dysfunctional family. I just hope we can come up with something at school that will help this kid."

Helen was a second-grade teacher at C. E. Conners Elementary School. Just two months into her first year of teaching, she had encountered the first rift in what had otherwise been a smooth and gratifying beginning. As a novice in the profession, she had hit the ground running, and her innovations had caught the eye of the central office supervisors, building level administrators, and parents. For the most part, her 27 second-grade students got along well with one another, and she was excited about the cooperative spirit that she had managed to cultivate in this average ability group.

At the beginning of the year, she had encouraged the students to select a name for the class—a name symbolizing strength, honor, and cooperation. The students decided to call themselves the Spartans, and at Helen's request the art teacher drew a picture of a warrior on horseback to post on the wall just outside the classroom. Helen then cut the backgrounds from students' photographs and meticulously positioned and glued each picture over the silhouette of the warrior, creating a beautiful collage. Across the body of the horse, in majestic red, was a salutation: WELCOME TO ROOM 204: HOME OF THE SPARTANS.

Helen tried to perpetuate a theme of cooperation throughout the course of each day. She took time during each week to teach, model, and have the students role play social skills that would encourage cooperation and citizenship. She praised students when she "caught them being good," and she routinely coupled this social praise with

137

"Caughtcha!" stickers that they could exchange for prizes from her treasure chest. She presented "Spartan of the Week" awards to students who worked hard to improve their grades in an area of weakness. Of course, there were times when curiosity and mischief spawned misbehavior and minor noncompliance, but for the most part Helen believed herself capable of using basic behavior management techniques to handle such occurrences.

And so it was that after just two months of teaching Helen was quite pleased with her performance and the performance of almost all of her students. She was greatly concerned about one of her little "munchkins," however. Justin E. Richardson II had transferred from another school in the county, and he was not keeping up with the rest of the students in the class. He daydreamed constantly, and he completed virtually no assignments. Against the advice of a colleague, Helen had scheduled a meeting with Justin's father, hoping to develop a home-school behavior management program that would motivate the child to increase his productivity. The meeting had been a complete disaster, and now Helen sat in her apartment, totally flustered by her first encounter with "irate parents." She was glad that Cindy was home, for she really needed to vent her frustrations, anger, and disappointment about what had just happened. She curled up in her recliner, gazed straight ahead, and began recounting her experience.

"After the first month of school, I reread Justin's cumulative folder and discovered that a confidential folder had also been sent from his old school. Justin's first-grade teacher, Judy Cole, had written on the referral form that Justin's behavior had started to deteriorate toward the end of the year. He daydreamed constantly, was inconsistent in his work habits, and refused to comply with her instructions. She also said that Justin was not an acting-out child, but that he was difficult to deal with because of his passive-aggressive personality. No one at Conners knew anything about this kid, so I called Judy, hoping she could tell me about some 'trick' that worked last year. I can still remember her response after hearing who I was: 'Oh, so *you're* the lucky one this year!' She told me she felt as if she was on a treadmill with Justin, his father, and the grandmother last year. It's really sad. Judy didn't think she could do anything to help Justin. She believed nobody would be able to help the poor kid until they eased up on him at home."

"Exactly what was happening at home?" asked Cindy as she kicked off her shoes, sat Indian style on the sofa, and began munching an apple. Cindy was an elementary school guidance counselor and a masterful listener. She interjected very little, but she frequently nodded her head and gestured to Helen to continue. For this, Helen was extremely grateful. Having a live-in therapist was great!

"Well," responded Helen, "I questioned Judy further about the home situation and discovered that Justin's parents had just divorced last summer. After the divorce, Justin and his father had moved in with his paternal grandmother, Ann Richardson—better known to school personnel as 'Brunhilda.' Judy also warned me that this grandmother was a real 'busybody' and would make herself a part of every interaction that took place between Mr. Richardson and the school."

"She told me that I'd 'really have to watch that lady.' Apparently, Judy's child study team recommended that Justin undergo a full evaluation, but his father refused to grant the school permission to go through with the testing. Judy didn't believe for a minute that the refusal came from Mr. Richardson. His mother has such a dominating influence over him that Judy was convinced that she's the one who blocked the testing. Grandma came to all the meetings with Mr. Richardson, and she was adamant that Justin's problems in school were all caused by his mother—'his no-good cheating, lying mother.'"

"Boy, it sounds like this Mrs. Richardson's a real charmer," Cindy concluded, rising to refill their mugs. She reclaimed her spot on the sofa and asked, "Is what she said about Justin's mother true, or did Judy give you conflicting information?"

"Actually, Judy wasn't aware of the causes leading to the split-up of Justin's parents, but she did know that the mother had relinquished custody of Justin and had left the state shortly after the divorce. No one at Judy's school knew exactly where the mother had moved, and this 'mystery woman' had made no attempts to contact any school personnel. Judy finally told me that because the mother was no longer in the picture I should follow her strategy from last year and try to get help from my school psychologist or guidance counselor. She told me to stay away from the father and grandmother because they're the ones mostly responsible for what this child is going through."

"I now realize that Judy couldn't have been more accurate in her assessment of the situation," continued Helen. "As far as I'm concerned, this meeting was a waste of time. Granny Richardson, even though I didn't invite her, came with her son to the conference and immediately started to blame Justin's mother for all of his problems. I couldn't believe it when she bad-mouthed her 'low-life' ex-daughter-in-law. The way she sat straight up in her seat reminded me of a drill sergeant, and the way she barked at me made me feel like I was a recruit!"

Helen sat bolt upright and proceeded to imitate Mrs. Richardson. Her voice took on a different timbre, and for a moment Cindy actually felt that she was being lectured by a sergeant. "'No matter how hard I try to make that boy realize that he has a no-account for a mother, he still wants to see his parents back together again. He wants them to be a threesome again, so he stages these little games and hopes that Jus will contact his mom.' 'Jus' is what grandma calls Mr. Richardson."

Helen stood, pointing her finger at Cindy, and continued her impersonation. "'Well, the last time he showed off like this, I whipped his ass good and took away his bike, and I know he shaped up for a while. I guess I'm just gonna have to do it again.'"

Helen took her seat, folded her arms, and nodded her head matter-of-factly. Cindy applauded this electrifying performance, concluding that this role playing was just the thing Helen needed to relieve some of the tension that she was feeling. She motioned for her counselee to continue, and they both giggled as Helen resumed her story, now somewhat more relaxed.

"Cindy, I could not believe what I was hearing or seeing! Just as Judy had told me, Mrs. Richardson monopolized every moment of the conversation. Mr. Richardson occasionally nodded and affirmed what his mother reported, but he contributed little else to the conference. I tried to direct questions his way, but every time I tried, 'Brunhilda' jumped right in. More and more, I realized that, because of his home situation, Justin was in jeopardy of developing some serious emotional problems."

"So, what did you suggest?" asked Cindy as she slid to the floor and rested her back against the base of the sofa.

Helen sat on the edge of her chair and shared her game plan. "At one point, I had decided to suggest that the family seek counseling, but after just a few minutes I realized that that recommendation would go over like a ton of lead. Also, I'd been warned previously by my assistant principal that such suggestions were frowned upon by the school division, because if Justin was found eligible for special education, then the system could be forced to pay for this as a related service. So, when I wasn't able to think of anything else, I decided to push for my idea of a home-school management program. I also tried to make these people understand that finding a solution to Justin's problems would require much more than spankings and scoldings. I described Justin's behavior, hoping that this would provide me with a lead into my management proposal."

"'Justin,' I said to them, 'sits and stares most of the time. He doesn't interact with the other students in the class. In fact, if they initiate a conversation or ask him a question, he usually refuses to even acknowledge their existence. He looks at one of his books or writes in one of his skillbooks, pretending to be hard at work.'"

"I also explained that Justin didn't respond to either praise or criticism, rewards or punishment. He hasn't completed any assignments. He's failed every section of every unit criterion test in reading. On one occasion, I watched him complete the comprehension subtest by merely going down the list and selecting answers at random. He hadn't bothered to read any of the passages in the section, and he failed the test miserably. After this, I thought that Justin was preoccupied and unmotivated. Later, I realized that, on the few occasions when he did try, Justin found it extremely difficult to decode unfamiliar words, and his oral reading was choppy and labored."

"Well, for what it was worth, I shared this information with Justin's father and grandmother. I practically begged these people to understand that we all needed to work together to help their child. Unfortunately, after hearing my concerns, Mrs. Richardson held on to her notions about what was best for her grandson. When I tried to ease into my proposal, I was interrupted abruptly."

Helen resumed Mrs. Richardson's position and voice. "'Justin don't need no kind of home-school program.' That was Mrs. Richardson's response to my plan. 'You deal with him your way here, and we'll deal with him our way at home. Like I already said, if push comes to shove, we'll just have to beat some sense into him. Once we help him get that woman out of his system, he'll be all right anyway. Just you wait and see, he'll be all right.'"

"There was no need for any further discussion," sighed Helen. "After this outburst, I thanked the Richardsons for coming and ended the meeting. As they were leaving my room I think I may have managed a half-hearted smile, but I couldn't help feeling sorry for Justin. This child is constantly being bombarded with negative information about a mother that he apparently loves, and he's being punished severely when his behavior and feelings are in conflict with those of his grandmother and father. I tell you, Cindy, I was exhausted and depressed after that meeting, and even though talking about it has helped I just don't know what my next move will be."

Cindy broke the silence that followed with the suggestion that they identify the most salient problems and rank them. The two then spent the next half hour trying to identify possible strategies that might improve the situation.

Is Kevin Bluffing?

CAROL YAKE

The moment seemed to float like a shimmering crystalline vision of eternity. A sensation of icy fear traveled up Carol Yake's extremities as she stood, chalk in hand, frozen at the front of her classroom on the school's second floor. Twenty-three of her sixth-grade students sat breathless and still, their eyes fixed on their classmate, Kevin. He was perched precariously on the top railing of the second story staircase just outside of the classroom door, rocking to and fro. His contorted mask of rage and desperate wailing gave Carol the sense that she was holding vigil over a hell-tortured soul who, in a futile attempt to alleviate his suffering, might at any second hurl himself into the darkened abyss below. What had ignited this sudden outburst seemed irrelevant. The right response eluded her. Her mind raced as her body remained immobile.

Like the frequent, preceding eruptions, this one was doubtless kindled by something as simple as Kevin's answering a question incorrectly or her not calling on him during class. Yet, Kevin's unpredictable outbursts threatened to rule her class by their sheer force and intensity. Carol found the perpetual fear that Kevin would injure the other students, himself, or her exhausting. After 14 years in the classroom, her keen intuition told her that Kevin must never sense that his outbursts frightened her, or how powerfully his behavior affected her. As a result, Carol often found herself in the position of having to call his bluff by ignoring his tantrums and carefully gauging her emotional reactions to them. So far it had worked, but the stakes had never been as high as they were at this moment.

Kevin had been diagnosed as psychotic and found eligible for placement in the behavior disorders classroom. But the logistics of the situation this year at Lockhaven Elementary School made it more suitable, in the judgment of the principal, Ms. Rice, for Kevin to spend most of his school day in Carol's classroom. She felt that the first-year behavior disorders teacher, Allison King, had neither the experience nor the necessary strategies to work effectively with Kevin in addition to a number of other diffi-

143

cult-to-manage students. Carol understood her reasoning and felt that, as an experienced professional, she should be willing to go along with the plan. As the year progressed, she felt that Allison did her best to help with Kevin; but, for the most part, Carol assumed the primary responsibility for him.

Carol and her students weathered Kevin's storms with stoic tolerance. The students were careful not to provoke him. Carol suspected that this was because they were very afraid of him. They had witnessed his screaming, cursing, and destruction of the classroom during his frequent outbursts. They watched quietly the many times that Carol found it necessary to restrain him physically and was pummeled and kicked by his flailing arms and legs.

Because she was aware that Kevin's behavior was frightening to her other students, Carol talked to them when he was out of the classroom.

"Kevin," she quietly explained to them, "has a handicap, just like a person who doesn't have an arm or a leg or is in a wheelchair. We can't see Kevin's handicap, but we must deal with it. I need your help and understanding."

So far, she had gotten it; but, she could only hope that one of these students didn't get hurt by inadvertently setting him off.

Because Kevin's tantrums were so frequent and violent, Ms. Rice had arranged for the maintenance man, John Patterson, to remove Kevin bodily from Carol's classroom when necessary. Carol usually signaled a student to find John as she struggled to restrain Kevin, and moments later he would appear to carry the shrieking, struggling Kevin to Allison's room. There, a wooden partition was erected to serve as a time-out site, where he was to remain until he became calm. Allison and Carol had written out a list of behaviors that would necessitate their placing him in time-out, and they had made sure that he understood them. This system seemed to work well enough, yet, it did not spare Carol from the apprehension and necessity of making critical, immediate decisions when Kevin exploded. She lived in dread of making the wrong choice.

Several weeks ago, Kevin ran, in a fit of rage, to the plate glass window that ran the length of the classroom doorway, turned menacingly to Carol and declared, "I'm going to kick this right out of here." Struggling to maintain a calm composure, Carol thought, he's trying to scare me, to control me, and I can't let him.

She heard her voice reply firmly, "You kick it, and your mother will pay for every penny it takes to replace it." It was more difficult to conceal her relief when Kevin pulled his foot back and didn't kick it in. She fully expected that he would. Nevertheless, she felt that the only thing to do under the circumstances was to call his bluff.

Carol's approach was to gauge her reaction carefully against Kevin's tantrums so that he would not be able to guess that she was being intimidated or frightened by them. Also, she worked hard to manage her own emotions in the aftermath. When he became calm, she made it a point to forget the outburst and put it behind her. In fact, she made a great effort to conceal from Kevin her true feelings about him.

As she explained to Allison, "I don't really like him that much, but I make him believe that I do. In fact," she added with a gentle laugh, "I think he thinks that he's one of my favorite students. I always treat him like I would anybody else, with the utmost respect. I take the time to kid around with him and talk to him. I never talk to him in anything that even hints at an authoritarian voice."

Carol had built what she thought was a good rapport with Kevin based on their talking about his circumstances. During some of their private conversations, often held on the playground during recess, Kevin confided in Carol about his real father, who used to beat him when he was small. She listened with quiet sympathy. She knew that his mother had remarried, and that he was no longer in danger of this abuse, though it had clearly left its mark. Carol was fairly convinced that this was where Kevin had learned to control others through terror. She also knew that he controlled his family this way.

Close to the beginning of the school year, after Kevin had nearly destroyed the classroom by throwing desks, books, and equipment all over, Carol told him that he couldn't leave until he straightened up. She called his mother and told her that she would have to come and pick him up. After many stalling tactics, Kevin finally did a passable job of restoring physical order to the classroom. His mother appeared and took him home. Carol thought she had scored a victory—until the following morning, when Kevin showed her a popular toy car that his mother had purchased for him on the way home. She interpreted this as Kevin's way of letting her know that she had not, after all, won.

It became clear at that point that she could not count on cooperation from home to support her efforts with Kevin. This conviction was further reinforced when Carol notified his parents that he had talked of committing suicide. Kevin's mother dismissed it lightly: "Oh, he's threatened to do that before."

Now, as Kevin swayed ominously on the thin railing high above the first floor, Carol again struggled to remain calm. If she took a step in his direction, he might instinctively jerk and fall backward. The tiniest little jerk, she thought, will cause him to go over the railing. Should I simply stand here and pray that he comes away? Will calling his bluff work this time? she asked herself desperately. Yet, the vacuous expression on his face made her doubt that this was a bid for control. As she struggled to make a decision, she heard the faint, stunned voice of one of her students.

"Mrs. Yake, if Kevin dies, will it be your fault?"

They Failed Derrick

MELINDA SMITH

Part A

I watched through my classroom window as Derrick and his mother got into their car and drove away. I tried not to cry as I gathered up Derrick's textbooks and returned them to the book room. I walked back to my classroom, sat down at my desk, and tried futilely to work on my reading lesson for the next day. I couldn't concentrate. Each time I tried to read something from my teacher's manual I couldn't help but think about Derrick and what I feared was going to happen to him.

And as for that placement team—that wonderful group of concerned educators—well, I was furious with those guys! The decision to transfer this child to a middle school and place him in a class for children with behavioral disorders was the worst possible thing that we could do to him! Even though he had taken me through some real changes since the beginning of the year, Derrick had made a lot of progress, and I really didn't feel that placing him in a special education class would improve his behavior. You would think that my previous experiences with children with disabilities would have counted for something, but it didn't. We simply didn't give this kid enough time. I will always believe the we moved too early on this one.

I came to know Derrick my first year back in a regular classroom after teaching children with mental retardation for over 15 years. Now that my own two kids were grown up and off in college, I felt that I was losing touch with how normal kids think and operate. I also believed that I was doing a disservice to my little handicapped kids. You see, because many of the classes for students with mental retardation were being phased out, my class had become a regional program. Students from all over the county were bussed to my school to receive services. I was teaching some of the same pupils for up to five years, and it finally dawned on me that this was not in their best interest—nor in mine. I considered myself a good teacher and I really cared about these students, but at the same time I felt myself becoming too routinized. I needed a change, and so did the kids. So, I decided to take the plunge. It was time for me to return to the regular classroom.

There were regular classroom vacancies at my school, Essig Elementary, but after considering my options I decided that I needed to make a clean break. Even though I got along very well with the faculty and staff at Essig, I just couldn't imagine watching *my* kids walking down the hallway with another teacher. So I talked with an old partner in crime, Greg Rodgers, who was the principal of Helmsley Elementary School. Greg and I worked together during my first five years as a teacher, and over the years it seems our paths always managed to cross. After he became an administrator, we were assigned to assist with the development of several county-wide inservice projects. I also served as his assistant principal during a few summer school sessions. Greg was a professional in every sense of the word, and I thought that it would be very rewarding to work under his leadership on a full-time basis. After taking care of all of the formalities, Greg offered me the position as the teacher of high average and gifted fifth-grade students. I looked forward to this change and challenge, and though it was difficult for me to walk away from what had been a major part of my life for 15 years, I packed up boxes of books, ditto masters, teacher-made games, presents collected over the years, and yes, even my drawer full of confiscated toys.

I started out on my new venture with a feeling of interest and optimism. During the summer, I enrolled in a course on teaching gifted children, and I read related books and journal articles whenever time permitted. I also spent a lot of time just thinking about my experiences and skills as a special educator and wondering how I could transfer these skills to my new situation. I was so excited! I wanted to be *ready* in September when those kids stepped off the bus and entered my classroom.

Well, even though I would be teaching higher functioning kids, and even though I was in a new school, I found that I had been type-cast. I don't know of any other way to put it. Other special education teachers who had returned to regular classroom positions often told me about their experiences. "Once a special educator, always a special educator," they'd say. It didn't take me very long to understand what they really meant. During the first day of teacher work week, Greg called me into his office and asked if I would consider taking a child who had some real emotional problems.

"This kid has shot holes through almost every teacher in this school," I remember him saying. "If there's anyone in the world who can make a change in him, it's you. Will you please consider taking him until we can get the paperwork done to have him placed in special education?"

"Flattery will get you nowhere," I replied. But in the end, I agreed to take on this kid. When I thought of having a student with emotional problems and academic deficits in a class with gifted learners, I felt a tingle in my spine. This would be a real challenge indeed, I thought.

The student was none other than the infamous Derrick Yates. He was 12 years old and functioning at about a third-grade level in all subjects. He had developed a notorious reputation around school. None of the teachers could handle him during the one year he had been at Helmsley. In fact, I found out that last year he hadn't even been able to stay at school all day. Greg had made arrangements with Derrick's mother to have him picked up after lunch until such time that his behavior improved. Greg had also written a contract with Derrick that outlined student, teacher, and administrator responsibilities. The contract also specified the conditions that would allow Derrick's time at school to be extended. Unfortunately, Derrick never made it past lunchtime. He defied and frightened faculty and staff members on several occasions. He never lasted longer than five minutes in physical education, art, or music because he would disrupt the class, curse or threaten a teacher, and be sent to the office.

Honestly, I hardly had time to hang my bulletin boards during inservice week because my room was buzzing with teachers who wanted to give me the low-down on Derrick. The other fifth-grade teachers talked about how their nerves had been frazzled all summer long because they feared that their worst possible nightmare might come true—that Derrick would be assigned to their classroom. Needless to say, they were quite relieved to know that *moi*—Melinda Smith, the new kid on the block—was also certified in behavioral disorders and fit all the qualifications to be the "chosen one."

"He has terrorized everyone," Karen, one of the fifth grade teachers told me. "His mother has absolutely no control over him at home, and so he thinks that he can also be the man in charge here. The weird thing about it is that . . . I think he's right."

At this point, I began to wonder what I had gotten myself into. The stories I heard about Derrick's home life were totally unbelievable. Derrick's father and mother were divorced, and Derrick was living with his mother and a younger brother and sister. He was angered by his parents' separation and the divorce, and he blamed his mother for the failed marriage. Apparently, he idolized his father, but these feelings weren't mutual. Unable to deal with this rejection, Derrick took out his frustrations on anyone and everyone with whom he came in contact. This included his mother, brother, and sister. Barbara Cole, the school social worker, told me stories that gave me goose bumps.

"This child actually butchered and killed the family dog with a knife. He cut off the poor dog's head and extremities and lined them up in a neat row in the back yard. His mother had locks installed on the kitchen drawers because she was afraid that he would use the utensils as weapons against her and the other children. She's also installed a double bolt lock on her bedroom door, and she lets the two younger children sleep in the room with her at night. Some people would consider this absurd, but she was wise to take this action."

To say the least, Barbara had aroused my curiosity. "What do you mean?" I asked.

"Well, on one occasion, Mrs. Yates reported that Derrick was angry with her because he was convinced that she had not allowed him to speak with his dad on the phone. Actually, Mr. Yates had called about child support payments and had expressed no interest in speaking to any of the children. That night, Mrs. Yates awakened to the sound of Derrick jabbing a large butcher knife against her bedroom door. After she threatened to call the police, he finally stopped his terrorizing and returned to his room.

I tried, but I couldn't get a word in edgewise. Barbara continued to share her experiences with Derrick.

"Shortly after that, I was sent to the Yates's home to conduct an interview with the mother. I found Derrick home alone that day. For no apparent reason, he was absent from school. Now, Derrick is a large kid for his age, and coupled with those bucked and crooked teeth, and that uncontrollable sick kind of laugh, he really looks like something scary. To see this kid in action is like watching a scene from an Alfred Hitchcock movie. Anyway, Derrick opened the door, stared at me, and asked in a threatening voice, 'What you want, Bitch?' Honey, I just politely turned, walked to my car, and got out of there."

As I listened to these horrendous stories, I realized that this would be the case of all cases. But still, I wanted to give this one a whirl. I had a few tricks up my sleeve that I hadn't even tried yet, and from the way everybody described Derrick, I figured that I would finally have the chance to use them. And so my special education training and my natural inclination and desire to work with troubled children prompted me to accept Derrick Winslow Yates into my fifth-grade classroom.

On the day the students arrived in September, it didn't take me two minutes to realize which one was Derrick. Aside from the descriptions that my colleagues gave, one could not help but feel this child's presence. There was a certain "looseness" about him. From the way he moved about the room, I could tell that he knew he could frighten people, and as I told the class to sit down and get settled I could feel his eyes on me. He took his time getting to his seat, and I had the feeling that he was trying to let me know that he expected me to fear him, too. Just as the other teachers told me, I could see that "look" in his eyes. So, I realized the very instant I met Derrick that I would have to handle him with kid gloves. Even though I had a little fear, I was determined that I would not let him see or even sense this fear. As usual, I tried to think positively, but I also made plans to expect the worst.

Well, to my surprise, the first three weeks of school went by without any major hassles. In fact, Derrick was not really a problem at all. He was talkative, restless, and obviously frustrated because the work was way over his head. I modified his assignments, however; and I kept a careful watch on him when I assigned independent work or work in cooperative learning groups. I also used proximity control and, sometimes, if he were getting restless or starting to harass one of the other children verbally, I would simply walk over to him and calmly put my hand on his shoulder, and he'd straighten up. Still, he maintained the "look," and I resigned myself to the fact that I could not let down my guard—that I had to watch him every minute he was in the room.

I don't think Derrick knew how to take it that I was not yelling at him, isolating him, or sending him to the office. He really tickled me one day when he walked up to me and asked, "You don't know about me, do you?" When I asked what he meant, he stated that he had a bad reputation and that he had stayed in the office more time last year than he had stayed in the classroom. He told me that the principal, teachers, and the kids were all afraid of him and that he liked to do mean things. Boy, did he lay it on the line! I had to think quickly before I responded.

"Why, thank you Derrick," I replied. "Thank you. I appreciate that you told me special things about yourself that will help me plan for you." I also told him that I was pleased with his behavior so far, and that I looked forward to having a good year with him in my class. With that, he looked at me as if to say, "No such luck, Lady!" and returned to his seat with one of his eerie chuckles.

A few days later, his mother called me very upset because she said that things were getting worse at home and she didn't know how long she could keep dealing with Derrick. He was driving her crazy, and she was still very much concerned about the safety of her other children. Well, I felt that Derrick, by coming to me and exposing the negative side of himself, was letting me know that our little hiatus was about to come to an end. It was as if he was saying, "Now you know, I've talked to you and my mother has talked to you, and now I'm going to let it all hang out." This is precisely what he did.

I'll never forget the very first major incident. The kids knew about Derrick's reputation, and they came in really upset and a little nervous to tell me that he had a pocket knife on the bus. Joey mustered up enough nerve to make the report. He was shaking like a leaf when he came up to me. He looked over his shoulder constantly to make sure that Derrick wasn't in the room. "Mrs. Smith, Derrick had a knife on the bus, and he was waving it in all of our faces, and he dared us to tell the bus driver!"

Poor thing, he was gasping for breath by the time he finished, so I used an old tried and true trick—"antiseptic bouncing"—to help him get himself under control. This little technique had been a real life saver during my years as a special educator. I sent Joey to the office with a note to the secretary requesting that she send him back with some bond paper after letting him sit and calm down for a few minutes. Just as he left the room, Derrick entered as if nothing out of the ordinary had occurred. He walked over to the browsing table and started thumbing through a motorcycle magazine. As usual, I told everyone to sharpen pencils and prepare for work. Then, I breathed a deep sigh and walked over to Derrick.

The Fairy Godmothers

PAUL MILLER

Part A

Standing in the middle of the empty, cold, and dimly lit classroom, Paul Miller felt a sense of emptiness. It was the end of January in the small North Carolina town of Marion. School had been closed for the past three days due to an unexpected snowfall. It couldn't have come at a better time. He could really use this time to get organized.

Paul, a former English teacher, had taken an educational leave of absence to earn a master's degree in special education with an emphasis in learning disabilities. Although he had enjoyed teaching secondary English for the past seven years, he sustained a strong interest in the students who had particular trouble learning. This interest, in conjunction with a sense of responsibility toward these students, made his graduate work compelling. Now, he had an opportunity to work exclusively with this population of students in this modified self-contained class for students with learning disabilities. He counted himself lucky to have landed this job at Marion Elementary School in the middle of the school year. He needed to get right back to work because his wife, Elise, was expecting their first baby in June. But something in the stark atmosphere of this classroom gave him pause.

Although it was a larger classroom than he had expected for a special education class, the dingy floor and the haphazard arrangement of desks lent the room a sense of discord. Several of the commercially produced posters of the parts of speech and the cursive alphabet had fallen to the floor and had left gaping holes on the medium green walls above the chalkboard. A perusal of the students' desks revealed a tangle of textbooks, crumpled papers, disorganized notebooks, pencils, and small toys. Paul noted that the textbooks were the same as those used in the regular classrooms; yet, for the 11-, 12-, and 13-year-old students in this class, second- and third-grade textbooks seemed inappropriate and out of place. What possible interest might a 12-year-old fifth-grade student have in a social studies text entitled, Our Neighbors and Our Community? His predecessor must have assigned their textbooks on the basis of norm-referenced assessment results.

As he set to work cleaning and rearranging the room, Paul speculated about what this class had been like and how he would work with this group of students. He had been told by Jane Abbott, the principal, that the nine boys and one girl whom he would be teaching had, "developed some bad habits." She had hastened to add, "But they are not bad kids." Paul had sensed that she had understated the situation, but he felt that he could expect as much. Both of them needed him to take this position, so he did not press for details. When his aide, Irene Walker, arrived in a quarter of an hour or so, he would have an opportunity to find out more. In the meantime, he began excavating the textbooks from the students' desks and stacking them on a long work table so that he could send them back to the school textbook depository.

Although he did not quite know what kind of person Irene might be, she was somehow not what he had expected. At 30 or so years of age, something in her demeanor suggested a child-like quality. A large woman with short, frizzy hair, Irene was exceptionally plain in appearance. She reminded Paul of the large panda bear embroidered on the front of her oversized sweater. After they exchanged introductions, Paul explained to her that he intended to make drastic changes in the students' curriculum.

"The first thing we need to do is get rid of these textbooks," he explained. Irene rolled her eyes heavenward in approval and went to work immediately, dislodging more textbooks from the tightly packed desk compartments.

Great, Paul mused approvingly. She was quick to deduce my reasoning about the textbook problem. I wonder what other insights she can offer. He tentatively decided to press her for more information regarding the class's history.

After about five minutes of procedural small talk, Paul broached the big question. "I know the teacher who had this class at the beginning of the year resigned unexpectedly. Was she ill or something ...?" His voice trailed off at the end of the question.

An expression of caution clouded Irene's flushing face. "No one told you?" she asked in a small voice. "Well, no," Paul replied, consciously controlling his response.

"Told me what?" he queried lightly, continuing to unpack a box of supplies on his desk.

With that, the information floodgates opened. "Oh, Mandy [the previous teacher] was awful," Irene declared. "The kids hated her, and so did I." Irene continued without Paul's bidding. "These kids have been all over the place. Everyone thinks this is the worst class in the school. Mandy tried to force these long, boring lessons on the kids, and she just kept on and kept on, and when the kids didn't get it, she got mad at them. She just kept drilling and drilling. And she didn't like them either. Don't get me wrong, they're not angels; but she just didn't know how to handle them. She had Glenn's mother, who is a very religious person, come to class one time to scare the kids into behaving. His mom told the kids that they would all end up in jail if they didn't start doing better. After that, it got so that they were climbing out of those windows and running out on that blacktop."

Irene swept her hand toward the long row of ground-floor windows. Paul and Irene stared out at the bleak asphalt-covered play area adjoining the parking lot.

"Sometimes they'd come back in through that door out in the hall and hide in the big cabinets in the library," Irene continued after a brief pause. "Mandy would be wandering the halls looking for some of them while the others just sat around waiting for her to get back. I never knew what to do, so she would get mad and yell at me in front of the kids. Toward the end, they were cussing her and she was cussing them back. Brian and Randy sat in the window sill and shot the middle finger at her a couple of times, then jumped out when she came after them. Once, she got so mad at Shane that she grabbed him, and before I knew it she'd wrestled him to the floor. Shane is 12 years old, but he's small for his age. He used to go to the special education class next door crying and begging Mrs. Flint to let him be in her class. But Mrs. Flint and her assistant made a point of staying out of the situation. They knew Mrs. Abbott was trying to do something about it. One day, right before Christmas, Mandy came back to the room from morning bus duty all furious, grabbed a box from the closet, and started packing her stuff from her desk. Then she told the kids that she couldn't take them or this place anymore and she was leaving. The kids were shocked. I think it hurt them a lot, because she was their teacher, and she was telling them what a worthless bunch of kids they were. She pretty much told them that nobody would want to teach them. Since then, they've had a substitute."

Feeling a little sick, Paul had listened quietly as Irene offered her account. So, that is what Jane Abbott meant when she said that the students had acquired some "bad habits."

"Where were the parents when all of this was going on?" he asked with a hint of incredulity in his voice.

"Oh, a lot of these kids come from broken homes. Cynthia ... she's the only girl. I feel sorry for Cynthia. She's my little friend because she doesn't have any other girlfriends. She's real lonely at recess. Her mother is a single mom. Her dad's in prison for shooting another man. They were drunk and playing cards, and her dad accused the other guy of cheating. You get the picture. So, her mom, she's concerned like the others; but, Mrs. Abbott told them that she was doing the best she could to get the situation under control. Mandy'd been teaching a long time. She was at the middle school before she came down here this year, so they sent her back to the middle school. She's got tenure, so what're they going to do? All the parents are so glad you're here. Mrs. Abbott has told them what a great teaching reputation you have. We're all so happy you took this job."

With that concluding remark, Irene smiled broadly at Paul. He offered a kindly smile in return. Irene continued to work as she related small details about each of the students. He marveled at her candor. Still, he was grateful to get the unabridged account of the situation.

The next morning, Paul arrived at 7:00 for his first official day as teacher at Marion Elementary. Shortly before the students arrived, a young woman entered the room with an inquiring expression on her face.

Paul introduced himself. "I'm Paul Miller, the new teacher."

"Oh," she faltered, looking troubled and confused. For a brief moment, Paul thought perhaps this was his student, Cynthia, because Irene had described her as being 13 years old but having a much older appearance. Dressed in blue jeans, a cotton knit sweater, and running shoes, this person seemed to fit the description.

"I'm the substitute, Cathy Hansen. I've been working with this class for the past several weeks. Nobody told me you would be here today. I had to drive for 45 minutes to get here. I wish someone had told me." By the way her eyes threatened to overflow with tears, Paul guessed that the 45-minute drive wasn't all that she found upsetting.

As if on cue, Irene arrived and greeted Cathy. "Mrs. Abbott didn't tell you?" she gasped. With that, Irene and Cathy retreated to a corner of the classroom to discuss the matter, leaving Paul to attend to his preparations.

As the students began filing in, Paul made it a point to greet each of them by name. He had found—in the teacher's desk—a yearbook, which he used to learn each student's name. Knowing their names on his first day seemed to be effective, he observed with satisfaction. The students seemed a bit awed by his knowledge of them. But then he noticed that they clamored around Cathy as she revealed the contents of a brown paper shopping bag she had brought with her.

One by one, Cathy brought forth games (Connect Four, UNO, checkers, etc.). "I got these for you guys over the weekend," she announced cheerfully. She beamed happily as the boys grabbed for the games and began tearing them open.

Watching the spectacle from the front of the classroom, Paul began to grasp the situation. For the past three weeks, this young woman and Irene had been trying to make up for the past with these students. They had become the good "fairy godmothers" who filled their days with fun and games. He surmised that little had been accomplished in the way of academics; and now, here he was. The young substitute did not seem to realize that she must step aside. Apparently, she had become very emotionally attached to these students; and, more importantly, they to her. "Oh hell," Paul thought, "What do I do now?"

The Phantom Pregnancy

BARBARA THOMPSON

When Barbara Thompson went home to her own two children, nine-year-old Shawn, and four-year-old Keshia, she often brought home lingering worries about her students. Teri Leigh was the one who troubled her the most. Her concerns were intensified by the new Family Life Curriculum. Barbara had warned Bob Farris, the principal, that the new sex education program recently adopted by the state would present some problems in her class.

Remembering that she had forgotten to prepare anything for tonight's dinner, Barbara absent mindedly opened the freezer door, only to find it empty except for a long-forgotten package of hotdogs. "Oh well," she thought, "this will have to do." Placing them in the microwave, she could hear Shawn and Keshia downstairs arguing over which television program to watch. She decided almost subconsciously not to intervene unless the argument escalated to physical blows. Her thoughts were on Teri Leigh.

Barbara had known since the beginning of school about Teri Leigh. Her confidential records and her special education teacher had given Barbara a great deal of background information about her. Several years ago, Teri Leigh was removed from her home when it was discovered that she was being sexually abused by her mother's boyfriend. The boyfriend had gone to jail, but when he was released her mother married him and left Teri Leigh and her two little brothers in separate foster homes. Recently, Teri Leigh's brothers were adopted, and she had cried several times in class, telling Barbara that she was upset because her family would never be together again. Barbara's heart went out to her, but she knew there was no real way to console her about her loss.

Teri Leigh's records indicated that she had both learning disabilities and emotional or behavioral disorders. In fact, Teri Leigh had been diagnosed as psychotic, and court records stated that she heard voices. Although Barbara had never seen evidence of this,

157

she did notice that Teri Leigh seemed to have a very imaginative inner life. Sometimes, Barbara was unable to determine whether Teri Leigh was telling her about an event that had really occurred or whether it was something she had only imagined. Beyond this, Teri Leigh was a well-behaved student; and Barbara was fond of this grown-up looking girl who sought her affection like a child much younger than her 12 years.

While she stared absently at a can of pork and beans revolving steadily on the electric can-opener, Barbara became aware that all was quiet. Apparently, Shawn and Keshia had come to some agreement about the television. Her mind slipped back to Teri Leigh and the time she had spent with her earlier in the day. Barbara had felt strongly that, given Teri Leigh's background, any sex education program for her should be handled with special care. Still, neither the administrators nor the special education teacher, Kay Middleton, had offered her suggestions or alternatives for Teri Leigh. It's not that she blamed them, but now her concerns were being realized.

Several weeks ago, in the family life class, Barbara had taught the basic lesson about pregnancy and childbirth. Two days later, three girls in her class approached Barbara on the playground and surreptitiously informed her that Teri Leigh was claiming to be pregnant. Consciously hiding her alarm, Barbara thanked the girls for telling her and sent them off to play. Could this be possible? Teri Leigh was certainly physically mature enough, thought Barbara. Because Teri Leigh had not come to her personally, Barbara felt that she should not approach her about the issue. Instead, she watched and waited.

She noticed that Teri Leigh had begun bringing baby clothes to school, and there seemed to be a great deal of secretive talk among her and the other girls in the class. Finally, one rainy day during recess, Teri Leigh confided to Barbara that she thought she was pregnant. Barbara asked Teri Leigh what made her think so. Teri Leigh explained matter-of-factly that she would probably be pregnant because of what her mother's boyfriend had done. Barbara explained to her several times in the course of this conversation that it was impossible after so much time had passed, but Teri Leigh clung resolutely to the conviction that pregnancy was inevitable. If this had been the end of it, Barbara would have continued to feel sorry and concerned for Teri Leigh, but she probably would not have felt the need to intervene. It was too big for one teacher to handle. Unfortunately, this was not the end of it.

Two weeks later, Teri Leigh gave some nude photographs of herself—photographs that her foster sister had taken—to two high school boys who rode her bus. Fortunately, the boys gave the pictures directly to the bus driver, who immediately brought them to Bob Farris. Bob called Teri Leigh's foster mother, who claimed that she had told the girls to tear up the pictures. Obviously, they had not obeyed. Further, her foster mother told Bob that she was unwilling to discuss the problem with Teri Leigh.

Because Barbara was responsible for teaching the Family Life Curriculum to Teri Leigh, Bob thought that she was the best person to address this issue with her. Calling her into his office, he told her what had happened with the photographs and provided her with some pamphlets to assist her in the counseling session she was to have with Teri Leigh.

After discussing the issue with Kay Middleton, Barbara arranged to have Teri Leigh stay after school with her so that she could spend as much uninterrupted time as necessary with her. Despite all of the advice and pamphlets she had received, Barbara relied on her intuitions to guide her. "I'll talk to her as if she were my own daughter, and tell her the same things that I would tell Keshia," she thought.

She began by asking Teri Leigh why she had given the boys pictures of herself. Teri Leigh responded frankly that she wanted to have sex and to have a baby. She went on to explain that she wanted the boys to like her, and that this was a good way to be popular with them. Barbara responded by discussing the seriousness involved with having a baby.

As she later related to Kay, "I talked to her about how much my children mean to me and how much I love them, but how much time they take from me. And I told her I was 27 when I had my first one, and had developed into a person. So I was ready to have my children, but I have very little spare time for myself. And that, how, at times, it takes all of the love I have to keep going with the children."

Barbara also talked to Teri Leigh about AIDS. Because Teri Leigh seemed to believe her warnings about the deadliness of the disease, Barbara drove this point home, hoping that it would help to deter her from seeking sexual encounters. She also talked about herpes and other sexually transmitted diseases, trying to be as explicit as possible. Unfortunately, Teri Leigh was equally candid as she insisted that she wanted to have a baby. As Teri Leigh talked, it occurred to Barbara that Teri Leigh's tenacity had a role in helping her deal with the abuse she had suffered. Because she still thought, despite Barbara's refutations, that she would eventually become pregnant as a result of the experience with her mother's boyfriend, Teri Leigh's assertion that she wanted to have a baby was her way of gaining some sense of control over, and therefore reconciling, what had happened to her. Maybe, Barbara thought, it was Teri Leigh's way of making it all right. As the clock in the empty classroom ticked toward 4:30, Barbara did her best to persuade Teri Leigh that trying to become pregnant would be a mistake, but she sensed that she was failing to get through to her.

After driving Teri Leigh home, she stopped at the babysitter to pick up Keshia and Shawn. Now, as she poured milk into glasses for the kids, the sound of her husband pulling up in the driveway drew her thoughts back to the present.

Dinner was eaten, homework was completed, and the children were made ready for bed. Throughout the evening, Barbara reviewed portions of her talk with Teri Leigh. Where would she go from here? What could she do to help this desperately troubled child? As much as she wanted to help, Barbara truly felt at a loss about how to proceed.

Stealing Time

ROBERT CARTER

Part A

Robert's seventh year of teaching began like most of the others. As a fourth-grade teacher, he had learned the value of setting his standards early in the year, letting students know in no uncertain terms the range and limits of acceptable behavior in his classroom. He felt strongly about strict but fair enforcement of rules, and he found that his students soon conformed to the standards he administered. He believed that if he was fair with students, they would be fair with him. As a result, his classroom became like a small community where everyone knew what to expect and how to behave at all times. Robert found that even his most unusual or troubled students soon fell in line with his expectations, and he believed that his classroom management benefitted these difficult students as much, perhaps even more, than the other students. In his classroom there was a comfortable predictability based upon the mutual understanding of, and adherence to, the ground rules.

Fall semester progressed just as he had assumed it would. He had worked hard to set his "precedents" and, before the conclusion of the first six-weeks grading period, his students had settled in. He was pleased that students like Andy and Martin, both children from very deprived, troubled backgrounds who also had behavior and academic problems, had shown much improvement in their ability to fit in. Kara, a mainstreamed student with behavior disorders, also appeared to be progressing nicely with the help of her special education teacher. So was David, a student from the self-contained learning disabilities classroom who was mainstreamed for short nonacademic periods of the school day. David came to Robert's class for morning homeroom period, which included roll-call, lunch money collection, the pledge of allegiance, and the like. David also went to art, music, and physical education with Robert's class. With the exception of minor and infrequent student transgressions, all was well.

Shortly after Christmas vacation, David's special education placement in the self-contained learning disabilities classroom was submitted to the required three-year reevaluation. The eligibility committee decided, based on his recent assessment results, that David should now be placed in the regular education classroom for at least 51 percent of the day. In other words, he was to receive special education services in a learning disabilities resource room, but more than half of his instruction was to take place in the regular classroom. Robert now had David for mathematics, a subject in which David possessed relative strengths, as well as for science and health. In addition, David ate lunch with Robert's class and attended the regular fourth grade social studies class with Ms. Gleason across the hall. Because David's participation in his class had not presented a problem before, Robert had no apparent reason to anticipate what was to come.

Within a few days Robert sensed the beginning of the end of what he had considered a pleasant school year. In mathematics, David did not turn in assignments and was soon far behind in his work. While Robert instructed the class, David alternately made strange noises and interrupted Robert and other students by blurting out declarations such as, "I know that," or "Let me do that." He dropped books loudly and deliberately on the floor, banged his pencil rhythmically on his desk, and probed noisily in his desk for lost objects. When Robert requested that he stop these disruptive and highly annoying behaviors, David ignored him. Robert considered David's behavior a relentless onslaught of interruption and rudeness aimed at him and the other students. He reasoned that David was attempting to regain the attention he had been accustomed to in the special education classroom. After all, in there he had been one of only five or so students with one teacher and a teachers' aide; he had been spoiled by receiving so much individual attention. Robert was certain that he was capable of successfully completing his assignments and that he was simply choosing not to do so, just as he was choosing his outrageous misbehavior. Whether David had taken his Ritalin, or had taken it at the proper time, did not seem to make much difference as far as Robert could see. Robert felt that David did what he wanted to do; and, most of the time, he wanted to show off and interrupt the class.

As both David's work and his behavior continued to worsen, Robert's loathing and resentment of him grew. This one student was ruining everything he had worked so hard to accomplish. To add insult to injury, David often stated loudly that he wanted to go back to his "real" class and to his "real" teacher. He was not even giving Robert a chance to be his teacher. He did not like Robert, and he did not like the other students. Robert felt that somehow he had failed to gain David's respect, but he was at a loss to explain why. In the meantime, David's relationships with the other students were deteriorating.

Because Robert's mathematics class was set up in a cooperative learning format, the students were compelled to work together in small groups, the success of which depended upon each member's productive contributions and hard work. David's refusal to complete assignments naturally lowered the average of his group. When some of the other students tried to help him, he rebuffed their efforts. Soon, his classmates began to complain. Robert began keeping David in from recess when he refused to complete his assignments; but he continued to neglect his work.

The day David took an assignment which Robert had just distributed and "chucked" it immediately into his desk, deliberately signifying that he had no intention of completing it, Robert went to his desk to sharply declare, "That's not what we do in here, that's not what's expected of you in here, and I've had just about enough of it." David retorted that he wanted to go back to his old class and that he did not like the way the other students *looked* at him. Robert replied that the other students *looked* at him because of the way he was acting. He went on to explain that these kids had never seen anybody act like this before, and that if he didn't want them to look at him, he would just have to change his attitude and change what he did in the classroom. At this point, Robert dismissed his class for lunch.

After lunch, David's behavior reached extreme proportions. When he reentered the classroom, he was "bouncing off the walls." He began making noises, pulling on the window blinds, and telling his classmates to "shut-up." Robert had planned to have the class prepare some answer sheets for the upcoming standardized testing. Because David was not to be tested with the rest of the class, Robert told him to go to the back of the room (to the time-out seat) so that neither he nor the class would disturb each other. David picked up his materials and went to the designated seat; however, when he reached his destination, he slammed them onto the desk with such force that his pencil bounced off the wall. Robert seized him briskly by the arm, informing him, "You are not going to throw things in this classroom." David replied, "It didn't hit anyone." He was anxiously repeating this assertion for the third time when Robert jerked him up by his arm, pulled him down the hall, and placed him forcefully into a student desk in the principal's office.

After instructing David not to return until he had completed his work, Robert returned to his classroom. David remained in the office until late afternoon. Because school rules dictated that students were not to be kept in from P.E. during formal instruction from the physical education teacher, David was to attend. Before leaving the classroom for P.E., David commissioned a classmate to tell Robert that he wished to talk with him. When Robert received the message, he told his class that David would just have to wait until the rest of the students went out for P.E.

When the others had left, Robert went to the back of the room where David waited. David said, "I hear you wanted to talk to me." Robert replied that he had understood that David had wanted to speak with *him* and that he was willing to listen to what David had to say. David's response to this was to tell Robert, "Forget it." After sitting quietly in the back of the empty classroom for a while, David approached Robert's desk and explained that he was sorry for his behavior but he didn't like the other kids in the class staring at him. Robert reiterated previously offered reasons for their staring. He went on to ask David if he might work better if the other students were told not to stare at him. David allowed that this would help him work better, and Robert followed by inquiring whether he or the class could do anything else to help him. David said that it would help if Kevin did not fuss at him in math groups. Robert explained that Kevin wanted his group to do well and that he fussed at him because David was bringing the group's average down. Finally, David agreed that it might be all right if Kevin fussed, but that it would be much better if he did it quietly. During these negotiations, David agreed to bring his materials to class, to treat Robert and the other students with respect, and to complete his assignments. After this discussion, David's behavior and schoolwork improved for the next several days. The following week, however, the situation regressed to its previous state.

Once again, David behaved as if he were angry with everyone. Robert kept him in from recess for not completing assignments, and he spent more time sitting in the principal's office. As Robert explained it, "He was just angry at everything, and the other kids in the class are just so angry at David, and I'm angry at David, too, because of what he's doing with us. He's just pushing my buttons, and it's just like a power struggle between the two of us. He wants his way, and I want my way. As long as I'm the adult in the classroom, its going to be my way, because it benefits the rest of the class. I can't have David disrupting everybody else in their work just because David's special. Well, as far as I'm concerned, I have 25 other kids who are special, who want to learn, and David has shown me so far that David just wants to learn when he feels like it; when he doesn't, he wants to disrupt everybody else."

While David was out of the classroom one day, one of Robert's students broached the subject of his behavior. Several of the others joined in, asking such questions as: "Why is he disrupting our classroom? Why isn't he doing his work? Doesn't he know he's going to fail if he doesn't do his work?" They told Robert that the day he had jerked David out of the classroom, they had laughed. Robert responded by admitting to the students that it must have looked "pretty comical." When they inquired, "Why did you have to do that?" Robert replied, "I don't think it's fair to you for David to sit in here and disrupt you." He followed this statement by asking, "Do you think it's fair?" The class concurred with his conviction. He went on to explain that he did not understand what made David "tick." By holding this discussion with the other students, Robert felt that he was being honest and "up-front" with them. Robert could see that the class was beginning to see David as a renegade and a social outcast, as many of them made statements like, "We don't like David to come in here." David was to provide further fuel for this opinion in a few weeks.

One afternoon, Robert did not allow David to attend recess because he had not completed his assignments. As David was working on one assignment in the empty classroom, Robert stepped out for three or four minutes to copy a worksheet David had not completed. When the class returned from recess, Bob, whose desk was near Robert's, reported that his watch, which he had left on his desk, was missing. Robert instructed Bob to check his locker and his desk. He had the other students look for the missing watch, too, but no one found it.

The following morning, David immediately rushed up to Robert's desk and announced, "Look at this watch that my daddy gave me!" Robert asked David to take the watch off so he could see it. As Robert examined the watch, he felt his anger, hurt, and suspicion growing. He was virtually certain it was Bob's watch.

The Truth About Alice

JANET LANE

Janet Lane often found her algebra 1a and 1b courses a challenge. These courses were designed for ninth and tenth graders who were comparatively slow to grasp the fundamental concepts of the subject. Janet noticed that this course sequence—algebra 1a (pre-algebra) first semester in preparation for algebra 1b (regular algebra) second semester—was generally selected by lower performing students and that she often had particular difficulty managing students' behavior in these classes.

Janet had dealt with her share, or more, of low motivation, inattention, and overt attempts to disrupt the class. In her 16 years of teaching, she felt that she had handled these problems more or less successfully. She had never encountered a problem that, over time, she was unable to resolve—until recently.

During the first semester in algebra 1a, Janet's class consisted of the usual mix of students. One student, however, distinguished herself from the others on the basis of appearance alone. When Janet looked at Alice, she could not help thinking that she was the most unattractive child she had ever seen. Although she was not from a poor home, Alice wore a pair of baggy dungarees (rolled up at the ankles) and a polo shirt to school every single day. She apparently had three sets of this "outfit," but she always looked the same. To magnify the frumpy style of her apparel, Alice's physical shape was . . . well, unusual. From the waist down, she was proportionally much larger than above the waist, giving her a peculiar pear-shaped appearance. The way she turned her feet in when she walked made her look almost as if she had an orthopedic deformity. Very thick glasses, dental braces, stringy, oily hair, and a general unkempt appearance all added to her misfit look.

If only Alice performed well academically, Janet thought, her odd appearance could be somewhat compensated for; but, in fact, Alice was also a weak student. Her parents had recently decided to remove her from the learning disabilities program because they did not want her to be in special education in high school. No one had

165

brought this fact to Janet's attention. But she did not customarily seek such information, choosing instead to "let the kids tell me what they are." As it turned out, there was a lot Janet didn't know about Alice.

Alice had been in Janet's class only a few days when she approached her and stated, "I'm going to have to be late for class." This soon became a frequent occurrence. Because the class met directly after lunch, the first several times Alice was late Janet didn't see it as a problem. After all, she reasoned, Alice had been nice enough to tell her each time she was going to be late.

When Alice's lateness became consistent, however, Janet became concerned and decided to have a talk with her. When she told Alice that her tardiness to class was becoming a problem, Alice became quite agitated and repeatedly insisted in a squealing voice, "I *have* to be late for class." Deciding that she must be firm, Janet replied, "I don't care if you're late occasionally, but you can't be late every single day. We have a class to run, you know."

Perhaps she should have expected the earnest flow of tears which ensued, but in fact, Alice's weeping caught her off guard. At the moment, all she could think to do was tell Alice not to worry, that they would discuss it later.

That afternoon Janet decided that it was necessary to seek some information and advice concerning this situation. Noticing Martha Keys, the sophomore guidance counselor, in the main office, she greeted her and began an account of the problem she was having with Alice. Almost immediately, Martha began to laugh so heartily that Janet felt a mild surge of confused annoyance. Noting the bewildered look on her face, Martha managed to ask mirthfully, "You don't know?" Janet shook her head "no" while Martha proceeded to direct her toward the guidance office. After closing the door, Martha explained the situation. Alice, she recounted, had attracted a great deal of attention last year as a result of an incident in the girls' restroom that had become, in a short time, almost legendary.

It seems that Alice's mother had insisted that she brush her teeth after lunch daily and had sent her to school with a neat little kit with which to accomplish this task. Too embarrassed to brush in front of other students, and too compliant to disobey her mother's orders, Alice solved her dilemma by brushing in the toilet stall. By all accounts, Alice was observed by another student using the water in the toilet to carry out her dental hygiene.

Word of this "incredibly grody act" spread quickly among the students, and when Martha got wind of it she called Alice into her office to discuss the matter. They resolved the problem by allowing Alice permission to be late for class after lunch so that she could brush her teeth at the sink after the other students had gone to class. Unfortunately, the incident had resulted in tremendous social damage and now presented Janet with some unusual behavior problems in her Algebra 1a class.

Janet had been aware that Alice's late arrival to her class caused some disturbance among the other students; yet she was unable to fully grasp the situation until she had discovered the reason for Alice's tardiness. It seemed that everyone had been in on the joke except Janet. When Alice entered class late, she was met with greetings such as, "Hello, Alice!" or "Watcha been doing, Alice?" These remarks were conveyed in ironic tones which held, for the informed listener, thinly veiled reference to Alice's past bathroom misadventures.

Now that she understood what lay behind these "greetings," Janet became increasingly aware of the disruption instigated by Alice's late arrival. The problem had grown to the point that three of the boys were so consistently ugly to her that Janet was compelled to go to the assistant principal and say, "I want those three boys, myself, and you to sit down and have a little talk." The "little talk," however, didn't amount to much. Just the usual, "I can't believe you are picking on this girl! Leave her alone! Act your age! Pretend she's not there . . . " During the meeting, Janet decided that she would definitely have to separate these three and Alice in class, surrounding her with a shield of nice kids. This worked well—for about a week.

Having decided that the boys were the instigators, it came as quite a shock to Janet when she discovered that notes were being passed between these boys and Alice. The particular "love note" that came to her attention was written to Alice by Mitch, the ringleader of the boys who were entertaining themselves at Alice's (and Janet's) expense. The note consisted of a simple message: "I like you, Alice. Would you like to go out sometime?" Alice had replied affirmatively and enthusiastically, and the note was on its way back when Janet intercepted it. Several students exchanged meaningful looks as Janet returned to her lesson.

Disgusted and frustrated, Janet took both Mitch and Alice to the office after class and had them assigned to in-school suspension. She tried to reason with Alice that she was guilty for having participated in the note-passing. How could she get Alice to understand that the boys were making a joke of her without hurting her feelings? Alice just didn't seem to "get it," and this made Janet worry even more. Alice, believing that the boys really liked her, could be played for the fool by them. In the back of her mind, Janet also worried about the possibility that the boys might easily take sexual advantage of Alice. There seemed to be no way out of this situation that would avoid Alice's eventual humiliation or further loss of social status.

One Bad Apple

After 26 years of teaching, Elaine Brown had developed a guiding philosophy which helped keep her goals as an educator in perspective. She believed that, as a teacher, she should get to know each student's distinctive blend of abilities and set her expectations accordingly. As she expressed it, "My expectations are different, not only for different students, but for every subject. If a student has trouble in math, but is extremely gifted in English and reading, I don't expect As from him in math, but he'd better give them to me in English and reading because that's his field." As she began her 27th year in the classroom, this year teaching fifth grade, she already had a working knowledge of most of her students' strengths and weaknesses because she had taught this group as fourth-graders last year. She had only two new students, William and Eddie.

William had moved to Pine County from a nearby city because his mother had withdrawn him from the class for children with behavior disorders and sent him to live with his father. From the little information Elaine could gather, William's parents had divorced when he was a toddler, and his mother was employed sporadically. Often, she and her three children slept in their car or floated from one friend's home to another between jobs. When she enrolled him in Pine County Public Schools, William's mother made one thing clear: She did not want him placed in a class for children with behavior disorders.

Elaine had serious misgivings about William being so abruptly and completely mainstreamed, but she felt she had little choice but to make the best of it. So she approached the task with the same philosophy she applied to the other students—determine what is reasonable to expect, and then uphold those expectations while always aiming higher. With William, she found that she had to set her expectations far below the average. Although he liked to read, William's reading was approximately two years below grade level. During the first week of school, he absolutely refused to do work in mathematics. He simply would not pick up his pencil. As the first several weeks of school elapsed, it was also apparent that he was not accustomed to attending school on a regular basis. In fact, he was absent two or three days a week.

Elaine reported this attendance problem to the visiting teacher (school social worker), Jerry West, who went to William's home on several occasions when William did not come to school. When Jerry had knocked on the door, no one answered, and everything seemed quiet and still. Jerry spoke with several neighbors who told him that as soon as he left, William—who had been home—opened the doors and windows and resumed watching television. These neighbors also explained that Mr. Payne, William's father, left for work at a pipe-fitting factory at 6:30 A.M.. and did not return home until 7:00 P.M. Jerry then went to Mr. Payne's place of employment and spoke with him during a work break. Mr. Payne, a small man who looked to be in his fifties, explained to Jerry in a soft voice that he wanted William to go to school. He told Jerry that he awakened William each morning; but, because he left for work so early, William was able to go back to bed and skip school. "I'll lose my job if I stay home to make sure he gets on the school bus," he explained.

When he did attend school, William was dolorous and withdrawn except when someone did something he did not like, and then he became explosive. Sometimes these temper tantrums came with no detectable provocation. It was through repeated tantrums that William cultivated his teacher's apprehension and classmates' fear of him. One such incident occurred on a warm September afternoon. The class was subdued from the stuffiness of the classroom and the heaviness of the school lunch. Elaine, perspiring and weary, nevertheless carried on with her lesson on the exploration of the New World. Without warning, William rose from his desk. Wielding the large fifth-grade social studies textbook far over his head, William slammed it forcefully on Chuck's desk, who sat directly behind him. Chuck reflexively jerked his hands from the surface of the desk and pulled his torso as far back as the orange plastic chair would allow before the book struck the desk with an explosive impact.

The class froze. The second hand on the plastic wall clock ticked laboriously before the spell of the moment was broken by William who, glowering at the class with malevolent intensity, shuffled to his seat and faced the front of the classroom defiantly. In those seconds which had elapsed, Elaine realized—and she knew her students also realized—that William had had no intention of altering the direction or velocity of the textbook even if Chuck had not removed his hands with such quickness. Her mind struggled against numbness in an effort to decide what to do. At four feet, eleven inches, she was not prepared for a physical encounter with William, and she was unwilling to risk further violence toward the rest of her students. Besides, she reasoned, although William had disrupted the class, he had not actually caused harm. Her instincts told her that it was best to let the moment pass, deciding that any immediate intervention on her part might send William completely out of control.

Because William was frequently absent from school, Elaine had the opportunity to discuss his behavior with her students, which she did on two occasions. During these exchanges, she acknowledged their fears and apprehensions, and as a class they agreed to treat William carefully so as to avoid provoking his anger. They would not tease him, touch his belongings, or correct him in class if he made a mistake. These were all things for which he seemed to have a very low tolerance. Elaine also asked the class to give William as much encouragement as possible by doing simple things such as nodding affirmatively after he read aloud. She had noticed that he seemed heartened by such approval, and she wanted to take advantage of this to make him feel a part of the class and feel better about himself.

Elaine took comfort in the trust she was able to achieve with this group of students. The bond she had established with them last year now stood them in good stead. This is not to say that the students became less frightened of William; they did not. What they did become, however, was much more astute in reading him and knowing when and how to hide their fear. Elaine quietly observed these developments with a mixture of pride and sorrow. However, she felt that they were all doing the best they knew how under the circumstances.

The only exception to this cooperative effort was Eddie, a small boy who seemed unable to resist attracting William's attention. Elaine believed that, in his own way, Eddie was at least as troubled as William. In fact, his records showed that he had been referred repeatedly to his previous school's child study committee because of behavior problems. His parents had refused to allow a formal evaluation by which the school could establish eligibility for special education services.

Because he was small, his behavior, although erratic, was more of an annoyance than a real problem, except when it came to William. Elaine's students were growing accustomed to Eddie's unexpected bids for attention. At almost any given time or place, Eddie would poke, slap, or punch classmates much larger than himself, apparently without heed of possible consequences. Any opportunity to get out of Elaine's eyesight provided him an occasion to provoke other students. Elaine remembered the day, that, returning from lunch, she found Eddie crawling around on the floor biting his classmates on their ankles. Reprimanding him for such behavior usually brought a blank smile to his face. Although she had attempted to provide meaningful consequences for his behavior, she had yet to find either a positive consequence or a negative one that really seemed to mean anything to him.

As with William, the class demonstrated more patience with Eddie than Elaine felt she could rightfully expect from a group of fifth-graders. To be sure, some students had more patience than others. On occasion, a less tolerant student would reciprocate Eddie's most recent annoyance with a sound slap or a decisive shove against the nearest wall. Because these retaliatory acts appeared neither to faze nor to hurt him, and because they rendered at least momentary results, Elaine usually ignored this vigilante form of justice.

It was when Eddie picked on William that Elaine could not ignore the repercussions. Unlike her other students, Eddie simply did not seem to understand that he should not provoke William, nor did he seem to realize that she could not guarantee his safety when he chose to incite William's ire.

That she could not ensure Eddie's safety was clearly illustrated on a crisp November day as she led her class in from their midmorning recess period. She had established the routine of having her class line up for water before returning to the classroom. After each student had gotten a drink, he or she was to proceed to the classroom to prepare for the upcoming lesson. On this particular day, Eddie, who appeared to be bursting with energy from the preceding kickball game, left his place in line.

Escaping Elaine's notice, he whizzed past William, giving him a playful push on his way to the end of the line.

Eddie's piercing scream caused Elaine's stomach to lurch and brought her rushing past the line of wide-eyed faces. There she found William on top of Eddie with his right knee planted squarely in Eddie's spine. His powerful arms were pulling Eddie's frail shoulders toward him, and his contorted features conveyed the full force of his anger and rage. Within that crystallized split-second, Elaine could almost hear Eddie's spine snap. Forcing a sense of quiet confidence, Elaine reached out, gently placed her hand on his taut shoulder, and whispered, "William." Almost instantly, William's muscles relaxed. He released Eddie's shoulders and slowly rose to his feet. His glaring eyes refused to meet Elaine's as he stated matter-of-factly, "I'm going to hurt him." Eddie rose to a sitting position and sat sobbing on the floor as the rest of the class stood in silent observation.

Turning her attention to Eddie, she asked him if he could stand. He nodded affirmatively, quickly got up, and wiped his tears on the ragged cuff of his blue flannel shirt. Watching William out of the corner of her eye, she reformed the line and directed the students to the classroom. No one spoke.

Arriving at the classroom, Elaine went to Katherine Ellis, the teacher next door, and asked her to watch the class while she made arrangements to have William taken home. She was hesitant to do this because she did not want to compound his truancy problem, but he seemed unable to compose himself. He continued to mumble threats, and his rigid bearing led Elaine to believe that he might explode again at any moment. She did not want to risk a second outburst in one day.

Upon returning to the classroom, Elaine noticed that Eddie's tears had long since dried and his memory of the incident seemed to have faded almost as quickly. She, on the other hand, would relive those moments frequently in the days to come as she grew increasingly aware of her tenuous control over the situation. She did discover, however, that she could protect Eddie from William's assaults by making sure that she was the first to intervene when Eddie misbehaved.

Although she did not believe in paddling, Elaine found that if she took Eddie out into the hall, borrowed a paddle from Katherine Ellis, and at least created the appearance that she was paddling Eddie for his misbehavior, that William would leave him alone. "It was really easy," she explained. "I would take Eddie out in the hall, take the paddle and come somewhere near him [hit him very lightly], and he would scream like someone was killing him. And William thought I was doing my duty. I'd go back in the classroom, and William would be nodding, and he'd leave Eddie alone." Although she felt that this was less than an ideal solution to the problem, her main objective was to protect Eddie from actual physical harm. This tactic seemed to work better than anything else. Therefore, Elaine resigned herself to getting along the best way she could, but she yearned for the school year to end without a tragic incident.

The Contract With Parrish and Son

REBECCA PHILLIPS

Frustrated and helpless isn't a good way to feel, Rebecca thought. It seemed such a long time since she had first met Bob Parrish, and she wasn't really sure that the strain was worth her investment of emotional energy she had put into trying to get through to him during the past three weeks. But there he was in her class, in her face, tearing at her heart, and the end of the school year seemed years away.

Rebecca Phillips had been teaching students with learning disabilities for six years. She felt confident now with her teaching techniques and with the progress of most of her students. She had learned the hard way, through trial and error, about discipline. She now understood the importance of setting up a consistent structure for behavior management from the very beginning of the school year.

This year, Rebecca had switched to a new behavior management program to enforce the rules that she and the students had decided on together. It entailed positive reinforcement in the form of free time or time to engage in preferred activities. She had set up a group contingency with which she was quite satisfied. The class or work-group began every period with ten minutes of free time "in the bank." She kept a chart on the board reflecting the current allotted time. If students followed the rules, the group had a chance to earn additional time at Rebecca's discretion. She was careful to award additional time intermittently so that her students could not anticipate when their good behavior might pay off. If a student was not following the rules, however, Rebecca simply pulled out her stopwatch and timed the student until he or she complied. She did not say anything to the student, nor did she stop her instruction. When the student complied, Rebecca stopped the watch and wrote the amount of time it had taken the student to get back on task in a "time lost" column on her chart. The total

173

minutes and seconds lost would then be subtracted from the group's accumulated minutes of free time.

Rebecca felt her group contingency worked very well because she didn't have to interrupt her instruction with reprimands or reminders. Her students began urging each other to stay on task, a kind of peer pressure Rebecca judged to be effective and appropriate. When she started her stopwatch, one or two students always seemed to notice and either let the offender know that he or she was not behaving as expected or helped the misbehaving student comply. For instance, another student might give the offender paper if he or she came to class unprepared. Even chronic offenders began coming to class with needed materials, participating in class, and helping others make sure they were behaving as expected. Only one of Rebecca's students did not appear to be affected by the fact that he was losing free time for the group by misbehaving. As a matter of fact, Bob seemed to thrive on the negative attention he drew from his peers.

Bob was an uncoordinated, slightly overweight seventh-grader, what some might call "husky." He dragged a large book bag around from classroom to classroom, usually tripping over it at least once in each class. Rebecca wondered whether this was an attention-getting device or simply adolescent clumsiness.

Bob had moved into Monroeville in early January, bringing with him a confidential file indicating that he had previously received instruction in reading, math, and English in a self-contained class for students with learning disabilities. While reading through his file, Rebecca noticed that Bob had a history of frequent moves—five in his eight years of schooling. Almost every teacher had remarked on Bob's attention-getting antics—inappropriate comments, yelling at the teacher, and refusing to remain on task, for example. Rebecca had made a conscious effort not to prejudge Bob because of his history, hoping against hope that he might have learned some coping skills in his last placement. Her hopes were dashed the day she met him. In group situations from the beginning, he volunteered a running commentary on anything she said that could be twisted into a double entendre. In a class of eight adolescent boys, his comments inevitably created a commotion.

"No matter what the topic during my language arts class," Rebecca recalled, "Bob managed to twist the words around in order to get his classmates' attention. One time when we were discussing Prohibition, I asked for a definition of "speakeasy," and he said, 'Isn't that where people used to get sex in the 1920s?' The rest of the class responded with laughter to Bob's comments at first, then began to ridicule him as 'dumb' and 'stupid.' The more the class got upset with Bob for each 'stopwatch' episode, the more Bob seemed to continue and intensify his efforts to get everyone's attention."

Rebecca quickly realized that Bob should not be included in the group contingency, as he was both thriving on the negative attention and reducing the effectiveness of the program for the other seven boys in the class. After only one week, she pulled Bob out of the free time program and set up an alternative individual contingency for him. She also felt that his parents needed to be made aware of his problems in the classroom. Two weeks after he joined her class, she found herself calling Bob's home.

What she learned from her call led Rebecca to believe that Bob's home life played a significant role in his behavior at school. As far as Rebecca could ascertain, Mr.

Parrish had obtained custody of his two sons, Bob and his younger brother, after a lengthy search to locate their mother and the children, who moved frequently. Bob's father had finally won custody a short time before their move to Monroeville. Mr. Parrish and the boys lived with Mr. Parrish's parents in an upper-middle class neighborhood. Bob's grandmother had a history of mental illness and was frequently in and out of "rest homes." When she was home, she apparently did not get along well with her husband. It was in this setting that the boys had begun to build a relationship with the father they had never known.

Mr. Parrish had definite ideas about how Bob should be raised. He intended, as he put it to Rebecca, to "make him into a man." When Rebecca had called to suggest that they discuss Bob's misbehavior, Mr. Parrish had not hesitated to agree to a parent-teacher conference.

At their first meeting, Rebecca was struck with how much Mr. Parrish looked like Bob—an older Bob with a clear edge of toughness, she thought. Mr. Parrish was tall, tanned, and obviously lifted weights. It immediately occurred to Rebecca that this totally masculine father figure might present some problems for Bob. Mr. Parrish was cordial and appeared concerned about Bob. He told his story of recently obtaining custody of his sons, stressing how hard he had worked to get his children back from their mother. He informed Rebecca that he punished Bob's misbehavior with a belt—one with a buckle, of course. In addition, he gave the impression that he did not have much patience with either Bob or his younger son. Mr. Parrish felt that Bob's problems stemmed from being babied by his mother for 12 years. His parenting responsibilities, he explained again, included "making a man outta him." One step towards this goal, he believed, was to put Bob on the football team, adding that he attended a "few football practices to help the coach out and kick Bob's ass when he messed up."

Soon after her first conference with Mr. Parrish, Rebecca met with Bob and his father to set up a home-school contract involving Bob's homework and behavior. Bob seemed to want to please his father as much as his father wanted Bob to "act more like a man." Although she had some doubts about what would happen, Rebecca had hopes that the contract would work. She had no idea what the consequences would be. The day after setting up the home-school contract, Bob confronted Rebecca when he came through the door.

"How come you told my Dad I was bad in class? He beat me when he got home, and it's all your fault." He stomped to his seat and flopped down, slamming his book bag down on the desk. Rebecca was stunned. Her heart went out to Bob. She was incensed with Mr. Parrish and his "macho" attitude. At that point, she decided that contacting Mr. Parrish about any of Bob's misbehavior would only result in a beating.

During class that day, Bob participated reluctantly for a short time. But he soon began tapping his pencil loudly on his desk. Rebecca reminded him of their contract.

"It don't matter," Bob responded. "My Dad don't think I can do it. He said so."

Rebecca felt her anger at Mr. Parrish growing by the second. How could he sit there in the conference and agree that the contract was a good idea and say he would encourage Bob, then go home and tell Bob he thinks he can't do it! Sighing, Rebecca tried to focus her attention on her work with the other students, hoping Bob would return to his work. He didn't. A few minutes later, she tried another tack, suggesting that he follow along with a student who was reading aloud from the literature book. His retort was swift and firm.

"I don't care where we are."

Rebecca chose to ignore this comment and went to stand near Bob's desk, cuing him to the sentence the student was reading. Bob continued to play with his pencil. Gently, Rebecca removed the pencil from Bob's grasp. He yielded, and turned his efforts to getting another student's attention. Rebecca did not say a word, but she felt that Bob was trying to upset her because he held her accountable for the previous night's beating. Although she felt guilty about this, she refused to let Bob get the best of her. She had worked hard to get the other students to work as a cooperative group, and she didn't want them thinking she was playing favorites by giving Bob more than his share of attention. As the other students finished their oral reading, Bob informed them of his evaluation.

"Man, you guys are the lousiest readers I ever heard."

Always priding herself in accepting each student at his individual level of ability, whatever it was, Rebecca responded immediately in a slow, even voice.

"Bob, I would like to talk to you out in the hallway. Please follow me." She began walking slowly toward the door.

"What? Me? What'd I do? It's the truth!" Bob complained.

Rebecca paused at the door, waiting for Bob to comply. A few seconds later, Bob ambled to the doorway. Rebecca struggled to contain her anger, her voice trembling.

"As long as you are in my class, you will not make comments about the abilities of other students. We are all in this class because we all have different strengths and weaknesses, and we are trying to find the best way for us to learn. If you continue to make these comments, I will have to call your father."

Bob stood against the wall, avoiding her stare. He said nothing, nor did he acknowledge her warning.

"Bob, did you hear me?"

Still no answer. Rebecca stuck her head in the classroom and asked her instructional assistant to come out into the hallway.

"Bob needs a little time to think about what I just told him," she explained. "Would you please stay out here with him for a few minutes until he feels he is ready to rejoin the class?"

Reentering the class, Rebecca was surprised to see that the other boys were simply sitting there, waiting. She thanked them for being so quiet and calm, and rewarded them with two extra minutes of free activity time. Bob tried to follow Rebecca back into the room almost immediately; she waved him back. When he returned several minutes later, he was compliant. He completed all his classwork and showed it to her. Perhaps, Rebecca thought, I've my troubles with Bob are over.

When Bob arrived the next day, he immediately searched for his writing journal. Rebecca's students wrote in their journals each day. Rebecca agreed with her students that their journals were confidential, so she read them only if they were intentionally left on her desk. At the end of first period, Bob's journal was on her desk. What she saw when she opened it sent chills down her spine. Bob had drawn an effigy of himself hanging from a tree. On another page, a knife was thrust deep into the head of his likeness. Another page contained a headstone with Bob's name and birth date. Under these scenes, in Bob's characteristic scribble, she read, "I hat life. I wish I wer ded." Rebecca caught her breath. Was this one of Bob's attention-getting ploys, or was he serious?

Realizing that in Bob's best interests she was compelled to break the confidence of his journal, Rebecca consulted the school psychologist, Mr. Moore, at her first opportunity. Mr. Moore suggested that she question Bob carefully to see whether she could determine the reason for his drawings and statements. He also encouraged her to keep anecdotal records of Bob's behavior. Together, after a few weeks of observation, he suggested, they could decide whether there was reason for referral.

Uncertain how she should react, Rebecca did not write a response to Bob's entry as she usually did; she waited to see what would come next. The following day, Bob again immediately went to his journal. Rebecca watched him open it and quickly close it again. Later that morning, he chose not to write in his journal while the rest of the students did so. From across the room, where she was working with another student, Rebecca prompted Bob to get started.

"I don't have nothing to say," he grumbled.

Rebecca repeated her request and began to move toward Bob. He reacted immediately.

"Why do you always haveta come over here? I ain't doin' nothing!"

Irritated at the disruption of her work with a willing student, Rebecca responded, "That's why I'm coming over, because you're not doing anything."

As Bob's face reddened with rage, she regretted her words. Fearing an all-out scene, Rebecca quickly asked her aide to take over while she talked to Bob. The situation was escalating rapidly to a crisis.

"Why are you always picking on me? Hector doesn't always write in his journal, but you don't yell at him!"

Refusing to get caught up in a power struggle, she continued to move toward Bob. She heard him mumbling.

"I don't care, You can't scare me. I can't stand you anyway. I hate this f—ing class!

At the last comment, Rebecca became indignant.

"In my class, there is no profanity. You know the rule. I'll have to call your father."

"Go ahead," Bob retorted loudly, "maybe he'll kill me this time and I won't have to worry about you and this f---ing class."

The other students stopped their work, staring at Bob and Rebecca. Rebecca was desperately trying to figure a way to get Bob out of the room, but she was afraid he was too angry to attempt any kind of move.

"Don't think the f---ing principal can help me!" Bob yelled. "Nobody can. Everybody hates me, especially my Dad. And I hate you, you f---ing b----!" With that, Bob pushed Rebecca's aide aside and ran out of the room.

The Mascot

Mrs. Clem maintained a very relaxed classroom structure in her class of 11- to 13-year-old students with learning disabilities, all boys. Only five of the 12 students she served were present all day; seven were mainstreamed into regular education programs for a varying percentage of the school day. Mrs. Clem described her class as a family, and she shared with them the daily trials and tribulations of her home life. Her own children were well known by her students and had visited the classroom many times. She told them often of the burdens of her work—too much paperwork and a bureaucracy that overloaded her with too many rules, which she in turn had to impose on her students. It seemed to her student teacher, Cathy Anderson, that Mrs. Clem spent too much time complaining about real-life responsibilities in an effort to prepare her students to enter the big, bad, unfair world.

When Cathy began her student teaching in March, she had high expectations of learning a lot from Mrs. Clem, who had been teaching for 20 years. Mrs. Clem introduced Cathy to the class, acting as spokesperson for the boys in letting Cathy know that she had passed the criteria the boys had set for looks. Cathy was pleased that the students obviously approved of her, but Mrs. Clem's introduction left her feeling more like a pet than a professional. She got the impression that she might be seen as a mascot, not a teacher or even as someone to be taken seriously. Little did she know how her initial perceptions would be confirmed.

Mrs. Clem's reluctance to let Cathy take responsibility for the class soon became obvious. Until the third week of the eight-week student teaching placement, Mrs. Clem did not allow Cathy to plan and teach a lesson on her own. Cathy was confined to serving as line leader when the class went to lunch or recess, teaching lessons planned by Mrs. Clem, or teaching on a moment's notice without any preparation when Mrs. Clem had other things to do. Mrs. Clem seemed determined to keep Cathy cast in the role of nonprofessional—or, perhaps, professional "ditz."

Cathy recalled several incidents in which she had ended up feeling like a dunce. On St. Patrick's Day she had brought in green Jello Jigglers, intending to talk about the importance of this holiday to Irish Americans. Mrs. Clem had put her on the spot, unexpectedly requiring that she discuss not only St. Patrick's Day but various religious observances and holidays with which Cathy was unfamiliar. Another day, Mrs. Clem asked Cathy to teach a sex education lesson concerning body parts, then interrupted her constantly to discuss sexually transmitted diseases. To Cathy's utter consternation, Mrs. Clem told the boys they could catch AIDS from tears and saliva. Not wishing to be party to such misinformation, Cathy had felt compelled to disagree with Mrs. Clem as diplomatically as she could in front of the class. More than once, Mrs. Clem had changed the day's schedule after she and Cathy had agreed on specific lesson plans. Reflecting on these incidents, Cathy wondered whether Mrs. Clem was trying to teach her as she taught her learning-disabled students—preparing her for the cruel, real world—or whether she was being deliberately malicious.

Still, Cathy was not prepared for the worst. On Mrs. Clem's recommendation, Cathy planned a lesson using one of the classroom science kits. Learning from the difficulties she had already encountered, Cathy was careful to let Mrs. Clem know that she was planning the lesson for 12:50, the usual time for the class's science lessons, on Thursday, March 31. As Cathy feared, the lesson did not go as planned.

On the 30th of March, Mrs. Clem and Cathy attended a workshop on teaching science, to which they took one of their classroom science kits. They had not used the kit at the conference, and when they returned to the school the next day it remained in the trunk of Mrs. Clem's car. Cathy reminded Mrs. Clem Thursday morning before the students arrived that she would need the science kit for her lesson and offered to retrieve the kit from the car. Mrs. Clem assured Cathy that she would get the kit because, as she put it, "You have so much to do to get ready for the day's teaching." Although Cathy felt well-prepared, she did not press the issue. After all, she told herself, Mrs. Clem doesn't like to be corrected, and I don't want to seem too confident of my plans for fear she might throw me another curve—rearranging the schedule or deciding at the last minute that the students ought to be taught a different lesson.

That morning the students all worked together on English and social studies tasks, as one of Mrs. Clem's favorite teaching strategies was to emphasize cooperation. Periodically, when the students were on task or finished an assignment, Cathy gave them "good work tickets," redeemable for a variety of items at the classroom store. Jabar, who Mrs. Clem often swore would grow up to be a lawyer because of his argumentative nature, tried intermittently to distract the other students so that he could be the first to finish his work. Juny, his best buddy, was particularly susceptible to Jabar's invitation to engage in off-task conversations. Cathy did some quick thinking, quietly and politely correcting Jabar and urging him to continue working and leave the other students alone. Throughout the morning, Mrs. Clem made distracting comments from her desk at the back of the room—comments that Cathy considered "off task" for a teacher. These comments predictably threw Jabar off task, and Cathy found herself trying, in response, to guide Jabar back to his work time after time. At first, Jabar's reactions were agreeable: "Okay, Ms. Anderson, I'm sorry, I know . . . " As the morning wore on, however, he began responding to Cathy more sharply and to show signs of rebellion: "Don't get on my case. I ain't talkin', Juny is."

At lunchtime, Cathy sat with the boys, enjoying the unstructured time to chat with them. She noticed that Jabar ignored her attempts to pull him into the conversation, but she felt that if he was angry that was his problem; she thoroughly disapproved of the behavior he had been showing before lunch, and she felt she owed him no apology for the quiet, mild reprimands she had used to get him back on task.

As she and the students ate lunch and chatted amiably, Cathy wondered whether Mrs. Clem was fetching the science kit. Her science lesson was to follow a 15-minute period directly after lunch, a period that Mrs. Clem typically used to read aloud to her students. Cathy had assumed the responsibility for reading to the students, meaning that she would not have time to get the science kit if Mrs. Clem had forgotten it.

When Cathy took the students upstairs after lunch, Mrs. Clem was in the classroom. The science kit was not. "Not again!" she muttered to herself. "Why me? Why does something always have to be screwed up when I'm expected to teach!" Cathy's anger made it difficult for her to concentrate on getting a rambunctious group of eight boys settled and ready to listen to her read. Jabar, Isaac, and Thomas began wrestling on the floor. Cathy separated them, got them settled, and began to read. Knowing that the matter of the science kit was something she'd have to deal with eventually, Cathy took solace that at least she'd gotten the class under control and would have a few minutes to feel like a real teacher. "You boys are not being at all nice to Ms. Anderson," interrupted Mrs. Clem. "She is the teacher now, and you're supposed to be nice to her. Jabar, Isaac, and Thomas, I want you to write apology notes to Ms. Anderson right now!" Jabar refused and left the room. Mrs. Clem, who explained to Cathy her belief that students should have the freedom to choose how they will behave and experience the consequences, simply accepted Jabar's exit. He soon returned, much to Cathy's relief, and sat at his desk. By this time, the reading period had evaporated into confusion and conflict. Half the class was busy writing apology notes to her, the other half explaining to Mrs. Clem their refusal to write their apologies.

Exasperated, Cathy could barely control her voice. "Mrs. Clem, we need the science kit now."

"Oh, yes. But it's so heavy," mused Mrs. Clem, "you'd better take one of the boys with you to get it."

Cathy groaned. She knew that if she left the class at this point she would need to spend a lot of time and effort getting the boys settled down and ready to work when she returned. Mrs. Clem, she observed, was settling her large figure comfortably into her teacher's chair at the back table.

Deciding that she'd better choose a student and get going, Cathy motioned to Tai, a boy who usually refused to work but who had worked hard all morning. "Tai, could you go out to Mrs. Clem's car with me to get our science kit?"

"Jabar should go, too!" Mrs. Clem interjected. "He knows my car, and he always gets things out of it for me. He's trustworthy."

What did trustworthiness have to do with it, Cathy wondered. Besides, in her opinion Jabar hadn't been behaving well enough to be rewarded with a privilege the boys obviously relished. She had noticed, too, that Juny was never given any of the desired responsibilities in the classroom, even though he was often well behaved. She decided to make her stand. "Jabar's behavior hasn't been good enough today. I'll take Juny."

Her assertiveness was a mistake.

Looking Cathy squarely in the eye, Mrs. Clem was ready with a decisive retort as she handed Jabar her car keys: "Juny never behaves! Jabar will go!" Jabar and Tai ran out of the room, down the stairs, and into the parking lot without Cathy. When she caught up with them at the car and asked them to walk with her, Jabar took the kit (which, as Cathy recalled, was not really heavy) and ran ahead to the classroom, while Tai walked with Cathy. She and Tai arrived back in the classroom in time to hear Mrs. Clem say, "Go ahead Jabar, you know how to set it up." Cathy tried to direct the activity according to her lesson plan, but the science kit was full of gadgets and parts that were not even part of the lesson—and they were now in the hands of eight different children. As she tried to get control of the group, she became extremely frustrated with Jabar's behavior. He was not listening and did not stop talking when Cathy asked him to. Appealing to what she assumed would be his understanding of how his behavior was affecting her feelings and the class, she pleaded, "Jabar, I'm really frustrated with your behavior right now. We can't go on with this lesson unless you pay attention and stop talking." To her amazement, Jabar simply got up from his seat again and left the room. He soon returned, but only to make explosive noises and distract the group, which Cathy had finally gotten on track, and then to leave the room again. Juny, unfortunately, began imitating Jabar's antics.

Cathy decided to ignore Jabar and Juny. Meanwhile, Mrs. Clem began yelling threats and instructions from the back of the room: "Juny, Jabar, come back in here or I'll kill you! Jabar, get in here!"

Finding it impossible to continue the lesson because of Mrs. Clem's yelling, Cathy stepped outside the classroom, where Jabar was merely loitering in the hall, to inform him that he had lost his 20-minute afternoon recess for leaving the class without permission. He could earn back some of his recess, Cathy told him, if he returned immediately to the class and participated appropriately in the lesson. Reluctantly, he followed her back into the classroom. He did, however, participate in the lesson and remain in his seat. For this, Cathy informed him that he had earned back five minutes of his recess, but that he would need to stay in the classroom for the first 15 minutes of the recess period.

When the afternoon recess arrived, Cathy accompanied the other students outside, leaving Jabar in the classroom with Mrs. Clem. After 10 minutes, Jabar appeared, claiming that Mrs. Clem had told him it was time for him to go out. Following recess, Cathy questioned Mrs. Clem about Jabar coming out five minutes early. "Well," she said, "he told me his 15 minutes was up, so I let him go."

Feeling that she should confront Jabar about his behavior, Cathy asked him to step into the hallway. "Jabar," she asked, "Why have you been giving me such a hard time all day long?"

Folding his arms and looking at the ground, Jabar replied, "You don't like me, so I don't care." Cathy's heart sank as she wondered what had happened to the good feelings these students seemed to have about her four weeks ago. How could she convince Jabar that she did like him, even though she disapproved of his behavior and would not let it pass without correction? She could sense the negative effect her constant conflict with Mrs. Clem was having on her ability to teach and manage the class, but she had four more weeks to go in this assignment. She was not sure that she could endure it. Tomorrow is April first, and I feel like an April fool. "I wish this was all a bad joke and tomorrow things would be different," she thought as she pondered what to say to Jabar.

Whose Class Is This?

JANE LEE

Part A

Jane's transition from the special education classroom to a regular fourth grade had been uneventful. After three years in a resource room, she welcomed the change. Teaching regular fourth graders was just as challenging. Her confidence stemmed from the many hours of individualized work with her special education kids. She often joked that if she could handle what special education threw her way, regular class teaching was sure to be a breeze.

Sitting in her classroom this warm March afternoon, though, she wasn't sure where to go next with the surges of anger, frustration, and depression that washed over her. Her troubles had started only a few months ago, but it seemed like years. Ann Dean was not the problem; it was her mother, Belinda Dean. Jane turned it all over one more time. The battle was lost, and so was the war. She didn't want to deal with school politics, negative feelings, and emotional roller coasters. All she wanted to do was *teach*. But she felt she couldn't. Not, at least, here at Eugene Field Elementary.

Jane hadn't thought it odd that Mrs. Dean had been somewhat irate during a parent conference before the start of the school year. Several parents had been dismayed that the city schools had changed the language arts curriculum without letting them know. Being a parent herself, Jane knew how they felt. She tried to direct their legitimate complaint to the district's central office. Belinda, tall and attractive, was a schoolteacher turned homemaker who served as a substitute teacher at Field School whenever she could—which was quite often.

Although she had felt safe in the answers she had given Belinda at that first meeting, their conversation had alerted Jane to the fact that Belinda seemed dissatisfied with a number of other things that were occurring outside of the classroom. Issues, Jane resentfully reflected, that were way beyond her control as a classroom teacher.

Mrs. Dean's next complaint was not long in coming. Jane's substitute had mistakenly assigned classwork for homework, and Belinda's swift reply indicated another round of hassle. Jane reread the letter:

Dear Ms. Lee:
We spent far too much time on homework yesterday. I believe that when children are 9 or 10 years of age they should not be expected to spend more than one hour on homework. In order to assimilate, enjoy, and actually learn the meaning of some words, the task ought not to be overwhelming, frustrating, and tedious, which this homework undoubtedly was.

Sincerely,
Belinda Dean

Jane refolded the letter for the umpteenth time. She remembered making a quick call to Mrs. Dean to explain the substitute's mix-up. Belinda apparently accepted her explanation. Still, for some reason, Jane had the uneasy feeling that this scene would be repeated. Funny, thought Jane, there were no complaints from any of the other 18 sets of parents about the substitute's mistake. Jane tried to put the incidents out of her mind.

Not long after Jane had received the complaint about homework, Belinda appeared as a substitute in the fourth grade classes. In passing, Belinda made disparaging comments about the "chaotic," classes in which she was subbing, the clear implication being that the teachers were doing less than their best. Jane couldn't overcome her anxiety about Belinda's implied questioning of her fellow teachers' professionalism and, by association, her own. Knowing that Art Dean was an editor for the local newspaper and a newly elected member of the school board, didn't help Jane's feeling of uneasiness. Like most new board members, Art was keen on establishing a record of prompt attention to any problems in any school in the system.

Belinda's off-hand criticisms escalated to the point at which the four fourth-grade teachers collectively asked Jim Black, the principal, to assign Belinda to other grades. On one of her days of substituting, Belinda crossed the thin line between professional teacher or teacher's aide and parent. Jane had seen this happen before. What perplexed her so about Belinda was the fact that she expressed her criticisms in the lunch room for all the teachers and other school staff members to hear. Belinda appeared determined to voice her parental complaints to Jane right there at the lunch table.

"Jane, I think that Ann was treated unfairly last week when you held the fourth-grade reading auction. Ann never got to spend her tokens. I don't think this is a very positive way to deal with any child."

Belinda conveniently omitted the fact that Ann had been absent from the auction to attend a voluntary training program. "Look, Belinda, why don't we set up a time for the two of us to get together, and I'll see if we can't work something out." It was all Jane could do to keep from screaming.

Belinda, however, was relentless. She aired other complaints: Why weren't the fourth-graders going on an extended field trip like they did last year? Was this a punishment for the whole fourth grade? If so, why were all the fourth-graders being made to suffer for the unruly behavior of a few?

Jane's logical answers fell on deaf ears. Belinda was hearing only what she wanted to hear. To this point, Jane felt that although Belinda was being troublesome, the barbs were not personal. Good communication and reciprocal understanding would, she assured herself, solve these problems over time. But a change in Belinda's tactics was soon to come.

The next meeting between Jane and Belinda was less gratifying. Indirectly, but clearly, Belinda let slip that Ann wasn't as happy as she had been the previous year. It didn't take a genius to establish that Belinda saw Jane as the reason for Ann's unhappiness. Jane reminded herself that Ann had had some problems the year before, too, but her hurt and anger were on the rise.

"Belinda, I feel that we aren't achieving anything in going on like this. You are being very negative with me and very personal. Please try to see all the positive things we've done for Ann—for all the fourth-graders, as a matter of fact, like the reading auction . . . "

Belinda cut her off in midsentence. "Well, the reading auction really isn't Ann's thing."

Why then, thought Jane, were you so upset that she missed the auction to attend her voluntary class?

Belinda leaned closer, as if to challenge Jane. Outraged, Jane nevertheless felt her intimidation by Belinda starting to show.

"If all of this started with the change in the Language Arts curriculum, you should speak with the Language Arts Committee. They made that decision. Really, it's hard to be expected to carry on, you know, instruction at everybody's level when you're the one in charge."

Jane knew this was crazy, but she couldn't help defending herself. Realizing that she was swiftly losing control of her anger, she abruptly ended the conversation. Nothing had been solved, and the gap between herself and Belinda had widened.

Two days later Ann handed a letter to Jane. Now more disbelieving than ever, Jane reread the neatly hand-lettered lines.

Dear Ms. Lee,
After our talk the other day I wanted to encourage you to foster a more positive classroom environment. Children like to feel good about themselves, and I think that feeling good about oneself is very important for future development and growth. Perhaps I can help you. I would be willing to deliver treats or small gifts at random times to the students, a reward that will tell them that they are wonderful human beings just the way they are. I hope we can work together.

Sincerely,
Belinda Dean

Jane realized that she was in danger of losing her class. She was trapped between letting this situation escalate out of control, and of wanting to assert her authority as the classroom teacher. It was time to relay what was happening to Jim Black. Jane poured out her story. Jim was empathetic. He had had some problems with Belinda before. Belinda had complained about a situation with her son in the second grade. A day later several other parents who lived in the same subdivision as the Deans complained about the same issue. Jim suggested that Jane no longer meet alone with Belinda, and offered to sit in on subsequent meetings.

For the next week Jane wrestled with her meager alternatives. She was sure, though, that she didn't want to start the random flow of noncontingent treats and repeated visits to her class by Belinda.

Two days after she received Belinda's last letter, Ann approached Jane's desk during homeroom period.

"My mother sent these," Ann said, handing Jane a pack of brightly colored pencils. Belinda was clearly serious about implementing her plan. The gauntlet had been thrown. Jane was adamant about not allowing Belinda to dictate what happened in her classroom. She put pen to paper.

The Ghost of School Years Past

JEANNETTE SLOAN

Part A

The initial weeks of her first year of teaching constituted a whirlwind of people, places, procedures, paperwork, meetings, and organizational activities. She had long anticipated her first year of teaching students with learning disabilities. Since her teenage years, Jeannette Sloan had wanted to teach special education. Having two brothers who had received special education had made her aware of the difficulties exceptional students face and the challenges involved in teaching them. Now, after completing her degree in special education and taking her first teaching position, she had finally arrived.

As the weeks wore on, Jeannette made a conscious effort to get to know the other faculty members. Because her ten students were mainstreamed for some subjects, she knew it was important to develop good working relationships and communication with the other teachers who worked with them. But more than that, she wanted to feel a part of Clearview Elementary School and to share a sense of collegiality with the regular classroom teachers.

It seemed a bit easier to get to know the other three special education teachers at Clearview because she shared their concerns—scheduling, paperwork requirements such as developing Individualized Education Programs (IEPs), and school district meetings. Although each of these teachers had taught for more than five years in the Seminole School District, they were all relative newcomers to Clearview Elementary School. Joan, who taught students with hearing impairments, shared the same partitioned classroom with her. On the adjacent hallway, two preschool special education teachers (Christine and Karen) shared adjoining classrooms. A sense of comradery came easily with these teachers. They listened to each others' concerns and held informal conversations before and after school about everything from current events to family, friends, and daily life. On the other hand, Jeannette realized that she had more in common with the regular classroom teachers with regard to students and curricular issues, and she wanted very much to share teaching methods, ideas, and materials with them. Yet, it seemed more difficult, somehow, to get to know them.

Most of these teachers, Jeannette had come to learn, had grown up in this small community. Their social and professional bonds were deep and longstanding. She also discovered that her predecessor, Cynthia Hudson, and her current teacher's aide, Pat Hughes, shared these ties with the faculty and community. Cynthia and Pat had worked together for the past eight years and still shared a close friendship since Cynthia had returned full-time to a nearby university to earn a master's degree in speech therapy. Also, Cynthia continued to send birthday cards to her students. Even in her absence, her presence was still very much felt by all.

As the fall semester progressed, Jeannette began to feel a vague sense of isolation. Although she was pleased with her class and her teaching in general, she also felt a nagging uncertainty about her teaching practices. Were her students progressing fast enough? Was there a better way to teach reading? Should she stick to the basal reading and spelling programs so that her students would be familiar with them in the event they were mainstreamed, or should she take an entirely different approach? If so, which one? Was she making the appropriate choices about behavior management? Who could help her find answers to these questions? Who would it be appropriate to ask? The school district's supervisor of special education seemed like a logical choice; but the current supervisor had recently taken employment elsewhere, and a new one had not yet been hired. Joan, Christine, and Karen did not share the same curricular concerns as she. And, for some reason, Jeannette did not feel comfortable expressing her self-doubts to the other teachers. After all, she was supposed to know what was best for her special education students. To admit her uncertainty to them might undercut their confidence in her, making it less likely that they would consult with her regarding the mainstreamed students with learning disabilities.

Jeannette thought she was managing to conceal her uncertainty from the other teachers, but Pat seemed quick to pick up on her every misgiving. With each decision she made, Pat was quick to interject, "Cynthia usually did _____," and "This was how we did it before." Coupled with the fact that she heard repeatedly from the principal, Mr. Owens, and regular education teachers about how wonderful Cynthia's behavior management and academic programs had been, these assertions became a source of discouragement to Jeannette. More and more, she found herself conforming to Pat's suggestions. In fact, because Pat knew how to implement Cynthia's behavior management program, Jeannette usually observed while Pat explained and administered procedures. Although she felt somewhat eclipsed in her role as teacher, she had come to discern that classroom control was held in high esteem by the faculty at Clearview Elementary. She had overheard murmurings about the few teachers whose classrooms were said to be "out of control." Jeannette wanted to avoid becoming the topic of those whispered exchanges at almost any cost.

She soon came to realize that she did not get what she bargained for on any level. Pat's burgeoning sense of power made her a force to reckon with as she became more and more authoritarian with the students. She shouted at students and ordered them to comply with such directives as, "Get over here," or, "Get in your seat." Sometimes these ejaculations startled both Jeannette and the students when they erupted without warning in an otherwise quiet and busy classroom. The students usually complied immediately. They seemed to be intimidated by these outbursts. Jeannette herself burned with indignation after such incidents; yet, she felt it was unwise to confront Pat about them.

At one point, it became obvious to her that Pat considered herself more competent in the instructional arena as well. One rainy November day while Jeannette was teaching money-counting skills, using coins and the blackboard for recording amounts of money, Pat interrupted her lesson and proceeded to take a different instructional approach. Her disapproval of Jeannette's teaching methods was obvious. As she stood watching Pat, she suppressed her sense of outrage and made a half-hearted decision to "let it slide."

Slowly, Jeannette became aware that the regular education teachers had begun consulting with Pat about the mainstreamed students. She realized this when Pat began to convey information about what should be done for individual students in hers as well as the other teachers' classrooms. Pat always seemed to be "in the know" about students' progress; and, apparently, she had tendered recommendations to the other teachers regarding academic and behavioral interventions.

About this time, Joan began to hint to Jeannette that Pat was assuming an inordinate amount of authority. One afternoon as they were watching students get on the school busses, Joan declared, "It's your classroom, Jeannette. If I were you, I would really watch Pat. It looks like she's taking over." Jeannette replied, "Oh, I don't think so. She just enjoys having more to do than run off papers. That's mostly what she did before."

Jeannette did not reflect much more about Joan's comments until one day in late December, when the extent to which Pat had assumed authority became crystal clear during a lunchtime incident. Earlier, in the classroom, one of Jeannette's students, Carrie, had refused to complete her morning assignments. Carrie had employed a number of avoidance behaviors, but finally completed most of the work in a somewhat slap-dash fashion. Jeannette had pulled Carrie aside before going to the cafeteria and told her to sit at a lunch table by herself and think about how she had behaved.

After all of the students were seated with their lunches, Jeannette joined Pat and Judy Rowe, a fourth-grade teacher, at the teachers' table. As Pat seated herself across from them, Judy used a large manila envelope which had been lying on the table beside her to hide her face as she inclined her head toward Pat, continuing what obviously was a private conversation. Jeannette's confusion turned to fury when she overheard the gist of the conversation. They were discussing her handling of Carrie's behavior. Jeannette rose and went to pour herself a cup of coffee.

Standing at the coffee maker in the corner of the cafeteria, her face burning, she felt like a 10-year-old who had overheard herself being discussed among adults. Who did they think they were? How could they be so uncouth? She knew she just had to do something to turn this situation around.

Winnie

PATTY GRAY

Part A

8/27

Well, journal, it's my first day back at school. I'm beginning my second year of teaching and I think that this time I'm in for a real treat. This year, I'll be teaching a group of "at risk" first-graders. When my principal first asked me about this class, I wondered, "What in the world do you mean by at risk?" I'd heard so many different definitions while I was in college. Well, as he explained the situation, it didn't take long for me to understand. The students I would have were in our pre-kindergarten program, our kindergarten program, and most of them had been retained in first grade. My goodness! I had taught a class of average students last year. This year, most of my kids would be eight years old in first grade. Mr. Brown (my principal), the reading specialist, and the Chapter 1 teacher decided that instead of using the standard phonetic reading program, I'd use a basal series that combined phonetic and whole word approaches. I was also told that I should contact the consulting teacher at our school to find out about supplementary materials and behavior management techniques that I'd probably need.

9/1

Wow, it's Friday already. I haven't had time to do much writing. We've been running from one inservice program to the next all week long. Boy, these work weeks are real killers! I'll get my bulletin boards up before Monday if I work all day on Saturday and Sunday. Fortunately, Mr. Brown will be here to let us in. Oh well, such is life in the fast lane.

Betsy, the kindergarten teacher who had many of my kids last year, gave me the low-down on many of the students during lunch today. Man, I'm going to have a class

193

full of boys—eleven of them and only three girls. Half these guys are on Ritalin. With such an active bunch, at least I don't have to worry about being bored this year!

Betsy also schooled me about one kid in particular. He's called Winnie. His real name is Winslow. He is seven years old and the only student in the class who was not retained in first grade. He's really tiny for his age, but he's also a real pistol. Betsy shared that Winnie could be so obnoxious that last year he was passed around from one kindergarten teacher to the next. She could only tolerate him for so long and then she'd have to send him to another teacher for about thirty minutes just to catch her breath. Winnie followed her everywhere—even into the bathroom. Many times she would use the class bathroom so that she wouldn't have to leave the room. The door wouldn't lock, so Winnie would just walk right in. Betsy would be sitting on the commode and he'd just walk right in.

I kid you not, Bets had me in stitches when she told me about this. She would look at Winnie with an I-can't-believe-you're-doing-this stare on her face and say, "Winnie, I'm using the bathroom." This didn't phase him in the least bit. He'd just simply respond, "But Mrs. Thompson, I have to tell you something." And then he would just say what was on his mind, turn, leave, and shut the door behind him. That's just one of the things he did all year that almost drove poor Bets crazy. I hope that knowing all this will help me cope with these problems. I'm also hoping that Winnie has matured some over the summer. Well, must get back to making the name tags for the kids. I'll try to write again soon.

11/3

My, how time flies when you're having fun! Sorry, I know it's been a while. I must be more consistent with my writing. Someday, when I'm old and gray, I'll be able to look back at these entries and have a laugh or two. For now, though, let me fill you in on how things are going.

It's now been about two months since school started, and although I'm really enjoying my class, I've already had to get some help to deal with both their academic and behavioral problems. Everybody told me at the beginning of the year that I needed to talk with Jackie, the consulting teacher at our school, for help. And so I did. Jackie has a very interesting job. Unlike regular classroom teachers, she is not assigned to teach a group of students each day. Instead, she's available to provide consultation to those of us who have students with academic and behavioral problems. We meet with Jackie on a one-to-one basis or with a group of teachers referred to as a teacher assistance team. Frankly, I've preferred working with her on an individual basis and you know what—she's really been great! We've been meeting, planning, and implementing for only a couple of weeks, and already I can see a difference in my group.

First of all, Jackie really helped me with the reading program. It didn't take me long to realize that the basal reading program I was given to use was not the answer for my children. I mean, my kids have such limited experiences and vocabularies that they simply can't relate to the material. I needed to make reading more relevant for them. So, I talked to Jackie, and she agreed to help me supplement my reading program with a whole-language component. We're going great guns with this approach.

For Halloween, for example, we made a witch's brew. This was really neat because we were able to build on what the kids already knew to increase their vocabularies. Jackie brought in this huge black pot and a long wooden spoon and I brought the ingredients for our brew. We had all kinds of nuts, raisins, yogurt raisins, pretzel sticks, malted milk balls, and—you know—the stuff you use to make granola. Both Jackie and I were dressed in witch's costumes, and we started the lesson by having the kids identify the ingredients and taste them. As they munched, we had them come up with words that described the taste—words like salty, sweet, crunchy, chewy. As they sampled each ingredient, we poured that ingredient into our "caldron." As we stirred, we danced around the "caldron" and sang a tune about witch's brew. This continued until each student had "taste tested" all of the ingredients. Finally, we had them sample the brew to note the difference in taste after all the goodies had been mixed together. The kids thought this was great! They were having fun and they were building their vocabularies at the same time.

Jackie also helped me with behavior problems. In other words, she helped me with Winnie. From the very beginning of school, he would never raise his hand. Whenever he had something to tell me, he would just blurt it out. Jackie and I talked about this, and together we came up with a plan. We decided that we would try to modify Winnie's behavior by ignoring him when he did not raise his hand and wait to be recognized. Of course, we sat Winnie down and told him what we were planning to do. To draw attention away from him, we told the class that this was something that we were doing with everyone. We expected everyone to raise their hands when they wanted to speak. Jackie did a few demonstration lessons to show me how to react to different degrees and variations of the target behavior and then I followed through with implementation of the procedure. She was—and remains—available to observe and coach me when I'm trying a new teaching strategy and this really helps me refine my skills. I really do hope this plan will work. I'm already beginning to feel the way Betsy did last year.

11/19

Well, it's been two weeks since I last wrote. We've been using our B-MOD plan with Winnie and it seems that things are getting worse instead of better. You won't believe this, but as I walk around the room, he continues to call out my name constantly. If he calls my name and I don't answer him right away, he forgets what he's planning to tell me. When I finally do acknowledge him he'll say, "Mrs. Gray," and then he'll snap his fingers and go "uhh, uhh, uhh." I guess that's why he feels he has to blurt out whatever he needs or wants to say—if he keeps quiet, the poor thing knows that he is going to lose whatever's floating around in his little head. The kids have started to pick on him when he does this. I really can't afford to let things get any worse, so I'll plan to meet with Jackie and develop a modified strategy. Will try to see her tomorrow if I have the time.

11/21

Boy, it's really nice to have someone around who is so readily available. Today, I met with Jackie after school and we modified Winnie's behavior management plan. In addition to ignoring his call outs, we also came up with a chart system for Winnie. I made a chart and divided it up into sections for reading, language, spelling, social studies, and science. If at the end of one of the blocks, he hasn't blurted out an answer or called my name without acknowledgement, he'll get a plus (+). If not, if he does call out, he'll get a minus (-). If he's gotten no more than three minuses in a day's time, I'll let him do something special like read to the class. He's coming along nicely with his reading and he really enjoys showing off his skills to the rest of the class.

12/30

I know, I know. I've been bad. I said that I would write every day. Things just got so hectic after Thanksgiving that I just could not get to you. I had a wonderful Christmas! Went skiing with some friends and had an absolute blast! Got some really nice presents, too! Jerry gave me a new compact disc player. I really love the sound. Will really enjoy it.

Well, I guess I'm writing because it's getting close to that time again. On Monday, vacation will be over and I'll be back at school with my class. I'm sure Winnie will be in rare form the minute he steps off the school bus. Honestly, you'd think he'd miss a day once in a while. He's the only kid in the class who has perfect attendance!

I mentioned on November 23 that we started using a chart with Winnie. Well, before we got out for Christmas break, it finally started working to where we could get him to raise his hand before he yelled out for help or just blurted out whatever was on his mind. But you know, with all the nervous energy that this kid has, the problem just started to manifest itself in other ways. One day the psychologist came into the room to observe another student. It seems that each and every one of them has some problem or another. Anyway, Winnie raised his hand, but I didn't call on him. Well, as loudly as he could, he just slammed his hands down on his desk top. I kept on ignoring him and the longer I ignored, the louder he got. He was tapping his pencil, kicking his desk, and he continued to slam his hands against his desk top. Finally, I just looked at him and said, "I simply refuse to speak to you while you are acting this way. When you can start to act like a seven-year-old, then I'll look at you." At that point, he was really angry. He put his head on the desk and pouted. He wasn't disturbing anyone else so I just let him sit there until he cooled off.

By our last day before the start of Christmas break, I just wanted to SCREAM! I just wanted to change my name because even though he was raising his hand more often, now Winnie was really into the same act that he so artfully performed in Betsy's class last year. He was constantly out of his seat, following me around everywhere I went. He followed me to the office. If I left the room to get something from another teacher I'd look back and there he was behind me. I didn't dare use the class bathroom when he was anywhere in sight. One day, he called my name so much that I just started to count the times. By the end of the day, he had called my name 37 times without raising his hand. Can you believe it? It seems like this was an improvement over his performance before we started using the chart, but he also has regressed to the point where he can never be wrong. If you tell him that he has missed two words on a spelling test—TWO WORDS—he just loses it! He bangs his head against the top of his desk, he crosses his arms and pokes out his lips, or he'll simply sit and sob incessantly. Oh, what a kid! What a kid!

I tell you about all the problems I have with Winnie, but you know, this kid is no dummy. He is the sharpest reader in my class. He can sound and blend like a champ and his comprehension is not at all bad. In math, he's a little slow with word problems, but he's great with computation and he's learning his facts with no problems. I honestly don't think that he has a learning problem. He's the youngest kid in my class, but academically, he's the strongest. Well, I'll see how he's doing in just a few days. Give me strength.

You Had Better Get on Them

BOB WINTERS

Although he had majored in teaching preschool children with handicaps, Bob Winters took his first teaching assignment in a middle school classroom for students with mild mental retardation. He had recently graduated from a small northeastern college and his choice of career options looked limited because he had decided to return with Kathy, his fiancee, to her hometown. She wanted them to make their home near her family, and because this was important to her, he agreed. Although teaching middle school students with mild mental disabilities seemed a far cry from his teacher preparation, he felt reasonably sure he could make the necessary adjustments. He reasoned that his principal, Mr. Dudley, wouldn't have hired him if it were an impossible transition to make.

During the interview, Mr. Dudley told Bob, "You're the expert. We'll give you a lot of leeway for making decisions about these students because you're the one who's been prepared to work with exceptional students." Bob appreciated Mr. Dudley's confidence and resolved to do his best to live up to his principal's expectations. He surmised from the ensuing discussion with Mr. Dudley that a key requirement was that he maintain strict control of the classroom. Mr. Dudley warned him that his class included several students who presented serious discipline problems. "The previous teacher had a lot of difficulty with them," Mr. Dudley explained. "You'll have to come down on them hard."

Throughout the first weeks of school, Bob spent a great deal of time in and out of school trying to develop and implement a viable instructional program for his students. This was a big challenge for him because he found that they were far more academically capable than he expected. He had assumed that he would need to concentrate on self-help and daily living skills; he now found that his students were ready for remedial work in reading, written expression, mathematics, and content area subjects. Several of them were mainstreamed for some of these subjects, and the sixth, seventh, and eighth-grade teachers were now coming to him for advice on academic and behavior management issues.

Keeping up with the everyday demands of his job became nearly impossible for Bob. He fell into a basic pattern of assigning class work, which he placed on the board every morning, and worksheets, which he selected every afternoon for the following day. Because he was unfamiliar with academic instructional materials and curriculum at this level, he tried to stick to familiar things like capitalization and punctuation worksheets. In mathematics, he made up problems involving the basic operations (addition, subtraction, multiplication, and division). Bob tried to give his students enough work to keep them busy, because as the days and weeks rolled by his class was becoming more and more rowdy and he felt his classroom control slipping away.

Unfortunately, the students raced through their assignments and then proceeded to wander around the room, gathering in small groups to laugh, joke, and verbally abuse each other with mild barbs while Bob attempted to work with one or two students individually. Getting poor marks on their work did not seem to bother them. In fact, six weeks into the school year several of them had taken to holding up their graded work and proudly proclaiming to have scored the lowest grade. Increasingly, they ignored Bob's directives and resisted his instruction. The classroom always seemed in disarray. "They seem to have no respect and less motivation," Bob thought. "I'm not really teaching." Waves of discouragement, shame, and fear engulfed him during these moments of reflection.

These painful moments were made more acute on occasion when Mr. Dudley stepped into his classroom to quell the noise emanating into the corridors. The first time this happened, Mr. Dudley stood squarely in the doorway, glaring unremittingly at one student as he announced in booming voice to the class, "I can hear you all the way down the hallway. If you can't get quiet and do your work, we'll all make a trip down to the office and call your parents." The room immediately fell silent. Satisfied that he had accomplished his goal, Mr. Dudley continued on his way. Bob's face flushed with embarrassment. Although Mr. Dudley had directed his stern warning toward the students, he had obviously also meant to castigate Bob for not controlling his class. What's more, the students began to laugh and make jokes about Mr. Dudley. "He thinks he's bad," one of the students quipped. The others shook their heads in knowing agreement.

Bob resolved to get tougher. "That's all these kid's understand," he concluded. By now, he had begun to perceive that many of his students were from "deprived" backgrounds. Most of them lived with single parents, foster parents, or whatever family member had been willing to take them in. On the few occasions when he had contacted parents, he had gotten little of what he considered cooperation. Either his suggestions were ignored, or the parents or guardians became inordinately angry and punitive toward the student. Bob did not want to cause one of his students to catch a beating, so he began to steer clear of contacting their homes. "These parents just don't seem to care or value education," he concluded, "so is it any wonder their kids behave the way they do?"

Bob also discovered that his students seemed impervious to punishment. He tried several punishments: taking away time to work on the classroom computer, keeping them from enjoyable activities, and sending them to the office. Not even getting after-school detention seemed to faze them. The less responsive they were, the more Bob stepped up his campaign to "get tough," as Mr. Dudley had recommended. One day while Bob was trying to teach a reading group, Lawrence repeatedly chased Cathy around the room, both of them grinning and giggling and seemingly oblivious of everything else. The first time it happened, Bob looked up and declared in a tired and disgusted tone of voice, "Okay, Lawrence, that's enough. Why don't you try getting some work done?" The second time, he shouted, "Lawrence and Cathy! Cut it out!" Three minutes later when he caught them at it again, he stood up and thundered, "SIT DOWN!" Several of the students who stood socializing in a back corner of the room were startled. Lawrence and Cathy went to their respective seats and sat down quietly. "Get out your dictionaries," Bob ordered, "and copy three pages." Sullen and reproachful, they nevertheless did as they were told. "Well," Bob thought with satisfaction, "that did it." Their unexpected obedience gave him a seldom-felt sense of authority.

Although he was sometimes uncomfortable with his "tough-guy" approach, Bob was convinced that this was the only way to handle these students because they didn't care about anything else. He was tired of their insolence and lack of values. He was tired of having to worry about his principal and colleagues witnessing the chaos that frequently characterized his classroom. In fact, he was just plain tired.

Because copying the dictionary seemed to be one of the few things his students seemed to dread, Bob invoked this punishment frequently. That is, he did so until the Thursday he lowered the assignment on Ronnie for disrupting other classes on his return from the restroom. Ronnie responded with an impish grin and declared, "Okay, I *love* copying the dictionary." He proceeded to copy more pages than Bob had assigned. The next day, Linwood flatly refused to copy any at all. Bob ordered him to the office, realizing full well that it was Friday and he was back to square one with regard to finding something that made these kids behave.

The following Monday, in desperation, Bob decided that if he did a better job of separating his students, he could also improve his chances of controlling them. He therefore drew a portable divider across the room, separating it into two smaller spaces while leaving just enough opening for his desk. With this arrangement, he was the only one who could see everyone at once. He assigned them individual seatwork and did no instructional group work the entire day. He watched them so carefully that no one had the slightest opportunity to become disruptive. It was a very quiet, very long day—but, he felt, an improvement.

Later that week, Bob decided that although the room divider had helped him establish a semblance of control when he desperately needed it, the divider was not feasible for the long-term. Nevertheless, he judged that the principle of "divide and conquer" was a valuable one. He removed the divider but arranged the students' desks two feet apart and facing the classroom walls. He reasoned that now they had little opportunity to become distracted with each other and would get more work done as a result.

When they entered the classroom, the students cast doubtful looks at one another and stole furtive glances at Bob. Aware of their surprise and disbelief, he feigned a "business as usual" demeanor and proceeded to make assignments. "Great!" he reveled inwardly, "I've got them now!" And, for a few days, it seemed as though he did.

On Monday of the following week, an early morning snowfall caused an hour's delay of the opening of school. When his students arrived, they were very animated and excited. Bob felt a sense of dread wash over him. He had trouble getting them seated and settled; and, when he did so, they scooted their desks together whenever the opportunity to escape Bob's notice presented itself. They met his reprimands with saucy comments like, "Oh, big man!" and, "Yeah, he thinks he's going to do something!" Even the somewhat quieter and more tractable students seemed to turn conspiratorially against him. Sensing their collective rise of power, they ignored his efforts to get them to work.

Bob realized in an instant that the stakes were high, but he was also furious. "Little jerks!" he thought to himself. When Gerald jumped out of his seat and ran over to whack Mike playfully in the back of the head, Bob lashed out. "GET YOUR ASS IN THE CHAIR!" he bellowed. Gerald froze, and the students stared silently at Bob as he strode over to his desk and sat down resolutely. Continuing, he stated in a determined voice, "I don't give a damn what you all want to do; you're going to do as I say." Cathy nudged Linwood, who sat beside her, and began giggling. Bob descended on her immediately. "Go to the office!" he ordered. Flashing angry eyes, Cathy stalked out of the room and slammed the door. The other students shook their heads and exchanged scowls.

Bob busied himself at his desk while the students sat idly but quietly. No one seemed to know what to do. Five minutes passed, then ten. The opening of the classroom door broke the stillness. It was Cathy, followed by Mr. Dudley. Cathy sauntered in and took her seat. "I told him," she announced to the other students.

"Mr. Winters, may I see you outside?" Mr. Dudley's request was more a command than a question. As Bob walked to the door, he overheard Amber state, "He's going to be in trouble." Bob guessed that she was right. A sense of defeat overwhelmed him as he closed the classroom door behind him and stood to face Mr. Dudley.

Index

Notes